Doing the Business

DOING THE BUSINESS

Entrepreneurship, the Working
Class, and Detectives in the
East End of London

DICK HOBBS

Oxford New York
OXFORD UNIVERSITY PRESS

This book has been printed digitally and produced in a standard design
in order to ensure its continuing availability

OXFORD
UNIVERSITY PRESS

Great Clarendon Street, Oxford OX2 6DP

Oxford University Press is a department of the University of Oxford.
It furthers the University's objective of excellence in research, scholarship,
and education by publishing worldwide in

Oxford New York

Athens Auckland Bangkok Bogotá Buenos Aires Cape Town
Chennai Dar es Salaam Delhi Florence Hong Kong Istanbul Karachi
Kolkata Kuala Lumpur Madrid Melbourne Mexico City Mumbai Nairobi
Paris São Paulo Shanghai Singapore Taipei Tokyo Toronto Warsaw

with associated companies in Berlin Ibadan

Oxford is a registered trade mark of Oxford University Press
in the UK and in certain other countries

Published in the United States
by Oxford University Press Inc., New York

© Dick Hobbs 1988

ISBN 0–19–825832–1

To Jack Reynolds, Alice Porter, and Fred Hobbs.
To those too expensive for wages.
To Sue and our sons Pat and Nik.

To Skulduggery.

Acknowledgements

The debt which I owe to my family is enormous, and extends far beyond the usual rather patronizing acknowledgements referring to 'tea-making', 'proof-reading', or 'support and encouragement'. While digging out the history of the area, and when exploring the contemporary options available to East-Enders, I made ridiculous demands particularly upon my immediate family. Dead and alive, the quick and the salaried; my family, often unknowingly contributed a great deal to this book. I must acknowledge the time and trust afforded to me by various police officers. In particular DI 'Oaks', DC 'Stout', and especially DC 'Simon', whose patience and loyalty were unrelenting at a crucial stage of the research.

Tony Goldman and Dave Hooper were responsible for getting me into the academic business, and once there Gerry Rose, Mick Mann, and particularly Terry Morris prevented me from falling out with it. Thanks are also due to David Jenkins, for his relentless support, and to Betsy Stanko and Clive Norris who, at a particularly depressing time, struck the right note in the worst pub in Britain. Also sincere thanks are due to Asher Tropp, who cast aside academic orthodoxy to talk about his East End, and supported me throughout what was for both of us something of an odyssey.

I am indebted to Paul Rock for the advice and comments that he offered in such characteristic discerning fashion, and to Joanna Shapland, Roger Hood, Geoff Pearson, Tim May, and Roger Silverstone for commenting on early drafts. Carl Klockars and Stuart Henry also provided helpful suggestions from afar. Particularly warm thanks are due to Robert Reiner and to Mike Maguire who read the manuscript and offered detailed criticisms, and to Jane Morgan for her advice and support. Thanks also to Georgina Marson for typing part of the manuscript and to Agnes McGill for organizing the text not once but twice.

Nigel Fielding supervised the original thesis on which this book is based, and his respectful treatment of my field-notes (and by association of my informants), despite the fact that some of the behaviour described must have been offensive to him, is a rarity in a profession increasingly prone to terminal timidity. Likewise to David

Downes who as both teacher and friend has put up with abusive letters, begging phone calls, and finally 'the book' with grace and good humour. A positive influence at every stage, he tolerated probably more than he should have done.

The final acknowledgement must be to 'the chaps'; notably Mr T., Harry the Fish, Smudge, Tony the Phone, the late John Hurley, Stanley Bambi, Doberman, Odd Nob, and Graham Hurley. Without their co-operation, patience, good humour, and friendship I would have nothing to write about. I hope that I have not let them down. Long may they prosper by the half-light shed upon them by free enterprise, and may all their 'little-earners' be big ones.

DICK HOBBS
London
1987

Contents

List of Illustrations

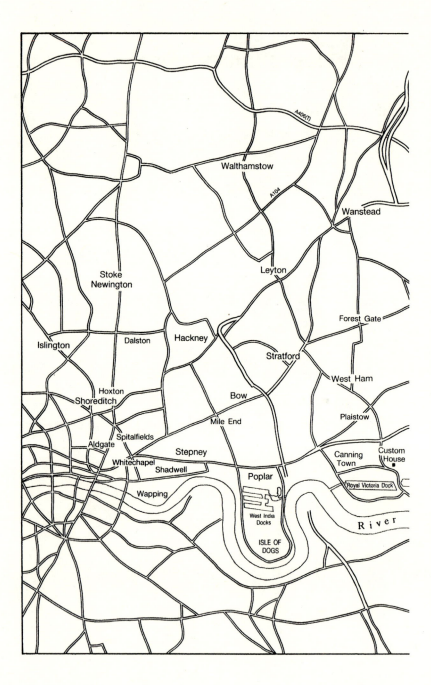

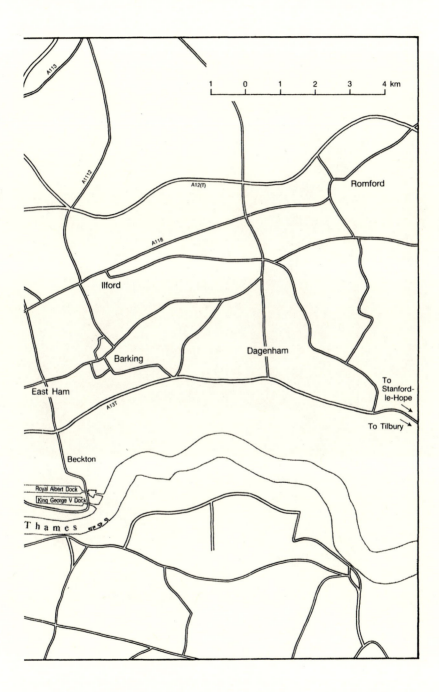

1

A Biography of a Research Project: Perusing Plod with a View from the Chaps

How's business? Fine yeah. You know, bits and pieces but things are moving; it's the time of the year really. You just can't tell. People either want the gear or they are throwing it in your face. It's a case of get the stall out, any weather, and punch away, turn over what you can, knock it out, put the frilly stuff on your head and shout and holler. It's a living and I really think that I am going to crack it. This time next year my son, this time next year.

Sammy, who sells ladies' underwear from the back of a van.

It's been quiet; not a lot going on. But what you've got to remember is, I can't just sit back and do nothing. Even if there's not a lot about I still put myself about. Sooner or later I'll get something, a little trade, a deal. Just so long as I'm busy eventually I'll get a little tickle and then it makes it all worthwhile, so long as I keep grafting.

Martin, a Detective Constable who works in East London.

This book is about entrepreneurship, an area, and a specific police culture. Both the area of East London and the culture of the Criminal Investigation Department of the Metropolitan Police are distinctive cultural, geographical, and institutional entities in their own right yet they share certain key characteristics. These characteristics can be located in the anomalous development of one section of the British working class, and in the evolution of a mode of social control that often appears to function in a contrary manner to that of the central police organization. Consequently, the book is about urban life, messy, haphazard, and ultimately perplexing. It is about both formal and informal control strategies and the coercive regulatory power of the market-place.

My analysis reverberates between East London and the CID, but it is not concerned with policing *per se*. Several excellent observational accounts of police work have emerged in Britain over the past few years, but understandably these studies have tended to concentrate upon uniformed patrol work (see, for instance, Norris 1987). However, in this book I have focused upon detectives not from an organizational perspective, nor from a conventional participant observer's perspective from within the organization (Steer 1980; Erikson 1981). Instead, I write from within the urban milieu. It is a view of policing largely from the point of view of the policed; policing from below. Yet no qualitative description of social interaction will make sense if it is not framed within a firm, structural base (McBarnett 1977, pp. 31-2). Consequently I also examine the historically determined enabling mechanisms of both East End and detective culture, for the style of the latter has parallels with the former. The area's deviant identity and economically determined traditions that stress autonomy and entrepreneurship have been compounded by market forces and the emergent cultural style finds favour amongst detectives of the Metropolitan Police who, despite their formal function as thief-takers, appropriate and acquire certain of the more tangible manifestations of East End culture for their own use.

In this book police work takes second billing to East End culture. Because of this and the methods I have employed to research the CID, the picture I paint of detectives is partial and this is acknowledged below. I also acknowledge the partial nature of my analysis of the East End. However, having held up my hands to a few of the more stark inadequacies of this work, it is probably prudent to provide some detail of how, and essentially why, this book came to be written.

Formally, this book started life as a Ph.D thesis in the winter of 1982. However, the real work on which both the book and the thesis is based began much earlier. I should stress at this point that I was very much part of the social world that I was to study: an ex-member who returned in order to conduct an ethnograpic inquiry. The reflexivity that is apparent in all forms of research is an obvious and essential element in the project that I subsequently embarked upon. Further, the methodology that I applied to the project was fully in accord with normative interactive processes and techniques that I encountered within both the area and the institutions that were to be the subject of my inquiry (Hammersley and Atkinson 1983, p. 15). The details of my biography are therefore crucial in understanding not only my motivation for engaging in research, but also in comprehending the importance of selecting a relevant methodology that exploits the researcher's inevitable participation in the ensuing social milieu (Hammersley and Atkinson 1983, p. 23).

I was born and brought up in East London, and on leaving school in the late 1960s worked in numerous occupations including that of clerk, road-sweeper, dustman, warehouseman, and labourer. In 1970 I left home and worked in the north of England for three years in a similar range of jobs and it was then that I became aware of both the diverse nature of working-class culture and particularly the uniqueness of East London. For instance, I had been accustomed to dustmen operating a 'job and finish' system, finishing their work as quickly as possible, and after a quick shower and change of clothing, spending the afternoon playing golf or running their own furniture removals, gardening, or window-cleaning business.

Had I moved to a northern city where sharpness of wit and tongue were prominent features of working-class life—Manchester, Liverpool, or Newcastle for instance—my experiences and consequently this book would have been very different. However, my colleagues in the cleansing department of 'Luddingford' were a very different bin of fish-heads. They worked extremely hard for appalling wages and put great store by physical strength and stamina. After clocking out at 2.00 p.m. (no 'job and finish' negotiated) the afternoons tended to be spent drinking in a local working-men's club, working on an allotment, or at home with the family. This was a way of life contrary to that to which I was accustomed. I thought that all working people were like my friends back home, but evidently not; working-class people were not all ducking and diving or wheeling and dealing. Only those designated by the trade union negotiated with management and formal social and occupational hierarchies tended to be adhered to, albeit begrudgingly. I had been accustomed to living and working with individuals who utilized a sharp verbal style and who were opportunistic and alert to the main chance. More importantly, I thought everyone else was the same. In 1970 before moving north I had never met a northener, a Tory, or a sociologist. The move north was a traumatic experience, the towns had rich and poor people, a polarized population, of which I had no conception coming from East London, a working-class city. In the north there were also students reading books, drinking, and leading generally pleasant lives. I knew of no universities in West Ham, Poplar, or

Stepney, and as I was not rich and hated dominoes, I started to attend night classes. This was followed by a four-year spell at a northern teacher training college where I found that the middle classes, as well as northerners, were 'different', and I sold cup final tickets to bourgeois soccer fans in order to keep my trading instincts sharp and maintain an essential gap between myself and cultures whose tenets remained obscure.

I subsequently returned to East London as a schoolteacher and during this period I reacquainted myself with the area's trading networks. Before I had any direct experience of northern culture, this trade and its incumbent networks were part of my life that I never had cause to question or regard as anything but normal, yet after the dour drudgery of life in Yorkshire, and the bland mediocrity of training college, the East End in comparison seemed like Batista's Havana. But my own involvements were now novelties, as my occupation had marginalized my class status to the extent that my position on the labour market no longer required me, as a condition of cultural membership, to display entrepreneurial qualities. It was as a coach to a local youth soccer team that I regained a measure of access to the entrepreneurial culture as an insider, for soccer was and remains a legitimate channel of upward mobility for working-class youth. As a coach I was regarded initially at least as an agent of mobility, and therefore someone of considerable status, possessing the ability to instil skills and habits that were of value in the market-place.

In any successful trading relationship it is essential for both parties to be satisfied with the goods or services traded, and the price negotiated. I traded my skills as a coach for access to a number of networks, into several of which I was able to renegotiate entrance at a later date for the purpose of my research. After four year's teaching I returned to full-time study and as I received no funding or grant, my ability to buy and sell, and my various legal and illegal contacts became increasingly important. My status as a schoolteacher was no longer a problem; I was now just another East-Ender scraping a living from the area's ever declining economy.

At this point I gave up soccer coaching in favour of my studies. I began to frequent The Pump, a pub that boasted a number of detectives amongst its clientele, and trading became established for me as a peripheral activity, secondary to academic pursuits; it was light relief from seminars on epistemology, an escape route. My studies at this time were helping me to formulate a broad base for my commonsensical concern with the uniqueness of the East End, and I wrote a dissertation on youth subcultures that was to form the theoretical frame for Chapter 6. A subsequent quest for research funding for a thesis on youth proved unsuccessful, and I arrived at the University of Surrey willing to put aside my interest in subcultures in favour of studying the police.

While engaged in the literature search I became interested in the relationship between the detectives who frequented The Pump and the rest of the pub's clientele, an interest that coincided with an approach to coach another soccer team. When I realized that one of the parents who followed the team was Simon, a detective who used The Pump, I willingly gave up one evening a week and my Sunday mornings to stand freezing in a damp field cajoling various Waynes, Damiens, Troys, and Justins to 'close each other down' and such like. My relationship with Simon steered the course of the research during those early months. Our relationship was most enjoyable and was initially a trading relationship; I had notional coaching skills that might complement his son's outstanding athletic ability, and he had knowledge of, and contacts in, the CID. Simon emerged as my principal police informant, granting me both formal and informal interviews, access to documents, and introductions to individuals and settings that would otherwise be inaccessible. My supervisor encouraged me to pursue this emergent strategy of informal access despite a recurring panic on my behalf concerning a desire to conduct 'real' research in order that I might metamorphose into a 'real' academic. Despite my misgivings, data began to emerge concerning the unique nature of CID policing, the commercial nature of their day-to-day work, and the reflexive nature of their occupational culture; that is, its parallels with East End culture. I went to pubs, clubs, and parties, and had to be willing to involve myself in heavy drinking sessions lasting many hours, or even as on one occasion, several days. The unstructured timetabling of my field-work meant that I could spend time writing up at leisure, usually 'the day after the night before', and without fail with a massive headache.

By the early summer of 1983, I had come to accept that my background, and particularly my London accent were major attributes and I became more confident in utilizing aspects of style, linguistic constructs, and my knowledge of the ecology and culture of the East End—all qualities that were acquired before my exposure to academe. There are precedents for utilizing knowledge acquired in this way (Polsky 1971; Douglas 1977; Alderson 1979, Benyon 1983; Parker 1974; Mars 1974; Holdaway 1983) and other writers have exploited their status as outsiders, the fact that they stood out, their very obtrusiveness often being regarded as a useful research foil, a way of attracting data (Ditton 1977, p. 11; Taylor 1984, pp. 11–12, 65–6, 169–70; Cohen and Taylor 1972, pp. 32–4). In CID offices my role was overt, and due to poor image-management during the early stages of the research I was extremely obtrusive. On one occasion I attended a semi-formal non-police function with Simon, and I dressed in a manner that I considered smart, yet comfortable: open-necked shirt, sleeveless Fair Isle sweater, and corduroy trousers. Simon told me I looked like 'a fucking social worker—where's your bike clips and bobble hat?' I retreated to the toilet, glanced in the mirror and, yes, I did look like a fucking social worker. Yet police contacts often accepted that I was an outsider and were pleased to inform me about 'real' police work, while I assumed an open-mouthed expression of wonderment as they told me about 'real' villains on their 'manor', men who I knew had trouble holding up their trousers.

In pubs and clubs I had to blend in sartorially; I could not be obtrusive. As a consequence I now possess a formidable array of casual shirts with an assortment of logos on the left breast (Parker 1974, p. 216; Liebow 1967, pp. 255–6; Patrick 1973, p. 13). This awareness of my appearance, and acknowledgement of the importance of image-management held me in good stead for the next stage of my work. I had never intentionally tried to look like a CID officer, and found I was still regarded as 'one of the chaps' and for the most part I spoke, acted, drank, and generally behaved as though I was not doing research. Indeed, I often had to remind myself that I was not in a pub to enjoy myself, but to conduct an academic inquiry and repeatedly woke up the following morning with an incredible hangover facing the dilemma of whether to bring it up or write it up.

My analysis of detective work has been limited by the decision not to seek formal access to the police organization. The degree to which detectives exposed both themselves and the nature of their work to me depended largely upon my ability to strike up a rapport with individuals. This meant that I became not so much a 'fan' (Van Maanen 1978) but more of a gumshoe groupie. I was fortunate enough occasionally to accompany officers while they were processing paperwork or making telephone calls. In addition, I spent the summer of 1984 alternating between various magistrates' courts and Snaresbrook Crown Court observing detectives. The most informative data from this exercise was gleaned from the waiting-rooms and canteens where much of the real work of the legal profession, as well as that of detectives, was carried out (see Chapter 8).

However, most of my analysis of detectives concentrates upon their occupational culture and although I did conduct a number of interviews with officers, the most valuable of which were carried out in their homes, the bulk of my material on detectives was gleaned from conversations and observation in pubs and clubs. I argue that this is where much detective work is conducted and further that the pub provides a suitable arena for the detective to justify, in indigenous terms, his existence (Chapter 9).

As the main emphasis of my argument is that the occupational culture and subsequent operational style of detective work in London, and more specifically East London, borrows stylistically from East End culture, the bulk of my field-work and subsequent writings is concerned with an analysis of that area. While engaged in this part of my study my strategy was to exploit contacts who were acquainted with my pre-academic self and 'blend in with the human scenery so that you don't chill the scene' (Polsky 1971, p. 132). This necessitated total flexibility on my behalf, and a willingness to abide by the ethics of the researched culture and not the normative ethical constraints of sociological research. When someone telephones at six in the morning with the cryptic message that: 'I got a parcel going to Felixstowe; need a hand. I'll be round in ten minutes—all right?' the response, if richness and depth of data are at all important, can only be 'yes'. A refusal, or worse still an enquiry concerning the legal status of the 'parcel', would provoke an abrupt conclusion to the relationship. Consequently, I was willing to skirt the boundaries of criminality on several occasions, and I considered it crucial to be willingly involved in 'normal' business transactions, legal or otherwise. I was pursuing an interactive, inductive study of an entrepreneurial culture, and in order to do so I had to display entrepreneurial skills myself. Because of my background I found nothing immoral or even unusual in the dealing and trading that I encountered. However, I do not consider the study to be unethical, for the ethics that I adhered to were the ethics of the citizens of the

East End. To comply with basic common sense and decency I have attempted to camouflage individuals, situations, commodities, and places so as to make legal action as a result of any of my informants' indiscretion extremely unlikely.

The crime that I have knowledge of does not feature an élite of professional criminals whose social and economic status sets them apart from the rest of the parent culture (Taylor 1984). Professional criminals were around and indeed were at times highly visible, yet they do not exist in a velvet-lined sub-universe. Taylor (1984, p. 7) defines the professional criminal as 'all those whose livelihood for a period of at least five years has been based primarily on persistent criminal activity'. I found this definition vague and hardly applicable to a population who were constantly moving from legal to illegal enterprises and back again. My own research revealed that in the East End everyone was 'at it' and some were 'at it' more than most. They were the professional criminals. However, their actions were marginal in the overall context of the entrepreneurial culture, the stakes were higher, and their trade subsequently more secretive. My access to professional criminals then was subsequently more limited than to those committing 'normal' crime.

In a similar manner, and for parallel motives, other groups are missing from my analysis. I am white, male, and of working-class origin, and I traded this profile with others who were dealing in the same market-place, ignoring women, Afro-Caribbeans, and Asians. With more time and the structuring of a research strategy with a substantially more formal approach, I could have examined the socio-historical parallels to be drawn between the Irish peasantry, who arrived in East London in the mid-nineteenth century, and the descendants of slaves who settled in East London during the 1950s, 1960s, and 1970s. Likewise, potentially interesting parallels might be drawn between the Jewish immigrants who settled in East London during the latter part of the nineteenth century, and the more recent arrival of Bengalis, both groups apparently sharing an essentially entrepreneurial culture. At the point of arrival all four of these groups had little direct experience of industrial capitalism and an analysis of these later arrivals would I feel, despite the probable abandonment of my favoured interactive strategy, enhance my research. Yet my gut reaction is summed up by Corrigan (1979, p. 14) that the experience of being black and in Britain should be written about by 'someone who has experienced these oppressions'.

Correspondingly, a female researcher needs to analyse the role of women in the entrepreneurial culture (Foster 1987). My gender prevented me from the kind of close, collaborative relationship that I believe I achieved with the men (Morgan 1981). Further, my feelings are that the East End remains a traditional working-class society in that paternalism and not maternalism provides the focal concern and control dynamic (see Young and Willmott 1957 for a contrary view). As Corrigan (1979, pp. 13–14) has noted, this is not an excuse for the 'total exclusion of half the population', so much as an acknowledgement that I draw heavily upon my own experiences and it would be grossly patronizing of me to attempt to impose the theoretical implications of a male ethnography on to women (see Burgess 1984, p. 91).

Not all the business enterprises that I became aware of went smoothly or without anomaly. One man, when planning a theft from a warehouse, asked his wife to pack him some sandwiches in order to sustain him on his night's work. He went to work that night with a parcel of cheese and pickle sandwiches and it was not until he had broken into the warehouse yard that he informed his notoriously dog-fearing colleague that the premises were guarded by two canine equivalents of mountain lions. As the beasts approached, the accomplice cowed and the cheese and pickle sandwiches were fed to the dogs, apparently placating them. The two men quickly loaded their booty (two tea-chests of razor blades) and triumphantly made off, only to be chased by the slavering hounds who caught them at the first set of traffic lights, noisily demanding second helpings of their midnight snack.

One night I was taken for a meal by a thief who, as it later transpired, had robbed an office the previous night in the expectation of finding a safe full of cash, only to discover that the only commodity in the safe was a quantity of luncheon vouchers. We were both drunk by the time the bill arrived, it was past midnight, and we were the Indian restaurant's only remaining customers. My fellow diner examined the bill and, as my anticipation rose, reached for his wallet. He then proceeded to pay entirely in luncheon vouchers. The waiter hovered, and my anticipation turned to consternation as I realized that the £15 bill was to be paid entirely in fifteen-pence vouchers. He took what seemed like an hour to count and recount the bills, as I giggled nervously. Eventually we left the waiter to make some numerical sense of the heaps of paper and we disappeared into the night, not before my friend had commented icily: 'The trouble with you Dick, you don't take is serious.'

Indeed I did not. The entire entrepreneurial milieu at its best was a fascinating cornucopia of light and shade, dazzling repartee, and bizarre situations. Particularly towards the end of my intensive field-work I found great difficulty in taking much of what I experienced seriously. For example, when one man—a car mechanic—with perpetually oily hands, pontificated one night on his intention to open an old people's home ('take their pensions, give 'em a bed and some grub, and your doing everyone a favour'), my tolerance was at a low ebb and I could take no more. I laughed hysterically at the prospect of this dreamer in oily overalls doing the morning rounds at 'Fred's Rest Home for the Elderly' (No Spitting), wiping a greasy screwdriver, and consoling a concerned relative with such soothing patter as 'sorry darling the bodywork's kosher, but she's going to need a new big end'. That night I discontinued the field-work. I was hallucinating.

Ditton, in a most sensitive passage concerning the problems of field-work, has commented on his feelings about turning individuals, to whom he felt close, into sources of data: 'Sometimes I almost felt I was doing research on my own family' (Ditton 1977, p. 17). I was, in effect, doing exactly that. My family, friends, and neighbours were all potential sources of data. There was no social situation I encountered during the three years of this research that did not warrant some inductive analysis. In addition, the sections concerning the history of East London necessitated extensive literature and documentary searches as well as formal and informal interviews. On occasion I found this period of the research deeply disturbing as my family history unfolded before me and I discovered much about my own inheritance. It was as if the history of the area exactly paralleled that of my own family, my ancestors consisting of small business men, cabinet-makers, french polishers, dockers, barge-repairers, seamstresses, clerks, and cleaners. Their themes were poverty, poor education, crime, sport and violence, heroes and villains. I have no comforting, safe conclusion to report regarding my feelings in researching and writing Chapter 5, merely that it was both enlightening and painful. However, these feelings are, in many ways, indicative of the emotional investment that the research demanded of me, an investment that only the reader can evaluate in terms of return. I trusted those that I spoke to and had that trust reciprocated tenfold. When contentious issues were being discussed, a compromise was reached and I often kept my mouth shut in favour of acquiring information that I considered to be more important than the sound of my own voice.

When in the company of policemen, this was relatively easy as my emotional investment in such relationships was negligible. They were, on occasions, racist and sexist. I kept quiet, let them talk, and later noted their remarks and behaviour (Polsky's advice on researching criminals is even more relevant to researching the police, i.e. 'keep your mouth shut' (Polsky 1971, pp. 126–7). The institutional frame within which CID work is carried out helped to create a vacuum between members and myself (a non-member). I was marginalized by my status as a non-policeman, and while informing a policeman that he is in the company of a sociologist could have a dramatic effect on proceedings I found, particularly with senior officers, that the ensuing relationship could work in my favour. These relationships usually inspired correspondingly formal interviews in which it was appropriate to ask questions concerning points of law and institutional structure—issues that could not be satisfactorily dealt with by the application of covert techniques in the boozy ambience of a pub.

No such distancing devices were available in researching 'the chaps'. During the research process, relations died, friends and relations were stricken with sickness, several people were badly beaten, others arrested, three sent to prison, one man was murdered, and one committed suicide. This research is not a freeze-frame snapshot of culture. For a central point, which I hope I stress, is that cultures are fluid, adaptive responses and as a researcher I too was fluid and adaptive. Life went on and if life was entrepreneurial and sharp, then so would I be. Sexist and chauvinistic, no problem. Racist? Well, no. Racism is part of East London's ideological inheritance and is manifested in various ways including a long history of racist attacks on a variety of ethnic groups (see Samuel 1981, pp. 275–7; Fielding 1981, p. 92; Newham Monitoring Project 1984, pp. 10–17; Robins 1984, pp. 116–17; Husbands 1982a, pp. 3–26). I did not in the course of my research meet any avowed members of the National Front or any ideologically allied fascist organization; indeed voting behaviour in East London, like many other aspects of the area's social life, remains traditional, the National Front receiving little support at elections (Husbands 1982b, pp. 177–90).

However, many of the respondents were racist; all Asians were

'Pakis' and Afro-Caribbeans, 'coons', 'niggers', 'macaroons', etc. Once, someone described their prospective next-door neighbours as 'Pakis with turbans'. Another explained how he had 'clumped a lippy Paki'. Another had moved out of an area because it was 'overrun with niggers'. Yet another explained that his reluctance at doing combat with 'Pakis' was due to the fact that 'they always carry a blade in their turban'. Yet these men were also husbands, fathers, and shop stewards, and almost exclusively socialists of various political hues. These contradictions were difficult to live with; my education had instilled certain liberal values that demanded I protest at overtly racist comments. I did this several times, and on each occasion lost valuable data as I was no longer 'one of the chaps', no longer a man to be trusted. I will not comment further; racism marked the parameters of my involvement in the cultural milieu. As Polsky has noted, the study of criminals in their natural setting requires the researcher to break the law, even if this means the mere possession of 'guilty knowledge' (Polsky 1971, p. 138). However, I found racism abhorrent, and I chose to draw the line here, on the periphery of criminal activity observing both legal and illegal trading networks. The ethical conundrums that I encountered were those faced by any white male of East London. Consequently, this research reflects my own gender, race, and class position, my regarding racism timidly the chief restraint upon a reflexive research enterprise.

Ethnography and the Place of Crime

Recent studies of crime, as Young (1986) has noted, have moved towards either an atheoretical programme of administratively based strategies of control and containment, or a fundamentally timid approach from the Left that has attempted to structure an agenda around theories of the state, thereby ignoring causation in favour of a simplistic, 'taken for granted' set of precepts that are built into the quagmire of indifference that has traditionally been the stance of Left functionalism (Young 1986).

The emergence of 'Left realism' (Taylor 1981; Lea and Young 1984; Jones *et al.* 1986; Matthews and Young 1986), and the blossoming of law and order as a primary manifesto issue for all major political parties, should have put the agenda into the hands of those for whom crime is a major problem, the working classes of the inner city (Kinsey *et al.* 1986; Jones *et al.* 1986). This has been partly achieved, as has a gradual recognition that the relationship between victim and offender is somewhat more intimate than had previously been articulated (Phipps 1986). However, by concentrating almost exclusively on intra-class crime, 'Left realism' is in danger of going the same way as its predecessors. For it is essential to stress the variety of criminal opportunities that are available to the working class and how, on occasions, these opportunities can enhance rather than encumber inner city life. However, the dangers of romanticism should at this point be acknowledged; the only Robin Hoods in East London are pubs.

They also Nick from Those that Have

Not all working-class crime has working-class victims. For instance, although burglary appears to be a crime that is committed by working-class adolescents against their elders (Maguire 1982, p. 23; Baldwin and Bottoms 1976, pp. 132–4), few adolescents continue to commit the offence into adulthood (Maguire 1982). However, working-class adults are often involved in criminal activity of some sort and these activities constitute not an insignificant proportion of urban life. Yet having to consider the criminality of an entire culture is not a comfortable departure and the aetiological basis of such an account would, I argue, necessitate a deviation from routine 'them'-and-'us' class relations. For class relations in East London have been characterized by oscillation between conflict (Bloomberg 1979), negotiation (Samuel 1981), and symbiosis. It follows then that crime, as a feature of the working-class city, created by the same market forces with which it shares this ambiguous relationship, will also run the gauntlet of seemingly antipathetic options of conflict, negotiation, and symbiosis. Similar social processes will be put into action when coming to terms with unemployment, housing, health, and education as they are experienced by the working class.

While burglary and street crime in particular are undoubtedly intra-class, and understandably therefore feature strongly in studies of working-class victimization, there are other forms of criminality that are less problematic but far more ambiguous in determining ideological origin. This ambiguous dynamic for both East End culture and the CID is entrepreneurship: legal and illegal practices that are legitimized by normative commercial activity.

As Young (1986) has noted, Left realism needs to incorporate a wide range of methodologies, and ethnography is an essential tool in digging out the real nature of crime. For if the agenda does not provide some tactile quality, a qualitative base, then any ensuing policy is in danger of being essentially one-dimensionally directive. The essence of working-class crime is that it is contradictory and much pragmatic endeavour is now being put into motion to come to terms with these contradictions. I seek, through the examination of entrepreneurial culture and control, to tease out some additional contradictions. For while the causes of crime may be obvious, the nature of individual acts and the collective meanings of specific crimes in specific circumstances are far from obvious. Further, the status of criminal action needs to be looked at not purely from the high point of the criminal law, or even from the point of view of apprehended offenders (Maguire 1982), but from within the enacted environment where crime and control are negotiated day in, day out.

I have attempted to use my status as a member of the culture to show how action, which is mediated via the market rather than law, can incorporate many of those factors that have traditionally been regarded as oppressive. Consequently I have focused upon action that is relatively public and accessible (give or take burglar alarms, guard-dogs, barred windows, etc.) which within the East End is incorporated into a broad ideological frame and is not rendered isolated, in terms of moral culpability, by law. Crime is but one option available to individuals operating within the maelstrom of market forces.

The huge step forward that has been taken by the realists in identifying the seemingly contaminating effects of capitalism on the working class, needs to be framed within a context not merely of abhorrence of something called crime, but within a historical malaise of culturally kosher responses to social, environmental, and, most importantly, market forces. In attempting to improve our knowledge of crime and the relative performance of the criminal justice system, we must not isolate criminality and control, but must locate their origins and enacted environment. By emphasizing both crime and control in terms not of legality or due process, but in terms of adaptation and modification, it is possible to focus upon 'the subjective capacity of man to create novelty, and manage diversity' (Matza 1969, p. 44).

Pre-publication, this book was described as 'containing no data' and as 'old-fashioned' and it is a fact that if 'real data' can only be constituted by a statistical analysis then it should be pointed out that, numerically speaking, I have restricted myself to carefully numbering each page. As for 'fashion', I take this to mean that my work is concerned neither with administrative analysis nor with the war against crime. The Chicago School and its associated methodologies have endured sufficiently to have been an influence on a good many criminologists, ethnographers, and urban sociologists, and I make no apology for working in this tradition. Better writers than I have gone the way of the buffalo, leaving behind a body of work whose principal contribution has been to improve our understanding of social phenomena. However, I make no such grandiose claims for this work, other than what I have attempted is to understand East London. Not in order that its denizens might be controlled, but so that, through an appreciation of their culture, the true nature of their social world, including the forces that shape and constrain its boundaries, might be comprehended. I make no apologies for my methods or for my moral stance. Becker's (1963) well-worn question 'Whose side are you on?' is particularly relevant in the contemporary academic climate. It is not simplistic to portray the moral parameters of research in terms of day-to-day activity, for we are all constantly faced with dilemmas regarding moral culpability and the likely consequences of our actions. Yet academics continually put up smoke-screens, elaborating the mundane with heuristic dissection, or making special claims for the specificity of their sub-discipline when discussing the ethical implications of their enterprise.

Participant observation is fraught with problems particularly if crime is all or in my case part of the subject-matter. As a researcher I found myself oscillating between my common-sense knowlege of East End culture, and academic orthodoxy in both selecting field strategies and attempting analysis. I avoided 'going native' by 'going academic'. My direct participation in the trading culture was no greater than that of other researchers engaging in similar enterprises (i.e. Polsky 1971; Klockars 1975; Ditton 1977; Fielding 1981; Humphreys 1975). However my status as an insider meant that I was afforded a great deal of trust by my informants, and I was allowed access to settings, detailed conversations, and information that might not otherwise have been available.

In researching the East End I was faced with the moral dilemmas of both the insider and the researcher. However, I did know whose side I was on, and I have sought neither to assist nor to hinder detectives. Likewise I do not wish to expose any individual to the forces of law and order. The research reflects the writer, East-Enders, and East End detectives. We were all feeding off each other: all 'Doing the Business'.

2

A Natural History of the British Police: The Contradiction of Control

It would be an error to portray the emergence of the British police solely as an institutional by-product of the Industrial Revolution (Styles 1987). Localized precedents for latter-day control agencies existed in pre-industrial Britain, and while acknowledging the restraints of historical relativism (Foucault 1972, p. 40), I intend to explore these early forms of police in an attempt to place contemporary policing in the context of its inheritance of control.

The Inheritance of Control

The formation of the Metropolitan Police in 1829 was noteworthy in that it marked the first unified body of state employees concerned primarily with social control (Miller 1977, pp. 26–7). Until this time the police task had been undertaken by a variety of offices. Traditionally these offices were haphazard amateur appointments. From approximately AD 900 the constable, originally a Norman high military office, bore the principal burden of policing. Over a period of some hundred years the rank of constable was gradually demoted, eventually taking over the mundane tasks of the Saxon tything-man (Critchley 1978, p. 1). The emergence in the Middle Ages of the parish constable, as an annually appointed or elected peace-keeper, while ostensibly embodying the principle of collective responsibility long established by the tything-man, was notable in that his authority was sanctioned by the Crown. The constable was entrusted with keeping the King's peace and, as Critchley had noted, this served to mark him out from other offices, thereby establishing a direct link between the authority of the constable and the power of the monarchy. Law was regarded as coming from the inaccessible source of the Crown, and manifested in the constable.[1]

[1] Reith (1948, p. 2) notes that in some parts of the country as recently as the 1870s, the parish constable was known as 'headborough' or horseholder, which were Saxon equivalents of the 'tything man'.

The Statute of Winchester in 1285 introduced three measures whose object was to 'abate the power of felons'. Firstly, the town watchman was introduced to supplement the parish constable's role, and, as Critchley indicates, marks a differentiation between the policing of rural and urban areas (Critchley 1978, p. 6). A 'watch' of up to sixteen men, depending on the size of the town, was positioned at the entrance of all walled towns between sunset and sunrise. These watchmen were afforded powers of arrest during hours of darkness, and were recruited according to a roster of all available men in the town. In turn the watchmen were under the command of the constable, to whom they delivered any arrested persons. Secondly, the Statute of Westminster revived the ancient Saxon practice of hue and cry to deal with those who resisted arrest by the watchmen. This involved the fugitive being pursued by the entire population, and failure to respond to the call invoked the wrath of the community and the risk of being accused of siding with the felon.

The third measure called into effect by the Statute, designed to support hue and cry, was the 'assize of arms'. Every male between the ages of 15 and 60 was required to keep a hauberke and helme of iron, a sword, a knife, and a horse, while the poor were to have available bows and arrows (Critchley 1978, p. 6). Two High Constables were appointed to every 100 men and, acting directly under the sheriff of the county, supervised the activities of constables and watchmen.

The Statute of Winchester, embodying a fusion of Saxon and Norman ideas, may thus be conveniently regarded as marking the end of the first police system in England which can be seen to pivot largely around the part-time constable, a local man with a touch of regal authority about him, enshrining the ancient Saxon principle of personal service to the community and exercising powers of arrest under the common law.

Social control then was localized, and remained in essence as described above for over 500 years (Styles 1987, p. 21). However, certain roles declined in relation to others. For instance, the introduction in 1327, in every county, of 'a good and lawful man to keep the peace', and the recognition in 1361 of these men as Justices of the Peace eroded the status of the constable and reduced the status of the High Constable to 'that of a rate collector' (Critchley 1978, p. 7).

The JP was a crown appointee who in turn appointed the constable. As Critchley has noted, the JP was normally the Lord of the Manor, and as such the constable was very much his man. This decline in the status of the constable was accelerated by a growing reluctance on the part of the wealthier members of the community to perform the unpaid and sometimes distasteful duties of constable. The practice of paying deputies to act in their place grew, and the deputy would often pay a deputy and so on, until those who could find no other employment found themselves engaged year after year. The status of the post subsequently plummeted and, 'within a short period the office was commonly regarded as appropriate only to the old, idiotic or infirm' (Critchley 1978, p. 10).

However, it was not only the status of the constable that declined during this period, for, as Miller (1979, p. 15) has noted 'the JP abandoned any notion of impartiality that the constable had theoretically embodied, and the class rule of the landed aristocracy was direct and personal, delivered via the office of the magistrate'. The JP was in theory the physical embodiment of an abstract body of law intended to represent universal standards of conduct and general public interest. Yet,

it actually supported specific ruling class needs and interests. Consequently, the legal order was legitimated as a mysterious, impersonal realm, but it was administered very personally. Its majesty seemed to lie in the very unpredictability of its administration. It was enforced sporadically, and magistrates reached down from the mysterious realm of the law to punish or pardon as they in accord with their general class interests deemed appropriate (Miller 1979, p. 15).

The JP was able to protect the interests of his class by the imposition of harsh sentences, of which the death penalty was utilized with increasing regularity. Hay (1975, pp. 18–19) has noted the parallel between the growth in capital statutes (from 50 to 200 between the years 1688 and 1820) and the extension and deification of the institution of private property.

'The legal instruments which enforced the division of property by terror' (Hay 1975, p. 21) were implemented against the unpropertied labouring classes in the form of floggings, transportations, and death sentences.[2] But the JP's discretionary use of the law was only half the story. Justice went to the highest bidder in a manner that, for the

---

[2] Hay is not fully clear in his explanation of the 'coexistence of the bloodier laws and increased convictions, with a declining proportion of death sentences that were actually carried out'. Radzinowicz (1948, Vol. 1, pp. 151–9) shows a decline in the numbers actually executed from the 1750's onward.

labouring classes, served further to erode the mystery and majesty of the law. This activity was blatant, culturally sanctioned, and fully in accord with the ethics of commercial activity. What Ascoli (1979, p. 21) calls 'basket justice' was an accepted and crucial part of contemporary judicial practice, and if justice 'may be bought and sold as in the market-place' (Ascoli 1979, p. 22), it was in tune with the two dominant, prevailing ethics of the day, patronage and commercialism. With this in mind, Critchley's (1978, p. 19) label of 'corruption' is quite meaningless, for attempts retrospectively to impose twentieth-century morality as a historical template upon sixteenth-, seven-teenth-, or eighteenth-century magistrates, can only be a step through an academic looking-glass to a 'time the world forgot'. By concentrating his wrath upon the JP Critchley fails to identify the entrepreneurial activities of magistrates as by-products of British society's preoccupation with wealth and property. As a consequence Critchley's analysis takes on a sequential pattern (Manning 1977, p. 42) that ignores not only the changes that took place in British society over this broad time-span, but also the emerging central concerns of property, and the accumulation of profit that allowed and required the magistrates to 'trade in justice' (Landau 1984).

The demise of the status of the constable and the rise to power of the JP came about slowly as part of a gradual movement towards the centralization of power. For a while it was possible to ensure institutional stability by the imposition of sanctions, but the establishment of London as more than a seat of government was making new demands upon the ingenuity of the nation's rulers.

London: the Mother of Capitalism and Congenital Disorder

Nineteenth-century London was no longer, in the words of Stedman-Jones (1971, pp. 14–15), 'simply the home of the Court, the Parliament and the national government; it had also become the capital of a vast new empire, and just as Rome had often been at the mercy of its mob, so London, impregnable from without, might become vulnerable to an even more potent and volatile threat from within'. Stedman-Jones and, in more detail, Hall (1962) have noted that London's economic importance hinged upon the Port of London, the city's position as the largest consumer market in England, and thirdly its place as a centre of government. However, London's great distance from the centres of coal production and the exorbitant duty imposed by the Corporation of London on incoming consignments of coal (Stedman-Jones 1971, p. 19), along with the high cost of scarce land around the metropolis, meant that large-scale factory development was a doubtful proposition compared to the North where cheap land and labour were abundant. As Booth pointed out, 'The absorption of space for industrial purposes is not necessarily an increasing factor in city areas, and at their centres it is even a decreasing one' (Booth 1902, Vol. 17, p. 181).

The bulk of London's workforce was engaged in five major industries—clothing, wood and furniture, metals and engineering, printing and stationery, and precision manufacturing (Stedman-Jones 1971, p. 21). None of these industries was subject to large-scale factory production methods. Correspondingly, the discipline required by factory manufacture was not a major influence on London's working class. Men working in small workshops were normally employed on a casual basis. 'Job and finish' required the labour of the worker for a fixed period of time. This limited contract normally coincided with seasonal market trends, spasmodic supply of raw materials, or uncertainty of demand, and resulted in a worker–owner relationship more unconventional and inclined toward the independence of the worker than the traditional factory system could invoke. Consequently, there evolved in London, a breed of worker whose independence was a direct result of the relations experienced in the workplace (see Samuel 1981, pp. 93–105). This ethos of independence marked out the London working class as a breed apart from their counterparts elsewhere, particularly in the north of England where the rigours of factory work enforced a form of discipline that tended to inspire acceptance of the given order. Factory discipline complemented and enforced conservative notions of family, and the patriarchal hierarchy of early capitalist society found its stereotype in male–female shop-floor relations (Perkin 1974, pp. 150–7).

Those who made up London's casual work-force had few occupational reins upon their life-styles and consequently their moral and sexual habits along with their drinking and gambling were allowed to continue unfettered by the dull grind of a factory job. As a consequence London's vast army of casual and unemployed workers was regarded generally as a threat due to its often obstructive habits, disregard for property, and its frequent manifestation as 'the mob' (Silver 1967).

By Pistol, Foot, River, Horse, and Basket:
Policing as Pentathlon; Some Early Attempts

> A magistrate in the London area could expect his home to be besieged by people with requests for summonses and warrants, invitations to correct an error of the Poor Law authorities, or demands that he sign one or other of the various documents that needed a JP's endorsement
>
> Tobias (1979, pp. 28–9)

Additionally the increased incidence of crime in the Metropolis that accompanied the explosion of population required the magistrate to sit in court for longer (Brogden 1987, p. 7). The task tended to fall increasingly on men who looked upon the magistracy as a means of employment (Tobias 1979, p. 29). Various forms of bribery, payments, and inducements became established, mainly as a result of petty offences such as begging and prostitution, for offences against property as previously noted were dealt with with unflinching severity.

The constable and his watch were also under pressure in the early eighteenth century. Apart from his duties in relation to the supervision of the watch, the constable had acquired over the years responsibility for dealing with minor disorder, carrying out warrants, and many more duties under the Poor Law regarding vagrancy. Given the part-time nature of the post, and the aforementioned tradition of deputizing, it is of little wonder that the efficiency of the watch system deteriorated and became of little value in solving the problems of crime and order in London. Slack supervision and vague role definition, despite intermittent attempts at reform (see Tobias 1979, p. 38), resulted in an ineffective force of reluctant but, after 1735, professional, watchmen. The professional watchman was employed by the parish as a response to local problems and consequently the tasks of the watch varied from parish to parish and tended to reflect the fears of the propertied class who controlled the parish council. Watchmen appear to have spent their time guarding premises.

Thomas De Veil was, in 1729, appointed as Justice for Middlesex and Westminster, and despite his unofficial status as a 'trading justice', he proved especially diligent in his efforts against criminals, and encouraged the apprehension of wrongdoers committing offences within his jurisdiction. So successful was he in fact that he was soon awarded the position of Court Justice, a post which had existed since Elizabethan times. The post required the holder to carry out, in exchange for a salary from secret funds, confidential business that, while needing a magistrate's powers, did not require the attention of the Secretary of State. The general maintenance of order in the capital was deemed to come under this category (Ascoli 1979, pp. 32–4).

De Veil endeavoured to make a 'fair profit' yet administered justice with relish, rapidly acquiring a reputation as the 'principal scourge of the criminal class' (Ascoli 1979, p. 33). From his home in Bow Street, De Veil almost single-handedly conducted a campaign against crime. In seventeen years he ordered the execution or transportation of 'above 1900 of the greatest malefactors that ever appeared in England' (Ascoli 1979, p. 34). By 1748 when Henry Fielding took over De Veil's job, the post of Court of Justice was established as central to the apprehension and trial of London's criminals.[3]

In 1753, Henry Fielding acquired £600 from the Duke of Newcastle to pay for informers and what Ascoli euphemistically calls 'the encouragement of public co-operation'. The scheme run by a small group of operatives was a success, and crime did drop. This success prompted the benevolent Duke to continue paying an annual grant for the maintenance of what became the nucleus of the Bow Street Runners.

Policing as a Trade: the Emergence of the Thief-taker

Fielding originally recruited seven men, six of whom were Westminster constables. How—or even if—they were paid is a matter for contention. Tobias (1979, p. 46) claims that Henry Fielding paid the Runners, first from a secret fund, and later from the Duke of Newcastle's annual allowance. Ascoli (1979, p. 38), however, suggests that the Runners made their living quite legitimately from collecting rewards. Indeed while the services of the Runners were available to anyone who could afford them, the rewards payable for 'prosecuting to conviction' were considerable. For instance, a 'coiner' who had been working in silver or gold was worth £40 to a Runner, and

---

[3] For a fuller description of De Veil's career, see Armitage (1937, pp. 25–37).

highway robbery £40 also, plus the horse, furniture, arms, and money of the convicted felon (Dilnot 1929, p. 19).

This particular trade in justice was an open and lucrative market, particularly if the sums paid by grateful avenged victims are considered additionally. The most famous Runner, John Townsend, in answer to criticism levelled against him replied:

Officers . . . have it frequently in their power to turn the scale when the beam is level on the other side. I mean against the poor wretched man at the bar; why? This thing called nature says that profit is in the scale; and melancholy to relate but I cannot help being perfectly satisfied that frequently has been the means of convicting many and many a man (Dilnot, p. 19).

Townsend was indeed a remarkable man. On a guinea a week he had accumulated on his death in 1832 £20,000. According to Reith the Runners took a full and active role in crimes against property and became 'little more than a corrupt organisation for drawing the financial rewards offered for the conviction of criminals and for the return of stolen goods between robbers and robbed' (Reith 1948, p. 28). The Runners however, were corrupt only in relation to the imagery and rhetoric of twentieth-century British policing. Even then only the scale and bravado entailed distinguishes Townsend from certain contemporary 'thief-takers'. Reith omits to mention that in Townsend's day there was no unified police force, let alone a police mandate. He attempts, quite simply, to apply twentieth-century morality to an eighteenth-century scenario.

The Runner was a thief-taker, he was rewarded by the court and by victims of crime. He was also able to acquire additional sums by acting as a guard at certain prestigious institutions such as theatres, the Opera House, and the Bank of England.[4] The scope for augmenting his income in other ways was considerable. Runners set up burglaries, arrested the perpetrators, and collected the reward (Armitage 1937, p. 196). Bribery and blackmail were also available to the intelligent Runner with bills to pay, but all these activities, as with the activities of the trading justices, were carried out within the ethical parameters of commercial practice and traditional patronage.

In 1763 the Horse Patrol was implemented in an attempt to stem the rise in highway robberies on the approaches to the Metropolis.

---

[4] Townsend himself was, in 1814, employed by the court to perform special duties related to protection of the king, for which he was paid an additional £200 per year (Armitage 1937, pp. 264–7).

This consisted initially of eight non-uniformed men who were paid four shillings a night, plus expenses, to patrol on horseback. Despite its great success, it was discontinued after just one year for economic reasons.[5]

In 1798 the Marine Police Establishment was set up, consisting of sixty salaried officers, and as Critchley observes this was a larger full-time force than the other police offices put together. This is most certainly due to the fact that four-fifths of the total cost of the Thames Police was paid by West Indian merchants (Critchley 1971, pp. 42–3). Therefore they were able (until 1800 with the Thames Police Act) to function as a private security force employed to deal with the '10,000 thieves, footpads, prostitutes and pilferers at work' (Critchley 1978, p. 42) along the river. For as Tobias (1979, p. 53) has noted: 'There were no docks and quays for unloading ships at this time, and goods had to be discharged over the ships side into lighters lying alongside vessels anchored in the Pool of London. This complicated system provided endless opportunities for theft.' The most notable attempt at establishing a policing system not concerned almost exclusively with property crimes was made in 1782. Named the Foot Patrol and controlled by Bow Street, it was implemented as a response to the growth in street crime. Its members were not uniformed, but were armed. They were paid a salary and recruited from the ranks of the Runners and the force appears to have evolved from occasional patrols of Runners sent out spasmodically over a twenty-year period.

The force was augmented in 1821 by the interestingly named 'Dismounted Horse Patrol', an additional body of 100 uniformed men whose task was to patrol the suburbs. As a uniformed preventative force these men appear to have avoided conflict by limiting their actions to suburban areas for, as I will point out later, the uniformed presence of policemen was met in London with less than a whole-hearted welcome.

The addition in 1828 of twenty-seven men for uniformed daytime foot patrols meant that along with the constables of the various police offices, the patrols, and river police, there was a total force of 450 men concerned with the full-time policing of London, all under the overall command of the Home Secretary. Additionally there were

[5] The Horse Patrol reappeared in 1805 as an armed uniformed patrol, and appears to have been acceptable to the population as a deterrent to highwaymen (Tobias 1979, pp. 51–2).

approximately 4,500 watchmen within the Metropolis. Henry and John Fielding from their base at Bow Street had established that policing was not a parochial matter, and in utilizing the patrols built a disjointed system of policing that was centred on Bow Street. The patrols operated up to twenty miles from the centre of London, and as Ascoli (1979, p. 57) noted, they created, in the carrying of arms and wearing of uniforms a remarkable and successful precedent for preventative policing.

Despite the success of the patrols in limiting highway robbery, certain issues served to limit the effectiveness of the force as a whole. Firstly, there was an emphasis upon dealing with, or preventing crimes against property. Secondly, the police did not constitute a unified force. Despite control by the Bow Street magistrate and the Home Secretary, the roles of the various branches remained vague, and manpower insufficient. Thirdly, the policemen continued according to tradition to sell justice.[6] As James Townsend candidly noted 'nothing can be so dangerous as a public officer, when he is liable to be tempted: for, God knows, nature is at all times frail, and money is a very tempting thing' (quoted in Tobias 1979, p. 49). Or as a contemporary CID officer commented on an approach by a professional criminal: 'If he wants something from me, I want something in exchange. So I said "What have you got for me?" Nothing? No deal. It's business!'

The Political Philosophical and Economic Context of the 'New Policing'

My attention has been drawn to the political and philosophical climate from which the 'New Police' emerged, as a reflexive response to what I regard as a tendency by many historians to present the evolution of the police as a logical, civilizing inevitability (see Emsley 1983; Brogden 1987). Political action, of the scope involved in the introduction of a state-run police system, takes place within a political milieu whose conflictual parameters are determined by the perceived interests of specific groups. To ignore power as a vital

---

[6] The remarkably frank testimony of Townsend to the Parliamentary Committee of 1816 is extremely valuable in an analysis of the businesslike attitude of early police entrepreneurs. See Armitage 1937, pp. 263–7; Tobias 1979, pp. 48–49; Ascoli 1979, p. 39; Dilnot 1929, pp. 18–21.

component in the formation of the police, as Reith and Critchley tend to, ignores how intellectual activity can be exploited in the interests of those for whom institutional change would be an advantage (Brogden 1982).

One particularly influential thinker of the time was Blackstone, who in his concern for propriety and good neighbourhood coined the phrase 'preventative justice' (Radzinowicz 1956, p. 418). This was Blackstone's answer to 'punishing justice' yet, as Radzinowicz indicates, 'preventative justice' did not include any mention of the police, only vague references to medieval efforts at promoting order, such as pledges and securities. For Blackstone the 'concept of the State' was grounded firmly in the rule of law, yet in his suggestions regarding its enforcement Blackstone's concern shifts to a fear of standing armies. The standing army could threaten and not support the status-quo, and would constitute a dangerous tinkering with what was regarded as a natural system, whose imperfections were a small price to pay for liberty.

Adam Smith, however, was able to include a notion of policing within his proposed political framework. Smith's notion of policing was, it must be stressed, very different from any contemporary model that we might recognize. Smith's police would have been general regulators of the city, concerned with such issues as cleanliness, and he tended to disregard the police as effective controllers of crime.[7] For Smith, policing encouraged a state of dependency, which was in itself corrupting, as opposed to independence which in some way put the onus on the individual and increased honesty (Radzinowicz 1956, p. 422). In place of the police, commerce and manufacturing would create independence, which would, in turn, eliminate the need for individuals to commit crime: 'Nobody will be so mad as to expose himself upon the highway, when he can make better bread in an honest and industrious manner' (Adam Smith on highway robbery, quoted in Radzinowicz 1956, p. 428).

For Smith then, policing was not synonymous with security, nor in fact were police essential to public administration at all. Improved law and order could only be achieved through a rapid expansion in the scope of existing economic enterprise, thereby enveloping the

---

[7] Radzinowicz (1956, Vol. 3, p. 422) points out that Smith compared the rigid police system of Paris where there were many murders to the relatively unpoliced London where there were few homicides. Smith concluded that the police were an unnecessary complication.

individual in the healthy pursuit of profit and personal self-improvement.

Paley regarded the administration of criminal justice as a central issue and not as a peripheral concern. Even so, Paley's views on the police were disparaging. Paley tended to concentrate on the necessity of punishment as a preventative measure and his restraint on the issue of policing was due to the direct link that he identified between the police and despotic forms of government.[8] According to Paley, the police 'subtract from the necessity of severe punishment' (Paley, quoted in Radzinowicz 1956, p. 425).

For all three of these influential thinkers, policing was at best of secondary importance to issues of (a) the state and (b) the economy, and at its worst a direct threat to liberty. As Radzinowicz (1956, p. 425) has noted, their fears sprang from 'their concept of the proper province and powers of the state in relation to what they conceived to be the natural and unalienable rights of the individual, the political freedom which all should enjoy and the rule of law by which society should be governed'.

Penal reform, with ideals concerning punishment at the forefront, was the primary consideration of most reformers of the era. Problems regarding the relationship between the state and the individual were avoided by concentrating upon the relatively uncontroversial area of the liberalization of the penal system. In this way individual liberty remained sacrosanct. However, the utilitarians in general, and Jeremy Bentham in particular were, as Radzinowicz (1956, p. 431) explains, 'unhampered by the dead weight of traditional thinking'.

Bentham's concept of the state allowed for state institutions to make a reality of the utilitarian principle of creating the greatest happiness of the greatest number. Bentham was in favour of change and alteration of laws and institutions. He pronounced that antisocial actions should be restrained, and that virtuous actions should be encouraged by an overtly public-spirited legislature. In short, Bentham proposed an extension rather than a restriction of government power.

The Benthamites were given an ideological boost by Beccaria (1767), quoted in Radzinowicz (1956, p. 426) who argued that: 'It is better to prevent crimes than to punish them. This is the chief aim of every good system of legislation, which is the art of leading men to

---

[8] Despotism here is related to the Continent in general and the French in particular. I will return in more depth to this subject later.

the greatest possible happiness, or to the least possible misery, according to calculations of all the goods and evils of life.'

This opened the way for utilitarians to consider a means of prevention that might exclude the need to punish. For although the idea of punishment was to prevent similar offences being committed, 'the greater number of offences would not be committed if the delinquents did not hope to remain unknown. Everything which increases the facility of recognising and finding individuals adds to the general security' (Bentham, quoted in Radzinowicz 1956, p. 433).

There came about a general belief among the utilitarians that an element of coercion on behalf of the government was inevitable if security from crime was to be established (see Radzinowicz 1956, p. 442). The 'preventative principle' became firmly established by Bentham.

Under a 'Preventative Minister', the police function was defined under eight headings: (1) prevention of offences; (2) prevention of calamities; (3) prevention of endemic diseases; (4) police of charities; (5) police of interior communications; (6) police of public amusements; (7) police of intelligence and information; (8) police of registration and recording.

Chadwick inherited Bentham's ideas concerning preventative policing, but added an enhanced theory of criminal motivation. For Chadwick crime was merely another form of socially undesirable occurrence (Radzinowicz 1956, p. 450). Chadwick had, as Radzinowicz noted, written some years earlier on the subject of public health, and argued for preventative measures being taken against disease. Disease and crime, sanitation and prevention, provided a powerful mixture of metaphors with which to explain social problems. Vivid descriptions of the sanitary conditions of the eighteenth- and nineteenth-century London are not hard to find. Pearson (1975), Rogers (1972), Schoenwald (1973), and others have all given powerful testimony to the sights, smells, and tangible evidence of the appalling plight experienced by London's poor. More importantly, however, numerous writers have utilized sewage and drains as guiding metaphors for an examination of urban deviance. Pearson (1975, p. 161) sums up the mood of the era:

Foul wretches, and 'moral filth' lay heaped in 'stagnant pools' about the streets. When they moved they were seen to 'ooze in a great tide'.

The population was 'slime' which gathered in ghettos which were described as 'poisoned wells', 'canker worms', 'sinks of iniquity', and 'plague spots'.

Their houses were described as 'cesspits'; and their way of life was a 'moral miasma ...'. The City 'reeked of vice', the 'scum' and the 'dregs' of society was a 'moral debris' and 'residuum' the words 'pustule', 'fever' and 'wart' came readily to hand when describing the moral condition of the labouring and dangerous classes.

It is also worth noting that the new sewerage system, as with the lower orders, represented a financial commitment on the behalf of property owners, thus linking to an even greater extent in the minds of the emerging middle class the non-productivity of both kinds of human excrement. Sewage was as potent a threat as the labouring classes and consequently was accorded similar imagery. When Mayhew wrote of the costers as 'vast dungheaps of ignorance' (Mayhew 1952), the suggestion is that they should be dealt with accordingly. The term 'residuum' referred both to 'the offal, excrement and waste which constituted the sanitary problem and ... to the lowest strata of society that constituted the social and political problem' (Himmelfarb, quoted in Pearson 1975, p. 162).

The sanitary and moral conditions of the poor were regarded as one and the same problem, both emanated from the harsh reality of man at his worst, and the problems concerning the moral and physical conditions of nineteenth-century society were found in the sewers. The unemployable residue of urban society might at any time have overspilled into the streets, contaminating respectable members of society.

Control of urban man and his sanitary habits was vital if some semblance of order was to be maintained, and threats to an orderly healthy existence eliminated. 'The coincidence of pestilence and moral disorder' (Chadwick 1842, p. 132) was a potent political statement. Chadwick's call for a physical restructuring of the city was a deliberate attempt to eliminate those habits of the labouring classes that seriously hindered the type of working practices that were integral to the factory system of labour.

Chadwick's attempts at public health reform were more than efforts to improve the sanitary conditions of the working class. What was at issue was 'the regulation of disciplined work habits and reasonable political attitudes among labouring man, and not just a regimentation of their bowels' (Pearson 1975, p. 171).

Chadwick's shift in concern from sanitation to policing is, in the context of nineteenth-century political thought, a natural movement. The shift that led Chadwick to consider from where the disease of crime emanated was not inspired by an interest in the social conditions that inspired crime, for the rookeries and other such structures had been long associated with criminal behaviour, but in the moral sense: why did Man commit crime?

For Chadwick crime was an attempt by the individual to acquire leisure cheaply. Accordingly, if the individual was successful in attaining leisure with less effort than by honest work, the need to work would be negated. Chadwick maintained that if individuals were to continue to bother to engage in conventional employment, the consequence of crime should be pain, not pleasure. If the chance of being apprehended was high, Chadwick concluded, a greater number of people would be deterred and penalties would be less frequently imposed. To prove his point Chadwick cited the rarity of highway robbery as being due to the presence of the Horse Patrol on the roads leading into the metropolis.

The idea of a preventative police force was forwarded as a means of reducing the chances of a criminal escaping, and to provide generally a restraining influence on the population. As Radzinowicz has noted however, Chadwick did not adequately explain how this proposed system of policing should be organized. Issues of control and centralization, both crucial to the fundamental issue of state policing, were avoided. This omission was probably, as Radzinowicz (1956, pp. 469–70) has suggested, due on Chadwick's part mainly to expediency, for as the debate on policing progressed, the utilitarian camp acknowledged that the whole of their project could be decried on the grounds of these two contentious issues. Chadwick's reticence then was due to fear of antagonizing public opinion.

Chadwick, following Bentham, established the idea of policing within a centrally organized 'preventative service'. He identified criminal motives and postulated how these motives and subsequent actions might be countered. While 'preventative police' remained a vague term, the utilitarians injected the rhetoric of prevention into the growing debate on policing. The implantation of prevention into the police debate helped create an intellectual and political climate that could be exploited by Peel in his efforts to establish his 'New Police'. The continued use of the term 'prevention' during the late eighteenth and early nineteenth-century in relation to a proposed system of state-controlled policing, finds certain parallels with the use of 'community' in the contemporary debate concerning state control over the policing of the metropolis in the 1980s. Both terms were on their inception regarded as radical, yet became with time absorbed into the rhetoric of conservative policy. The original meaning is then lost, the offered definition no longer posing a threat, and the concept becomes an integral component of the pronounced philosophies of both radical and conservative groups alike.[9]

However, even the considerable tool of 'prevention' was sorely tested in overcoming the fear of 'Continental policing'. The antagonism towards Continental policing that was voiced by British politicians in the early nineteenth century, has had far-reaching implications for the form of social control that is dominant in Britain to this day. The constant state of war between France and Britain throughout most of the eighteenth and early part of the nineteenth century produced criticisms of French institutions in general, and French methods of policing in particular. Continental policing was used as a metaphor for threatening alien power in a similar way to the enduring utility of the Gestapo as a metaphor for oppression in general.

While this attitude may have found its roots in 'national xeno-phobia' (Whitaker 1979, p. 174), it was not entirely without foundation. The establishment of the Marquis d'Argenson's *mouchards* in the late seventeenth century, in order to penetrate lower-class criminal gangs, established a precedent for French policing that soon gained entry to well-established aristocratic family networks, and became no longer concerned purely with information to expose criminals (De Polnay 1970, p. 18). Sexual and moral habits were monitored by an elaborate network of informants employed in brothels, and by 1776 the police controlled the lives of many well-to-do families. As De Polnay (1970, p. 23) noted, many members of the aristocracy consulted the Lieutenant of Police as to the suitability of their children's intended marriage partners. Servants, newsvendors, and anyone requiring police co-operation in gaining employment were easily recruited into this ever-expanding network.

De Polnay (1970, p. 24) writing of the regime of Police Lieutenant Lenoir noted: 'If anybody had anything to hide, Lenoir spoke to him, and since Lenoir knew everybody's secrets, more often than not the man would agree to work for him. Thus, Knights, counsellors of Parliament and magistrates spent their time spying on each other.'

The French Revolution of 1789 brought the notorious Lieutenant

---

[9] For instance, all major political parties pronounced the virtues of 'community policing'.

Fouché to prominence, and the police informant network was strengthened and became explicitly political, adding the *agent provocateur* to the long-established French police institutions of informants and spies. British hatred of the French and the fear of revolution constantly fuelled the argument against policing. At its best the police idea was regarded as an alien-power element, and unnecessary to the functioning of the state, and at its worst a tyrannical evil.

The British ruling classes were able to deal with mass outbreaks of rural disturbance by utilizing the most powerful military force in Europe. Consequently, civil disobedience was observed at some distance by the rural rich, but in the cramped, expanding cities of early nineteenth-century Britain, the plight of the poor affected the rich, whether through cholera or pickpocketing, gin-swilling or sanitation. It was not long, therefore, before desperate efforts at distancing themselves from the great unwashed were being made by both the rich and the emerging middle classes.

Fear of a rampant urban working class, wracked by gin, and without the tight reins of factory discipline, resulted in residental segregation and discriminatory legislation (Rubinstein 1973, pp. 6–7). It also initiated a gradual movement towards a means of preventing crime to parallel improved control of cholera. The traditional landed gentry were still immune from this new dangerous class,[10] but the new middle class, whose power was based in emerging commercial interests, experienced the poor daily, and 'As government grew an administrative structure clustered in London, and the idea of state control began to emerge' (Manning 1977, p. 47).

This idea, as Manning has noted, indicates a slow evolutionary process towards a state-run police force, and any analysis should take into account as many factors affecting Britain as possible from the English Revolution onwards (see Styles 1987, p. 21).

The fear of a police force that represented the very essence of the republican threat[11] was only to be placated by conjuring up a representative of public good along the lines of an impartial socio-legal sanitary inspector. Miller (1977) has emphasized the deliberate

---

[10] See, Perkin 1969, pp. 170–1. Also Chesney 1968, pp. 102–24, and Stedman-Jones 1971, pp. 102–3

[11] Hay, in Fitzgerald *et al.* (eds.) (1981, p. 22), quotes Christian on the rationalization and clarification of law, who concludes that 'we should all be involved in republican gloom, melancholy and sadness'.

masking of the 'new police's' coercive power, and by adopting a visual image that was distinctly municipal and non-militaristic, the overt function of prevention, as symbolized by a benign, uniformed, obtrusive 'bobby', was established as the basis for the early British police mandate.

The emphasis upon prevention in the political rhetoric that led up to the formation of the Metropolitan Police is crucial (Reith, 1956, pp. 24–5, 135–6, 211–24). Reformers sought to manufacture 'a vigorous preventative police consistent with the free principles of our free constitution' (Peel, quoted in Radzinowicz 1956, p. 362). The dramaturgical presentation of civilian control in the form of a uniformed officer gained parliamentary approval in that the non-militaristic yet uniformed presence could only be preventative when it sought to act upon the populace on behalf of the state. Consequently, the early police presence was far from the threatening, insidious, unseen spy from the French system, and in forming a fully professional force of paid constables, visually accessible to all, the clientele were also easily distinguishable, and the internal binding of the organization assured (Manning 1977, pp. 128–9).

Enter Old Bill

The Metropolitan Police were formed in 1829 as a uniformed non-military force designed to prevent criminal activity, and as such were regarded by Parliament as an acceptable and uniquely British addition to the constitution. The essence of their power can be located in their uniformed presence as symbolic purveyors of the legitimacy of the state to intervene. As Rock (1973, p. 174) has noted: 'Their role is as much representational and symbolic as it is one centering on instrumental action.' The ideal-type uniformed 'bobby' represented the embodiment of an emerging system of law. In turn the law was to be regarded as neutral, and the policeman as the human representative of that unbiased mystical entity. If authorship of the law could be obscured, then any apparent bias could appear to be a misconception, and blame attributed to no one in particular. 'As a reified entity, law has an authority and concreteness which is independent of its creators' (Rock 1973, p. 127).

However, despite the fact that 'the law can be embellished by potent symbolism' (Rock 1973, p. 127), Peel's early recruiting drive spawned a force of men who were all too human. Despite his benign manifestation on the streets of London in leather top-hat and blue tailcoat, the Metropolitan policeman of 1829 displayed many of the frailties and habits of his clientele. The specifications for applying to the newly formed constabulary required men to be between the ages of 22 and 35 and of a minimum height of 5 ft 8 in.[12] The ability for an applicant to read his own handwriting was a requirement, and references from 'respectable people' had to be produced. Initially it was also policy to recruit men who 'had not the rank, habits or station of gentlemen' (Peel, quoted in Critchley 1971, p. 52). A deliberately low wage was set to deter officers from the navy or army from applying, thereby allaying fears of an organized standing army and ensuring the evolution of a force in which individual members would be subservient to the class who most feared its inception.

To ensure the PC's status as an agent of impersonal authority, free of local or class ties (Miller 1977, p. 26), Rowan and Mayne, the force's first Commissioners, preferred to recruit agricultural labourers (Gorer 1955, p. 308). There does not appear to be any official policy regarding the demographic origins of police recruits, yet Miller notes that of the forty-one policemen who gave evidence following the Hyde Park disturbances of 1855, only three came from the Metropolitan Police area. Brogden (1987, p. 11) notes that 'policing by strangers' is a common characteristic of colonial policing.

Once selected, strict rules regarding the living accommodation and private lives of the officers regulated all aspects of their existence. Any moral or residential anomaly was frowned upon, and officers were expected to live exemplary lives. It is of little surprise then that the turnover in manpower in the early years was extremely high. In the first two years of its existence over 8,000 recruits joined the force. However, in the same period, 4,000 resigned. By 1833 of a total strength of 3,389 only 562 were original recruits of 1829 (Reith 1948, p. 44; Ascoli 1979, p. 89). Incidences of drunkeness and incompetence appear to have caused this turnover, as the Commissioners applied the regulations with vigour. In enforcing these regulations, Rowan and Mayne were able to ensure that their men were isolated physically and culturally from the rest of the population, and so were able to appear as impartial purveyors of law and order.

[12] As Miller (1977, p. 26) notes, this was above the stature of most Englishmen at the time.

The uniform of the early policeman belied the military organization to which its wearer bore allegiance[13] and its conspicuous neutrality epitomized the preventative principle upon which the force was grounded. As Ascoli has noted, the men were dressed in a uniform that, while unmistakable, was not too different from standard civilian attire of the era. British policing was established from its inception to be the prerogative of the uniformed constable and, as a symbolic manifestation of law and order, his duty was to prevent crimes by his very presence. As Manning (1977, ch 1). indicates: 'Police are in symbolic terms the most visible representation of the presence of the state and the potential of the state to enforce its will upon citizens.'

When this presence becomes invisible, covert, and indistinguishable in appearance from the policed, it has been traditionally perceived as un-British, and therefore threatening. However, the original 3,300 uniformed men of the Metropolitan Police met with hostility from society in general and resistance from the working class in particular. The objections of the new middle class to Peel's police were not only ideological; they also objected to the expense of the force, and this economic consideration found favour in the press, whose vitriolic attacks on Peel and his men inspired more direct action against the police in a form that had previously been exclusively the prerogative of the lower orders. 'Peel's Bloody Gang' (Tobias 1979, p. 89) were whipped, beaten, stabbed, and killed, being fair game for all in the early years, culminating in the Cold Bath Field Riot of 1833, when the violent death of a constable prompted a coroner's jury to record a verdict of justifiable homicide. The verdict was subsequently quashed by a higher court, a verdict that had middle-class approval (Reith 1956, p. 166).

The ability of the police to control riots without military intervention swung political opinion towards an acceptance of the new police (Hall *et al.* 1978, p. 300). This came at a time when military action against civilians in the provinces was being employed with 'unprecedented vigour' (Tobias 1979, p. 90), and London's new police were slowly accepted as a preferable alternative to the 'cavalry

[13] Both Rowan and Mayne had distinguished military careers behind them, and many aspects of the police organization were borrowed from the army. For instance, the beat system was borrowed from the Light Infantry outpost training (Ascoli 1979, p. 85). The rank of sergeant came straight from the army, as did the tradition of teaching drill to recruits.

charges and volley firing by troops, and without blood letting and fatal casualties' (Reith 1956, p. 157).

The benefits of order to the commercial interests of the new middle class were becoming apparent.[14] Electoral reform in 1832 effectively marked the end of serious middle-class opposition to the 'crushers' by bonding them to the existing order and separating them from the interests of the working class (Miller 1977, p. 9).

All the long suffering in person and property from lack of police protection was promptly forgotten, but after some years of hostility, complaint, and agitation the peaceful citizen began to realise, almost unconsciously, that he could visit his neighbours in safety in the evenings, and that he need no longer fear seriously the menace of unruly mobs, or be obliged to rely on his own initiative and power for the protection of his house and his property (Reith 1938, p. 252).

The urban situation became simplified once the general support of the middle classes was achieved. In giving the new middle class a stake in the nation's order, it became apparent who constituted the police's antagonists. 'Active dislike of them, and active hostility against them, became increasingly confined to sections of the public and to individuals who were liable, in one way or another, to be frustrated in pursuit of their aims and activities by the police' (Reith 1956, p. 167).

The ethos of prevention when applied to the crucial areas of the mob, property crime, and street-trading, pitched the policeman into working-class areas, and with minimal opposition from the enfranchised middle class the problem of order was seen pragmatically as being associated wtih the life-style of the lower orders. In all cases, the essence of the policeman's authority was to be found in the wearing of his uniform. As Miller (1977, p. 33) notes, the 'scarecrow function' was a key element in the early emphasis on prevention.

The effectiveness of the British police measured in the early years in terms of their activities against the working class constituted action carried out without the restriction of a working-class presence in Parliament. This activity was resisted by the working class, especially the costermongers for whom police action meant loss of livelihood (Cohen 1979). The harassment of street-traders created,

[14] Miller (1977, p. 7): 'a shooting affray in the streets of the metropolis might destroy a substantial part of the nominal national capital'.

particularly among the costers, an institutionalization of opposition. The conspicuous nature of uniformed policing, the very essence of which is its high visibility, assisted this resistance. As Chesney (1968, p. 44) has noted, 'to "serve out a crusher" as they said was the most admired exploit a young coster could perform'. Popular working-class sports and pastimes were also dealt with by the police as a means of enforcing new public order legislation (Cohen 1979). However, the habits, livelihoods, and culture of London's urban working class were still firmly based on pre-industrial economies[15] and 'the police force was charged with introducing elements of urban discipline into a population which had not yet fully experienced industrial discipline' (Chesney 1968, p. 125).

Despite these daunting tasks, the uniformed policeman's success in controlling mass disturbances, working-class street-trading, and leisure (Cohen 1979) were sufficient to appease the propertied classes, yet as Stedman-Jones (1971, pp. 140–1) pointed out despite the 1834 Select Committee's report that the arrival of the new police reduced robbery and burglary, few people were arrested and only one-tenth of the property recovered. Manning (1977, p. 19) noted that the 'core' activity of the British police was defined in the preventative patrol. This was the basic visible activity of the police. However, the notion of preventative policing had been sacrificed early on in order that certain property criminals might be apprehended and certain political meetings infiltrated (Reith 1956, pp. 42 and 221).

Sir John Fielding had noted the prospective role of detection within a preventative framework (Styles 1987, p. 17). Yet unobtrusive police work was still officially frowned upon. The 'preventative principle', if not redundant, was certainly handed notice when in 1842 two inspectors and six sergeants founded the Detective Department. This acknowledgement of the police's role in unobtrusive plain-clothes detective work established an ambiguity between the police and the state on the one hand, and the police and the policed on the other, that has pervaded images of civil control in Britain to the present day.

I have already discussed the very real fear of Continental-style

---

[15] As Perkins reminds us: 'Although England remained predominantly rural throughout the "Old Society", by the mid-eighteenth century more workers were engaged in trade and manufacturing than in industry, and this was confirmed by the first census in 1801, when only just over a third of all families were allocated to agriculture as against two-fifths to trade manufacture and commerce. Some of these were self-employed, independent masters, but most worked for a merchant on his materials and often with his equipment under the domestic out work system.'

policing that initially hindered and then shaped the installation of a professional state-run police service in London. A covert style of policing using informers and spies corresponded, in British eyes, with invasion of privacy and restriction of individual liberty, and paralleled images of change and violent revolution. The early years of stalwart, uniformed 'bobbying' established the preventative principle and demonstrated to the propertied classes that they had nothing to fear from the new force. By allaying fears of alien despotism the new police were able to expand their activities into plain-clothes work. However, this was not without the periodic moral panic.

In 1833 a Sergeant Popay, who had been a schoolteacher before entering the police, disguised himself as a poor artist, and for several months spied upon a radical political group. When Popay's role was revealed there was a public outcry against police tyranny. Popay was dismissed, and a Parliamentary Committee, although they exonerated the police authorities from any involvement, were moved to condemn the over-zealous sergeant's conduct as, 'a practice most abhorrent to the feeling of the people and most alien to the spirit of the constitution'. The fear of a Fouché-style power network was real, yet the gradual realization that police action would be confined to action against the 'dangerous classes', created a new situation that was progressively amenable to an extension of police powers.

The key to this new-found trust can be located just four years after the foundation of the Metropolitan Police in the wording of the 1833 Parliamentary Commission: 'it appears to your Committee that the Metropolitan Police has imposed no restraint either upon public bodies or individuals, which is not entirely consistent with the fullest practical exercise of every civil privilege, and with the most unrestrained intercourse of private society.' 'Public bodies', 'individuals', and 'private society' were indeed untroubled by the presence of the Metropolitan Police's sturdy yeomen. Yet the working class, unrepresented in public bodies, disqualified from private society, and without the vote, property, or political influence hardly qualified as individuals in the sense applicable to the middle class. They encountered the police regularly as an added obstacle in an increasingly hazardous urban existence.

The emergence of the primary police role as that of rationalizers of the chaotic city, who would be concerned with controlling the working class, was accelerated by the Police Act of 1839. This Act, concerned with nuisance and petty disorders, established the service role of the police, and extended police activities into spheres of working-class life that may not have constituted a direct threat to the propertied classes, but were inconsistent with the dominant utilitarian model. The establishment of the service role, combined with the potent rhetoric of prevention, gave the police free reign to act against costers,[16] hawkers,[17] and pitch-and-toss players, (Cohen 1979) all of whom were regarded as being unable to enter into the normative exchange implied by the social contract. 'For social contract theory above all else insisted on the rewarding of useful activity and the punishment of damaging activity. Positive and negative characteristics were assigned to different kinds of behaviour in terms of their utility in a newly propertied society' (Taylor *et al.* 1973, p. 3).

Considering the hostility that greeted the Metropolitan Police on its inception, the speed at which it was accepted by the propertied classes is astonishing. The reason is quite simply that the new police served their interests in rationalizing social life by controlling a working class largely unaffected by factory discipline. As Gouldner has noted, 'the new middle class held in high esteem those talents, skills and energies of individuals that contributed to their own individual accomplishments and achievements' (Gouldner 1971, pp. 62–3).

The Evolution of the British Detective

Until the inception of the detective branch in 1842, the preventative principle as embodied in the uniformed patrolling officer was only violated by officers in plain clothes acting specifically against the working class. While the police could not legitimize detective work via the preventative principle, as it was not the working class who were sensitive to Continental styles of policing (Dickens 1986) and in any case no legitimate platform for working-class dissent was available, plain-clothes policing continued unabated and largely unnoticed by a middle class who were rapidly identifying any palpable threat to them as coming not from the police, but from the 'dangerous classes'.

The formation of the Detective Department in 1842 was only a

---

[16] The life-style of the costermongers and their relationships with the police is described by Chesney (1968, pp. 43–56); the hereditary nature of costermongering is referred to by Stedman-Jones (1971, pp. 61–2) and Mayhew (1952, pp. 76–9).

[17] The best example of the range of hawkers attempting to make a living on London's streets can be found in *Mayhew's Characters*, (ed.) P. Quennell 1951.

partial acknowledgement of the role of the plain-clothes policeman, and rigid rules of conduct designed to restrict the detectives' scope for action were enforced. They were, for instance, forbidden to mix with criminals, yet from its inception, 'A few detectives seem to have exploited qualities of native skill and cunning that matched the brains of major criminals' (Critchley 1978, p. 160).

From the early days the detective was caught between the demands of 'the job' and the official version of his practice. Initially this ambiguity resulted in the detective branch being pilloried for its inability to solve major crimes. Gradually the Detective Branch expanded, but its role was still viewed with considerable suspicion. When in 1877 the Criminal Investigation Department was formed with 250 men it was created against a backcloth of scandal. Three of the four chief inspectors of the detective branch had been found guilty of corruption (Ascoli 1979, pp. 143–6). Consequently the CID were regarded as requiring stringent controls and the newly appointed Director was ordered unofficially by the Home Secretary to bypass the Commissioner and report directly to the Minister (Prothero, 1931, p. 83). The Director, a lawyer by the name of Howard Vincent, was sufficiently politically astute to balance governmental interests with the prerogatives of policing practice.

Vincent studied and copied the centralized detective operation of the French Sûreté showing how quickly the 'Continental threat' had receded in the minds of the public. The CID was formed as a totally autonomous force with a structure and hierarchy bearing little resemblance to the uniform branch. Detectives could be recruited direct from civilian life, and received higher pay and status for CID duty.

The Metropolitan Police became a divided force, partitioned into two separate branches, each with rigidly defined functions. The higher pay awarded to the CID resulted in jealousy on the part of the preventative branch, and senior uniformed officers objected to officers operating on their patch over whom they had no authority (Ascoli 1979, p. 149). Vincent does not appear to have responded to the objections of the preventative branch and continued in his quest to 'abate the power of felons, so that where prevention failed, detection of crime would provide, an increasingly effective second line of defence' (Ascoli 1979).

However, the crude state of pathology, and lack of really effective forensic skills led to the popular conception of the CID as incompetent bunglers. This conception was inspired by the fictional detective Sherlock Holmes, who as an enthusiastic amateur was constantly outwitting the plodding professionals of Scotland Yard. As Ascoli (1979, p. 151) cogently points out: 'It is not without significance that perhaps the two most celebrated professionals in detective fiction were to be a Belgian and a Frenchman.'

Despite a gradual increase in arrests by detectives (see Ascoli 1979, p. 150) the CID was assuming a public identity that was part clown, part devil. The dark side was reinforced by the Titley case of 1880, when the sinister label of *agent provocateur* was again tagged to detectives' operations (Ascoli 1979, p. 150; Prothero 1931, p. 100).

The occasional scandal within the detective service reinforced the growing tension between the uniform branch and the CID. Both groups then as now considered that 'real police work' was the sole prerogative of their respective branch. This antagonism was never in the early years acknowledged by the heads of either branch. Sir Charles Warren wrote in 1883: 'The great aim of the present system is to keep up the most cordial relations between the uniform branch and the detective service' (Clarkson and Hall-Richardson 1889, p. 266). Indeed Warren as Commissioner appears actually to praise the CID and stresses the essentially English characteristics of the successful detective. 'Englishmen possess pre-eminently qualities which are essential to good detective work such as dogged pertinacity in watching, thoroughness of purpose, an absence of imagination and downright sterling honesty' (Clarkson and Hall-Richardson 1889, p. 266). It is difficult to reconcile these rather generous remarks with Warren's omission to make any mention of the CID in the Commissioner's Report just two years later! (Prothero 1931, p. 130.)

Vincent's progress in expanding the CID continued unabated and a special squad was set up to deal with the Fenian bomb campaign of 1883–5. Over this period twenty-two terrorist attacks mainly on prominent buildings took place. 'The Special Irish Squad' were successful where the uniformed branch's blanket protection of likely targets had failed. Consequently, the squad remained operational after the Fenian campaign, and formed the nucleus of the Special Branch, dealing with civil offences against state security (Allason 1983).

This specialization of detective work, accelerated by improved technology and growing expertise, appears to have enhanced the reputation of the CID officer as a more efficient authoritative image was constructed. In this respect 1901 was a milestone in the progression of the detective branch as Edward Henry introduced to the CID an efficient fingerprinting system which in turn facilitated the development of the Criminal Records Office that same year. This movement towards specialization and increased professionalization within the CID was furthered in 1902 by the setting up of a detective training school at Scotland Yard.

Information concerning the development of the CID is thin on the ground but it is aparent that periodic scandals concerning alleged malpractices occurred with almost predictable regularity, yet the insulation of the CID from the uniform branch has provoked writers of police histories to take an official view riddled with stock clichés concerning the abhorrent state of the detective force. This is due in part to the dearth of information regarding the CID and the control over official sources by the uniform branch (see Ascoli 1979, introductory chapter). In this light, his comment that, 'by 1922 the CID had become a thoroughly venal private army' (Ascoli 1979, p. 210), can be taken as a view typical of that taken by the contemporary uniform-dominated hierarchy of the Metropolitan Police, if not their predecessors.

One notable scandal that proved to be premonitory in terms of its location was that of Sergeant Goddard. Sergeant Goddard was stationed at Vine Street in the West End, and in 1922 was put in charge of a squad whose task was to deal with the increasing problem of vice that emanated from the area's burgeoning night-club industry. In 1928 after a series of anonymous letters, Scotland Yard began to investigate Goddard's affairs. Goddard was found to be living in a £2,000 house and driving an expensive American car. Additionally, he had amassed in two safe-deposit boxes some £12,471, the notes of which were traced to West End club-owners and brothel-keepers. Goddard claimed to have achieved both his life-style and fortune on his police pay of £6 per week. He received a hefty fine and eighteen months' hard labour (see Sherman 1974, p. 98).

Down these Dark Streets, Jeeves: The Early Imagery of the British Detective

The military structure of the Metropolitan Police perfectly complemented the well-defined duties of the uniform branch, and in turn reflected the militaristic careers of the Commissioners. Many senior soldiers were appointed to this post with varying degrees of success. Yet very few could come to terms with the detective branch, which continued to function as a separate autonomous unit, oblivious to the rigid structure imposed on their uniformed colleagues. Consequently, there developed a mystique around CID work. Without the predictability of shift work and freed from the strictures of pounding the same monotonous beat, the detectives developed a rogue identity that set them apart from the bumbling uniformed officer and his blimpish leaders. It is worth noting at this point that the 'rogue detective' finds dynamic, positive reinforcement in the portrayal of police work in the cinema of the day on both sides of the Atlantic. Yet in the USA J. Edgar Hoover's manipulation of the movie industry that marked the establishment of the 'G Man' as an acceptable model of law enforcement, found little comparison in Britain, where the cinema portrayed the detective as a gentleman amateur whose success was founded in a distinctly unprofessional methodology. (See Reiner 1985, pp. 146–63 for an excellent discussion of the meaning of fictional police work.)

Gideon's way was that of his ancestor in Baker Street, and the hero was not interchangeable with the villain. Cagney and Robinson could wield a 'Chicago violin' in the name of law and order or Al Capone, yet the very English, pipe-smoking gents of the 'Yard' remained typecast and were not to be confused with the criminal classes ('It's a fair cop guv'). Pat O'Brien and James Cagney emanated from the same tenement in the Bronx, or even the same impoverished family. Yet one grows up to be a dedicated detective (or priest or district attorney) and the other a gangster. Sexton Blake however had nothing at all in common with those he pursued, and Leslie Howard, George Sanders, and Ronald Coleman were all to inhabit a universe of English middle-class gentlemen, whose contact with the lower orders was purely professional, incidental, and conflictual. Crime was presented in the popular media of the United States as having a pathological base, resulting in a clash of good and evil. This clash was symbolized by actors whose differential roles owed nothing to their class, but was reliant on the individual pathology of the actors. The British detectives' qualities were those of the English middle class and those of his adversaries clearly to be attributed to the lower orders.

This dramatization of detective work is important in that it presents an image of the detective role that is in keeping with the prevailing social mythologies of the day, yet totally unrepresentative of plain-clothes work of that era. The lack of information about CID work leads the writer to utilize sources that are, due to their bias towards the establishment (uniform), unsatisfactory. It would appear then that the CID continued to function with minimum interference from the uniformed branch. The tension between the two branches however remained, and like the occasional corruption scandals, acknowledgement of this rift was periodically made.

An Old-established Firm

Commissioner Lord Trenchard, ex-RAF wrote in 1934, 'the state of jealous rivalry ... which has so long existed between the C.I.D. and the uniform branch is gradually being put to an end, and the two branches integrated into one harmonious whole' (Ascoli 1979, pp. 239–40). As Ascoli notes this was an empty threat and the CID continued as an autonomous service much as it had done from its inception in 1872. In 1938 the Detectives' Committee presented its findings after five years of research. It claimed that Britain lagged behind other nations, and paved the way for a general rationalization of detective work, involving systematic training, improved laboratory and forensic facilities, and a revamping of systems of communication. All these measures served to elevate the status and general efficiency of the CID and to isolate detectives still further from those police officers for whom prevention took priority.

Only the wartime measure of Special Branch expansion altered the CID function in the following thirty-five years. The ethos of prevention remained of primacy within the police service as a whole. Yet due to its structure on its inception in 1872 the CID remained a detective force, functioning as an autonomous body. Despite the occasional scandal, changes in the force served merely to bolster its isolation, and it remained an anomaly, a deviant group eventually numbering over 3,000 officers until Robert Mark was appointed Commissioner 100 years after its formation.

3

The 1960s: Investigation and Myth

The CID has evolved as a unique specialist branch of the police that is expected to perform duties and serve functions which are often interpreted not only as crucial to, but illustrative of, the very essence of good policing. The Metropolitan CID in particular have, through the dramatization of certain cases, gained an élite status. This is particularly true of the post-war CID which, in an attempt to challenge the hegemony of the preventative branch, has elevated the activities of key personnel to that approaching cult status. The three cases that I will focus on were selected because of the dramatic and bizarre detail of both the alleged crimes committed, and of the methodology or lack of it that is apparent in the subsequent police investigations.

These cases help us to understand how a formal organization evolves 'naturally' as a response to forces unrelated, or even opposed, to the formal rules and priorities of an administrative structure.

The Era of the Blue Lamp

After 1945 the uniform branch continued as the focal point of police work. 'Society has in our opinion a duty not to leave untried any measures which may lead not only to the detection of, but above all to the prevention of crime' (Introduction to the 1962 Royal Commission). The ethos of prevention was continually being reinforced. Debates concerning the police and the central issues of pay, police housing, recruitment, and relations between the police and the public, revolved around the uniform branch and the preventative function they were to perform.

Problems of public order dogged the Metropolitan Police throughout the late 1950s and 1960s, with political demonstrations in particular being carried out in the full glare of the world's mass media. Youthful disorder was centred mainly upon seaside towns as working-class adolescents took excursions to the coast. Consequently, the respective police forces of Southend, Margate, and Brighton in particular were able to acquire crowd control techniques beyond the scope and level of sophistication normally associated with declining seaside resorts. The pressure in the Met fell squarely upon the uniform branch. A.8, the branch of the Yard concerned with public order, was badly organized and inadequately equipped to cope with the demands made upon manpower and communications. Traffic control also required attention from the Commissioner Sir Joseph Simpson, and B Department, described by Ascoli as 'a highly professional team of specialists' and by one of my more eloquent informants in the CID as 'a bunch of wankers, no interest in crime, fucking Gestapo', came into being.

The CID continued to develop separately and the only alterations imposed upon it served to elevate its élite status still further. In 1960 the Robbery Squad was brought into being as an addition to the fêted Flying Squad (C.8), and in the same year Criminal Intelligence (C.11), and Stolen Vehicles Investigation (C.10) were formed. These squads promoted the image of the detective as a specialist and this image was boosted still further by the various activities of professional criminals, and by the subsequent investigations and prosecutions that followed.

The Great Train Robbery

The 1960s were marked by a series of dramatic and spectacular criminal episodes that served to emphasize the emergence of the Met CID as a specialist élite. In 1963 a gang of mainly professional criminals, most of whom were from South London, robbed a Glasgow to London train of over two and a half million pounds. Rumours concerning the robbery, fired by Fleet Street's desire to fill the void created by the parliamentary vacation, were as vivid as they were preposterous. Indeed, the media's continued references to the military precision with which the robbery was carried out prompted the robbers themselves to concoct a story connecting a notorious Nazi commando leader with the crime (Read 1979, pp. 53–69, 291–312; Biggs 1981, pp. 217–23. See also Biggs quoted in Macintosh 1971, p. 124).

Despite the fact that the 'Great Train Robbery' was committed outside London, the Met CID were called in immediately. The sum of money involved prompted a deluge of information, most of which turned out to be false, and the initial confirmation that a London 'gang' was involved came from an inmate of a provincial prison in an attempt to gain some additional privileges (Read 1979, pp. 141–2).

Brigadier Cheyney, the Chief Constable of Buckinghamshire County Constabulary, sought the assistance of Scotland Yard and Detective Superintendent Gerald McArthur was sent to Aylesbury to set up the investigation. When it became apparent that a London gang was responsible, the newly promoted Chief Superintendent Tommy Butler was put in charge. Butler had made his name by investigating the two pre-Kray bosses of London's West End, Jack 'Spot' Comer and Billy Hill. He had also been sent to Cyprus in the search for EOKA leader Colonel Grivas. In Cyprus, Butler was unsuccessful, whereas in London he appears to have received plaudits where they were not due. Spot and Hill were old-time villains who ruled with a heady mixture of money and diplomacy. When this mixture proved ineffective, and hostilities broke out in spring 1955, the up-and-coming Kray twins were able to stake their claim. The ageing Spot and Hill both retired around the summer of 1956, and for a while free enterprise boomed as various federations of their ex-associates tentatively established themselves. Eventually the Krays, under the tutelage of Billy Hill, were able to move 'up west' and with the assistance of the 1961 Gaming Act proceeded to amass a fortune.

All this had little to do with the efforts of 'Scotland Yard's greatest detective' (Pearson 1973, p. 184). Despite having spent a total of seventeen years incarcerated in various penal institutions, Hill retired to southern Spain of his own accord. Changes in the make-up of London's organized crime scene prompted the demise of both Hill and Spot, who retired to run a furniture business in West London, and the police had only bit parts in the action. Yet Tommy Butler somehow achieved a considerable reputation within the force, and his appointment to lead the train robbery investigation is indicative of the esteem in which he was held (see Williams 1973, p. 11).

It was, however, the local police who made the biggest break-through in the case by discovering the robbers' base for their assault on the train, Leatherslade Farm (Read 1979, pp. 142–3). A man named by Read as Mark was hired by the gang as a 'dustman' and was paid £28,500 to destroy all evidence at the farm after the robbers had left. Whether the fact that £10,000 of this sum was paid in ten-shilling notes in any way affected Mark's reliability we shall never know (Read 1979, p. 222). What is clear however, is that

Leatherslade Farm was discovered by the Buckinghamshire Police in the same condition in which the robbers left it.

The farm was littered with mailbags, bedding, vehicles and food, all festooned with the fingerprints of known villains (Read 1979, pp. 163–7; see also Biggs's opinion (1981, pp. 89–96) of the legality of some of the forensic evidence). The forensic evidence collected at the farm formed the basis of the police evidence against the robbers (Williams 1973, p. 13). Butler travelled the world for five years pursuing the robbers as they attempted to set up new lives for themselves and their families.

By 1968 Biggs was the only robber whose identity was known to the police who was still at liberty and Butler's name was constantly used by the 'media' as a byword for professional policing. Now head of the Flying Squad, Butler postponed his retirement to arrest Charlie Wilson in Canada and Bruce Reynolds in Torquay after the fugitives' flight from the south of France. Ronnie Biggs, however, after a successful conviction and his subsequent escape, continued to elude Butler, and another officer, Chief Superintendent Jack Slipper, arrested Biggs in Rio in 1974. Slipper was the last of the original train robbery squad still serving in the Met, and after a dubious collaboration with a national newspaper, eventually returned to London empty-handed due to the pregnant condition of Biggs's girl-friend, and Brazil's uncharacteristically liberal laws relating to extradition (Biggs 1981, pp. 190–209).

Butler died in 1970 one year after his retirement. Superintendent Frank Williams who had arrested Buster Edwards, another prominent train robber in September 1966, was regarded by many as Butler's natural successor as head of the Flying Squad, but had, in order to secure the conviction of Edwards, exhibited a certain amount of leniency in the presentation of evidence (see *Daily Telegraph*, 19 September 1966) in exchange for Edwards's co-operation. Edwards received a sentence of fifteen years, half the original sentences being served by many of those successfully convicted in 1964.

The CID hierarchy and Butler in particular were enraged at what they considered to be poor commercial practice by Williams when the evidence against Edwards, including finger- and palm-prints was so damning. Williams's leniency was a severe miscalculation and Slipper was eventually promoted above him. Subsequently, Williams left the force in 1971 to join Quantas Airlines as head of security.

The train robbers were apprehended as a result of their own incompetence. Yet despite the overwhelming forensic evidence gathered by the CID Biggs was never recaptured, and they were unable to uncover the identities of three principal participants (Read 1979, pp. 330–1).

The Richardson Brothers: A Model Investigation

From the late 1950s the brothers Charles and Edward Richardson had built up several lucrative businesses in South London. With a social and economic base in the scrap-metal trade they proceeded to expand their business interests into many seemingly disparate commercial areas including wholesale chemists, mineral-mining, fraud, blackmail, and extortion.

For the Richardsons, protection was especially lucrative mainly because of the lack of any real local competition. In East London the Kray organization constituted the dominant 'firm' and by the mid-1960s had established powerful alliances with potential rivals in North and West London, and had also formed associations with international criminal organizations (Pearson 1973, pp. 175–6, 236–8, 240–1). However, the Thames proved to be a more formidable natural barrier to criminal affiliation than the Atlantic, and the Richardsons operated unhindered by any interference from the Krays' more extensive organization. The Richardsons' various activities also went unhindered by the police; indeed, one of their illegal drinking-clubs prospered just a few hundred yards from a police station, and off-duty uniformed officers and on-duty detectives were valued customers.

The Richardson organization would probably still be prospering today had they not recruited some East End muscle, and gone on to underestimate what little opposition South London could offer. 'Mad' Frankie Frazer, the man who had 'striped' Jack Spot (Kray and Sykes 1976, p. 100), had joined forces with the Richardsons, and he still held grudges against the Kray twins from the mid-1950s when Frazer and the twins were on opposite sides in the Hill–Spot feud. Before the Krays had completed their succession of Hill's empire Frazer had posed a real threat to their organization. However, Frazer was imprisoned for the attack on Spot, and the Krays progressed without serious opposition until his release in 1964.

On his release Frazer formed a friendship with an ex-member of the 'Watney Street Mob' named Myers[1]. Apart from an enduring enmity between Myers and the Krays dating back to feuds about adolescent territorial imperatives, the Krays had destroyed a long fraud venture of Myers (Pearson 1973, p. 180). After meeting Frazer, Myers changed his name to Cornell, and in the search for employment the pair sought out the only alternative to the Krays and travelled south of the river to join the Richardsons. The South London firm promptly moved into the West End, Cornell and Frazer leading the vanguard.

Cornell took over a portion of a previously unaligned pornography business and Frazer took over a chain of fruit machines from the Krays. These insults were reinforced by Cornell's claim that Ronnie Kray was a 'fat poof' (Pearson 1973, p. 180; Kray and Sykes 1976, p. 170). Early in 1966 the twins were negotiating with the American Mafia over the proposed investment of millions of dollars in London's gambling industry. The twins would receive a percentage if they could guarantee that the clubs would be free from trouble. The South Londoners' sortie into the West End constituted a tangible threat to this new investment, and the Krays set out to eliminate the Richardsons, and in the process settle some old scores. Automatic weapons were acquired and old alliances reaffirmed as armed men took to the street. Before the two gangs could settle the matter, however, the Richardsons self-destructed. Mr Smith's Club in Catford was a very successful licensed gambling establishment. At 3 a. m. on 8 March 1966, a shooting occurred in the club involving a shotgun and an unknown number of hand-guns. The result of the shooting was one dead and five wounded. Among those arrested were Eddie Richardson and Frankie Frazer (Parker 1974, pp. 276–82). Nearly five months later Charles Richardson was arrested and charged with crimes of violence not directly related to the Mr Smith shooting. As a police officer who was serving in South London at the time remarked: 'They had to do something. It was out in the open; they couldn't ignore it anymore.'

Eddie and Charles Richardson received sentences of ten and twenty-five years respectively, and their trials were marked by bizarre accusations concerning their methods of retribution, including the

---

[1] The 'Watney Street Mob' were traditional adversaries of the 'Bethnal Green Mob' of which the Krays had been members. See Kray and Sykes (1976, p. 54); Pearson, 1973, pp. 97–9, 128–9.

use of pliers to remove teeth and fingernails, and attaching electrodes to the genitals of victims.

The police investigation of the Richardsons was significant in that it marked the introduction of certain tactics that were also to feature largely in the subsequent police campaigns against the Kray twins. Prominent amongst these tactics were arrest and detention without bail, giving the police the opportunity to gather together witnesses of doubtful character, who in turn were granted immunity and financial inducements to turn Queen's evidence. The similarities between the Kray twins' and Richardson investigations were assured when Chief Superintendent Tommy Butler was designated to take charge of the Mr Smith case, for just two days after the Mr Smith shooting an extraordinary event took place in Bethnal Green.

The Kray Twins: 1960s Chic and a Tradition of Violence

On the evening of 9 March 1966, Ronnie Kray walked into the Blind Beggar pub in the Mile End Road, drew a 9-mm. automatic from his shoulder-holster and shot George Cornell dead (Pearson 1973, p. 183; Kray and Sykes 1976, p. 171; Dickson 1986, pp. 26–34). Superintendent Tommy Butler was summoned and promptly put Ronnie Kray in an identity parade. The barmaid from the Blind Beggar failed to identify the killer and Ronnie was released. Tommy Butler proceeded to co-ordinate the two investigations north and south of the river and to assist him Assistant Commissioner Brodie enlisted another veteran of the train-robbery investigation, Chief Superintendent Leonard Reed.

'Nipper' Reed's first contact with the Kray twins came early in 1964 when he was promoted to Detective Chief Inspector, and posted to West End Central police station. By this time the Krays had established themselves in East, West, and North London and had fostered personal connections with all sections of society from villains to show-business personalities and members of the aristocracy. The twins were on the verge of making some potent international connections when Reed was ordered to head an inquiry into the Kray's involvement in protection, fraud, blackmail, wounding, and intimidation. The investigation was halted by a bizarre newspaper story concerning Lord Boothby and Ronnie Kray (Pearson 1973, pp. 165–9). The publicity that both the story and the ensuing libel action promoted stilted Reed's investigation and put the Krays on their guard against a possible police inquiry.

A man named McCowan, who part-owned a club in Soho, was threatened by 'Mad' Teddy Smith who, like McCowan, was a well-known homosexual in London's covert, pre-Wolfenden scene. Smith, who was described in court as a writer, demanded money from the club owner, supposedly on behalf of the Krays, and committed some £20 worth of damage.[2] The twins were arrested and kept in custody for three months pending trial. At the trial the twins were acquitted after the timely intervention of the Revd. Edward Foster of St James the Great in Bethnal Green on behalf of the defence. The twins promptly bought McCowan's club, renamed it, and celebrated their victory on the night of their release. Reed spent most of the evening outside the club noting names and faces as guests arrived. At some point that night Reed was invited into the party and was photographed drinking champagne with the twins. The effect of these photographs, which featured in both London evening newspapers, was almost disastrous for Reed. At the ensuing police inquiry Reed was cleared of improper behaviour and was immediately promoted (a mysterious decision in the light of this *faux pas*), before joining the train-robbery squad under Tommy Butler.

During this period the local police had little cause to become animated in response to the activities of the Kray twins (Dickson 1986, p. 11). Their 'business' enterprises served to reinforce a taken-for-granted sense of order built upon a solid foundation of independence, autonomy, and tough masculinity. The class solidarity of East London that had emerged from centuries of poor housing, casual work, unemployment, and individual entrepreneurial endeavour, emphasized these characteristics and, in turn, served to structure an informal but pervasive form of social control that by definition had tended to exclude representatives of society's master institutions (White 1983).

As integral agents of the indigenous social order the Kray twins were unproblematic to the local police force. In their world children, women, and old people were respected and kept in their place. The sense of decorum enforced at their establishments likewise rendered the police peripheral, their role being reduced to that of token representatives of the state. This is not to deny that the police did

[2] Charles Kray claims that this was a personal dispute between McCowan and Smith (Kray and Sykes 1976, p. 154).

have a role to play other than merely providing a symbolic presence, for as Mawby (1979) has shown and Taylor (1981) has suggested, there is a demand for policing from the white working class, particularly in response to street crime and violence: 'working class support for the police has appeared to increase the more that the traditional social controls of working-class community have been dislocated by post-war social and economic changes' (Taylor 1981, pp. 150–1).

While working-class resistance to the police has been diluted by social changes that preceded the Second World War, and negotiation took over from outright physical confrontation (Cohen 1979, p. 119), East London in the 1960s had retained sufficient of its heritage of dissent to maintain and support a thriving culture. Immigration to East London during the mid-1960s was minimal and inspired neither organized racist opposition nor demands upon the police for protection from black incursion (Taylor 1981, p. 151). Just as crucially, the rebellion of East London's youth was tempered by a relative boom in the local economy, particularly in the docks. The culture was still intact and the internal control mechanisms that drew so much upon the rich, autonomous isolation of East London's heritage before the dissolution of dock-work and the final destruction of the ecological base, took prime responsibility for the maintenance of the indigenous social order.

The Sport of Twins

The Kray twins were crucial to this social order. As Ronnie Kray said in an interview with the *Sun* newspaper: 'When Reggie and me looked after things in the East End there was never any of this mugging of old ladies or child killing. If anybody had started pulling strokes like that they would soon have been stopped' (*Sun* 20 July 1984). Whether they ever operated in such an altruistic manner is not entirely clear, but much of the Kray twins' activity was directed towards the reinforcement of a traditional social order that was as conservative, restrained, and self-confident in the defining of social parameters as that of the burghers of any leafy suburb or rural community.

Boys' clubs, charities, and the elderly all benefited from the Kray twins' business acumen and feel for publicity (Pearson 1973, pp. 152–3; Kray and Sykes 1976, photos, centre pages). They were frequently described as 'local sportsmen' in the press (Dickson 1986, p. 47).

They were tough, wealthy, and successful and the police had no cause to intervene. For as long as the Krays avoided project crime and their potential for violence remained discreet and integral to 'normal' economic and social order, the police were able to concentrate upon the indiscreet, the nihilistic, and the pathological. Indeed, it is the manifestation of the pathological that provides the most useful insight into police activity against the Kray twins.

In December 1966 they engineered the escape of 'Mad Axeman' Frank Mitchell from Dartmoor Prison. When the simple-minded Mitchell became an embarrassment he was killed and his body disposed of (Pearson 1973, pp. 189–200; Dickson 1986, pp. 95–107). In June 1967 Reggie's wife took her own life and, coupled with Ronnie's deteriorating mental state, this led to the murder of Jack 'the Hat' McVitie.

Since the slaying of Cornell, Ronnie had taunted his brother for his reluctance to commit murder. The more businesslike Reggie, while being an extremely violent man, had married and attempted to lead a more 'normal' existence. However, his wife's suicide resulted in Reggie drinking heavily and resorting to several vicious attacks on allies (Pearson 1973, pp. 205–8). McVitie, a well-known villain in East and North London, had been paid to murder someone on the Krays' behalf and had failed to carry out the mission. He had also pocketed Kray funds when involved in a scheme to distribute amphetamines. A feud developed and McVitie was seen searching for the twins, toting a shotgun. As a consequence of this indiscretion he was invited to a party in Stoke Newington and Reggie, encouraged by his twin, attempted to shoot him, only for the gun to jam. According to Pearson (1973, pp. 216–18) Reggie then butchered McVitie with a carving knife (see Dickson 1986, pp. 118–28).

In the autumn of 1967 Leonard Reed returned to Scotland Yard as a Detective Superintendent and joined the Murder Squad. Reed had behind him some successes under Tommy Butler in the train robbery investigations and he had also been in charge of a team of detectives dealing with crime instigated by the crowds visiting London for the 1966 World Cup. Early in 1967 Sir John Waldron was appointed Commissioner of the Metropolitan Police. Waldron was concerned with the publicity that the Richardsons had attracted and was embarrassed at the way in which the Krays flaunted themselves. An investigation into the twins' activities was ordered, headed by a Superintendent Walker. In the autumn, Walker was promoted and Reed was put in charge.

Reed was given his brief to operate an undercover team of fourteen investigators, with the headquarters at Tintagel House, a block of government offices in South London. The official line was that Reed was investigating a murder and that his team were looking into police corruption (Pearson 1973, p. 225), an issue due for its periodic airing. Reed began to contact villains and associates of the Krays and offered immunity from prosecution in exchange for any information rendered. This method produced little real evidence until Reed contacted the man that McVitie had been contracted to kill, Leslie Payne. McVitie's disappearance had terrified Payne and when approached he agreed to talk to the police (see Levi 1981).

Payne furnished Reed with 200 pages of evidence concerning fraud, assaults, protection, and Mafia connections. From Payne's statement, Reed was able to expand the investigation and began to achieve some positive results. However, most of those interviewed by Reed's investigators would only agree to give evidence in court if the Krays were safely locked up in custody. From Reed's position it became obvious that the entire Kray organization should be locked up to ensure that witnesses could not be intimidated.

At this point the police had no evidence connecting the twins with the murders of Cornell and McVitie, or the disappearance of Frank Mitchell. Reed's breakthrough was due entirely to Ronnie Kray's unbalanced mental state. Had the twins kept a low profile the costly police investigation would probably have petered out, but the stalemate was broken by Ronnie's dreams of grandeur. Pearson (1973, pp. 71–2, 78–9, 129–30) has noted how the Kray twins had attempted to model themselves on American gangster stereotypes and McVicar (1982, pp. 8–12) has noted the Krays' obsession with Hollywood gangsters. While the police kept a round-the-clock watch on the twins, Ronnie was able to leave the country and visit New York for a prearranged meeting with Mafia leaders. Despite the Mafia's failure to turn up, Ronnie was wined and dined and returned to London determined to reorganize the Kray 'firm' on the American model. Rumours that the mafiosi in New York no longer had faith in the Krays fired Ronnie's enthusiasm to make the 'firm' a potent force again. He promptly accepted a £1,000 contract for the killing of a Maltese club owner. The 'hit man' designated to carry out the murder was arrested in possession of four sticks of dynamite and the eight-month stalemate was over (Pearson 1973, pp. 241–8).

At this juncture, Reed's investigation was unexpectedly hampered by the presence of an *agent provocateur* working for the United States Treasury, who had set up the attempted murder (Pearson 1973, pp. 244–6). After the arrest of the hapless 'hit man', the twins again retreated and Reed was forced to take an unprecedented gamble. Shortly after dawn on 9 May 1968, all but two of the Kray 'firm' were arrested. Reed had enough evidence from the American Treasury agent and the would-be 'hit man' to keep the Krays on remand while a case concerning more serious charges was constructed. The remaining two members of the gang were arrested and potential witnesses emerged from the woodwork without fear of retribution. The barmaid from the Blind Beggar regained her memory and the twins were sent for trial (see Millen 1972, ch. 15).

By the time of the trial in January 1969, the entire structure of the Kray organization had crumbled. Several of those involved in the killings of Cornell and McVitie turned Queen's evidence. In total, some twenty-eight men gave evidence against the twins in return for immunity or much-reduced sentences. As McVicar has noted, most of the Kray gang appeared not in the dock, but in the witness-box (McVicar 1982, p. 12). One witness was actually present at McVitie's murder and, according to Reggie Kray, wielded the knife. Charles Kray also makes this claim (Kray and Sykes 1976, p. 225), yet despite admitting in court a part in the murder at least as important as that of Ronnie Kray, the man walked free from the Old Bailey as the result of a deal orchestrated by Reed (Dickson 1986, p. 159).

The twins got life imprisonment with a recommendation that this sentence should be not less than thirty years. Nipper Reed gained promotion to the rank of Commander in the Metropolitan Police and returned to his native Nottingham as Deputy Chief Constable, before retiring from the police to take up a post as Head of Security at the National Gallery.

The details of all three cases—the train robbers, the Richardsons, and the Krays—are important in that they give important clues as to how the CID presented itself in the 1960s and how they worked to gain crucial prosecutions against individuals who had committed crimes that were regarded as strategically important. Consequently those criminals were deemed to be especially dangerous and the subsequent investigations represented the dramatization of good versus evil and the affirmation of key roles among both criminals and the police. Deviance may well be a 'living insult to the gods' (Berger and Luckmann 1967, p. 117) but in the case of certain criminals who have rooted their activities firmly in the culture of the immediate locality, the police are well able to ignore such apparent blasphemy.

The Krays and Richardsons did not challenge social reality but reinforced it by conforming to behaviour traditional in entrenched urban working-class districts. I am drawn very briefly to Miller's class-based concept of focal concern (Miller 1958, p. 7). The Krays and Richardsons were able to take these focal concerns to the limit. Trouble, toughness, smartness, excitement, and autonomy featured prominently in the careers of both pairs of brothers. In the case of the Krays it would appear that when issues emerged from beyond the parameters of these concerns, then offences were committed that the police could no longer ignore.

Mental illness and homosexuality were two such alien issues. Whether Cornell would have been killed regardless of his 'fat poof' insult to Ronnie is a matter of conjecture. However, there is little doubt that had Reggie's disturbed young wife not been successful in her third attempt at suicide, Reggie may have rejected the pressures to succumb to the taunts of his insane brother and 'do his one'. As a consequence McVitie, albeit (perhaps) a maimed McVitie, would be alive today.

Despite the Krays' involvement in an array of lucrative criminal enterprises, the police were able to gain successful convictions only on these two unconnected, profitless murders. It is doubtful whether the charges upon which the Krays were remanded would have resulted in more than a three- to five-year sentence. These charges resulted from ridiculous schemes engineered by Ronnie and insti- gated by an American Treasury agent who later claimed to be working in collaboration with John Du Rose, the head of the Murder Squad.

While the Krays remained within the cultural parameters built upon the focal concerns of East London, the police were able to accept a state of truce with the twins. However, the issues of mental illness and homosexuality found no articulated precedent within the culture and led to extreme acts of violence that the police could no longer ignore. Once exposed, not as entrepreneurs and business men but as brutal murderers, the scene was set for the dramaturgical presentation of the Kray twins as the epitome of evil. The careers of the twins suddenly became 'interesting and set apart from other everyday evils' (Manning 1977, p. 23). Yet for some seventeen years the Krays' activities had been accepted as normal and unremarkable, except in the scope of their success. 'The human organism when it is working efficiently and experiencing no discomfort is said to be "healthy". When it does not work efficiently a disease is present. The organ or function that has become deranged is said to be pathological' (Becker 1963, p. 5). Murder carried out against a background of homosexuality and mental illness shifted the Kray twins' activities out of the normal and into the pathological and their inevitable prosecution constituted 'the selective presentation of behaviours for public view, and the symbolisations referring to these behaviours that can be interpreted as conveying a message or set of messages about the meaning of those behaviours' (Manning 1977, p. 23). As an experienced detective constable noted with more than a hint of regret: 'They went too far, as simple as that. They could have been millionaires, legit, by now, but they went too far.'

The Kray twins forced the police to act and it was not the CID's powers of detection that secured their prosecution but Reed's abilities as a negotiator. Reed secured immunity from prosecution for vital witnesses in exchange for damning evidence against the twins. This was due to an arrangement that Reed secured with the Home Office (Pearson 1973, p. 226) and while it resulted in prosecutions for the main actors, one of McVitie's killers and those immediately responsible for the escape and disposal of Frank Mitchell walked free.

Likewise, in the case of the Richardsons, the Mr Smith shootings forced the police to act. It was impossible to ignore a corpse and a brace of wounded gangsters. Once in court, however, the 'torture trial' unfolded to reveal a collage of evil as a backdrop to a morality play in which the police were portrayed as moral crusaders.

The local CIDs of both South and East London had coexisted with the Krays and Richardsons for many years, as had their predecessors with the likes of Jack Spot and Billy Hill. Occasional arrests had always been necessary for some misdemeanour but both the Krays and the Richardsons had made it impossible for the police to turn a blind eye in the case of murder. 'Outsiders' such as Reed then took over and the villains had to be seen to be punished.

Manning (1977, p. 107) has noted that: 'The responses of the police mark the limits of respectable segments of society, the boundaries of informal social control and the shapes and locations of evil.' The activities of the Krays and Richardsons were rooted in the working class and dominated by the previously mentioned focal concerns of that culture. By their limited response, the local police accepted that the Krays and Richardsons were not threats to societal boundaries and when they did respond to misdemeanours, the system of informal, social control of which the villains were an integral part was implicitly reinforced. As Manning (1977, p. 103) also notes, while the police force may be bureaucratically organized, much of police action is situationally justified. This can be illustrated by the police attitude to both gangs during the 1960s. 'They didn't mug old ladies or hurt kids; they only hurt their own. The "old bill" didn't want the "ag"; then they went too far' (CID officer on Krays). It suited the police to ignore the activities of the gangs at a local level and this could justify their inaction, both in terms of maintaining an equilibrium and the moral argument typified by the CID officer's statement.

The train robbers, in leaving so much evidence for the police, also made it difficult for the police not to prosecute. Large-scale project crime of this type has always attracted publicity, particularly in Britain where the vulnerability of safes and locks before the Second World War created a tradition of craft robbery in the theft of large sums of money. This vulnerability continued until the 1950s by which time improved technology had enhanced the security of large sums of cash so as to make the old-style safe-cracker or peterman all but redundant (Ball *et al*, 1978, pp. 68–70).

The boom in project crime was due to the almost impregnable conditions in which cash was stored overnight. Criminals had to attack banks or payroll deliveries. Project criminals unlike those involved in craft crime reduce the risk of retaliation by going to work armed, as their victims usually are aware that they are being robbed and may react aggressively. Initially this involved fists, coshes, or pickaxe handles, but as Ball *et al.* (1978, p. 73) have noted, this often led to pavement battles being fought between criminals and similarly armed security guards. Guns became commonly utilized to ensure the smooth running of hold-ups.

The sudden change from craft to project crime, from thermic lance to shotgun, attracted the attention of media and public alike. The Great Train Robbers, despite their relatively minimal use of violence, attracted vast media coverage and prompted an unprecedented police operation, basically for three reasons. Firstly, the audacity of the crime was a challenge to many ambitious policemen. Secondly, due to the amount of evidence left at Leatherslade Farm, the identity of many of the robbers was known within days. Thirdly, in robbing the Royal Mail, the state was offended. This meant that Tommy Butler could always justify a business trip to France, Canada, or Mexico on the premiss that those who rob Her Majesty must be caught. As Manning (1977, p. 105) has noted: 'Police are in symbolic terms the most visible representation of the presence of the state and the potential of the state to enforce its will upon citizens.' Armed robbers are prized catches for policemen generally. 'It's OK to nick a motorist; but the prize, the mythological prize is a bank robber. For a policeman to catch a bank robber is like a fisherman catching a 20 lb.-trout' (Bank robber, quoted by Taylor 1984, p. 76). In the case of the train robbers, there was the added incentive to the police of personal publicity leading to promotion. The fact that the case was solved by forensic experts did little to detract from the dramatic man-hunt that followed. Butler, Reed, and Slipper all enhanced their reputations in the ensuing investigation.

The selection and utilization of facts and events to represent the effectiveness of police action produces a dramaturgical effect (Manning 1980, p. 62). The three cases mentioned were especially crucial for the police in that the heady mixture of deviant behaviour they involved assured public attention. They included theft of the Queen's mail, robbery with violence, and the use of military uniforms in the train robbery; gangland shootings and torture in the Richardsons' case. The Krays, however, had everything including the hint of police corruption, murder, homosexuality, madness, show-business personalities, politicians, and the aristocracy. All these cases were presented as: 'A series of dramatic confrontations between good and evil in which the police possess the preponderance of resources, skill and virtue. We expect that they will emerge victorious, given adequate resources if they display sufficient courage and determination' (Manning 1980, p. 253).

It is, however, imperative to note that these three important investigations were carried out exclusively by the CID with the Metropolitan CID dominant in all cases. Consequently, the dramaturgical presentation of the CID produced a positive, efficient image of successful police work unmatched in any comparable period in the history of the detective branch.

However, there existed another side to the CID that produced an image of the detective branch far removed from the slick professionalism of the Leonard Reed. While in many ways it would be correct to treat what became known as 'The Challenor Case' as an aberration, the subsequent investigation was to prove the forerunner of many similar inquiries into CID malpractice.

4

A Natural History of the CID: The 1960s and 1970s—A Polarization of Policing Ideologies

The reinforcement of an already potent imagery that resulted from the successful prosecution of certain key criminals was not the only significant outcome of CID activity in London during the 1960s. Evidence of entrenched illegal practices and widespread corruption within 'the department' was emerging with increasing frequency. In turn the CID's strained relations with the uniform branch were further exacerbated by the appointment to the post of Commissioner of a man who more than any other served to emphasize the structural, operational, and ideological rifts between the detective and uniform branches of the Metropolitan Police.

A Recurring Problem

In July 1963 the King and Queen of Greece paid a state visit to London. This resulted in demonstrations being mounted against the Greek regime and several arrests were subsequently made. At Savile Row police station one man was charged with possession of an offensive weapon, half of a house brick. The prisoner claimed that this had been planted on him by the arresting officer, Detective Sergeant Challenor. Challenor had joined the Metropolitan Police in 1947 after distinguished war service during which he was awarded the Military Medal. The regimented life-style of the Met in the 1940s and 1950s suited ex-servicemen like Challenor and he quickly impressed senior officers with his 'zeal and industry' (Ascoli 1979, p. 285).

'Promotion' to the CID was a natural progression and Challenor was posted to West End Central police station where he served, eventually as a Detective Sergeant, for the rest of his career. Ascoli (1979, p. 285) has described Challenor as 'a difficult, abrasive character with a strong, if not always beneficial, influence over some of his younger colleagues'. Recently, an officer who served with Challenor at West End Central gave a rather more candid view of Challenor: 'He was ruthless. He would plant objects on suspects, abuse prisoners as routine matters. He could be violent. We would then have to sort it out, placating people and take the heat out of the situation. Meanwhile he would carry on regardless. A crude, ignorant man.'

The accused brick-carrier, who was subsequently acquitted in court, then issued a writ against the police and received £500 in settlement of his claims for damages for false imprisonment, malicious prosecution, and assault (Critchley 1978, p. 322). An investigation was set up and the Director of Public Prosecutions instituted proceedings against Challenor and three police constables for conspiring to pervert the course of justice. At the trial in June 1964 Challenor was found to be mentally unfit to plead but the three other officers were convicted. A barrage of accusations immediately followed. As Whitaker (1979, p. 253) has noted, Challenor had made a grievous error in planting the half-brick on an educated, articulate man, able to manipulate the law to respond to a citizen's traditional rights: 'Other, less articulate victims who had evidence planted on them had regularly been convicted: 24 were later pardoned but had already served a total of over 13 years' wrongful imprisonment.'

In June 1964 the Home Secretary appointed the Chief Constable of the now defunct Wolverhampton force to head an inquiry into: 'the circumstances in which it was possible for Detective Sergeant Challenor to continue on duty when he appeared to have been affected by the onset of mental illness' (Ascoli 1979, p. 286). Both police and medical officers were exonerated of any blame regarding the identification of Challenor's condition and all allegations of corruption were deemed to be totally unfounded and attributed to malicious intent. Challenor never stood trial and retired unfit on a full pension. The three mentally stable police constables who were charged with Challenor received prison sentences and were summarily dismissed from the force.

Challenor's case was yet another moral panic directed at the police similar to that of Goddard's in 1928 and it was dealt with as an isolated aberration. Meanwhile, the Met's unofficial public relations mechanism (Chibnall 1977, pp. 142–71) that promoted the exploits of 'Nipper', 'Slipper', and the rest, was complemented in 1967 by the formation of a new public relations office, as if acknowledging the spotlight that was about to shine upon 'the brightest jewel in the Met's crown' (Mark 1978).

Robert Mark

Individual biographies are intrusive factors in any study of the Metropolitan Police. In the recent history of the Met CID several names stand out, but none more so than the man who sought to do battle with 'the most routinely corrupt organization in London' (Mark 1978, p. 130).

Robert Mark was born in 1917, the youngest of five children. His parents were of middle-class Yorkshire stock who had moved to the suburbs of Manchester in their late thirties. Mark entered grammar school and proved to be a proficient sportsman who also participated in the school's cadet corps and was later appointed head prefect. He left school in 1935 and joined a firm of carpet manufacturers as a clerk. Dissatisfied with his lot Mark joined the Manchester City Police in 1937 and, while still a probationer, entered the plain-clothes branch dealing mainly with vice (Mark 1978, p. 26).[1] As war approached, Mark found himself appointed to Detective Constable in the Special Branch in 1938. The expanded wartime role of the Special Branch assured Mark immunity from military service until 1942 when he joined the Royal Armoured Corps. After basic training Mark received a commission[2] and served in France, Belgium, Germany, and Czechoslovakia. He stayed in Germany with the Control Commission until 1947 when he was demobbed with the rank of major.

On his return to the Special Branch in Manchester, Mark was soon given the rank of sergeant and claims that he found himself detached from the ordinary criminal. However, the harsh realities of CID duty were made apparent when Mark was 'on loan' to the detective branch. 'I admit quite frankly that there were some such occasions on which my hair stood on end when I discovered the difference

---

[1] At this stage in his career Mark appeared to have shown few scruples regarding what were evidently traditional forms of police violence. He routinely carried and used a concealed rubber truncheon and describes in sickening detail how, while dealing with a truculent drunk, he broke the unfortunate man's leg with a blow from such a weapon (Mark 1978, p. 28).

[2] Mark displayed great affection for Sandhurst (Mark 1978, pp. 38–42) and throughout his autobiography expresses his admiration for men who had distinguished military careers (see particularly pp. 48, 74–5, 111, 223).

between theory and practice in applying the rules governing police interrogation' (Mark 1978, p. 51).

Mark is also remarkably honest in his assessment of the courts' compliance with the malpractices he encountered in the CID (Mark 1978, pp. 51–4). Yet he appears to point the finger firmly at the detective, for it is he who must interpret Judges' Rules. This task is performed in the often fraught atmosphere of an interrogation and, as a detective sergeant, Mark had to have intimate knowledge, perhaps emanating from his own inevitable involvement in illegal methods of interrogation. However, Mark is able to interpret these malpractices as understandable when regarded 'in the context of policing at the time' (Mark 1978, p. 55). Why Mark could not apply the same logic to the Met CID some 20–25 years later is not entirely clear.

In 1950 Mark was promoted to Detective Inspector and in 1952 returned to uniform as Chief Inspector in charge of administration. His rapid progress continued and just one year later he was appointed Superintendent and Chief Superintendent in 1954. In 1957 at the age of 39, he took up the post of Chief Constable of Leicester. It is worth noting that his 'street policing' amounted to only ten years before arriving behind a desk as a Chief Inspector. Of those ten years all but a few months were spent dealing with the rarefied problems of the Special Branch.

Robert Mark's chief priority at Leicester appears from his autobiography to have been rationalizing the city's traffic system (Mark 1978, pp. 64–7). While this may not be indicative of the city's 'crime problem', it does give some insight into Mark's organizational priorities in his new command of 440 men. His stay in the Midlands was fairly uneventful and he took advantage of the spare time on his hands to lecture on a wide spectrum of subjects, becoming known nationally for his fervent lobbying for changes in the criminal law. He was particularly concerned that changes be made in cases tried by a jury so that majority and not unanimous verdicts might be required to establish guilt.

However, one outstanding incident appears to have been something of an omen for Mark's subsequent relationship with the Metropolitan Police CID. A gang of London villains commuted to Leicester and robbed a bank. They were apprehended, but not before a young pedestrian had been killed in an accident resulting from the ensuing high-speed pursuit. Subsequently a telephone caller from London offered a bribe of £1,000 for the Leicester police's non-opposition to bail. The caller's knowledge of police procedure convinced the listener that he was speaking to a CID officer. The offer was rejected and the robbers safely 'tucked up'. Coincidentally, Mark was in the CID office when the call was received and it gave the Chief Constable what he describes as 'a foretaste of things to come' (Mark 1978, p. 72).

Officer Élite

In October 1966 with force amalgamations looming, the Home Secretary, Roy Jenkins, appointed Mark as the police representative on the Standing Advisory Council on the Penal System. Soon after he was appointed as Assistant Commissioner in the Metropolitan Police, again by Jenkins. According to Mark, this appointment caused him genuine consternation: 'I reflected that only one provincial policeman had ever been appointed to such high rank in the Met, Arthur Young, and he only lasted three years' (Mark 1978, p. 81).

Indeed, the Met liked to breed its own. The police college at Hendon was set up by Trenchard in 1934 and in its five years of existence had 197 graduates. Trenchard's plan was to introduce an officer class into the police service and to establish Hendon as a Sandhurst for the training of the civil force's élite. Admission to the fifteen-month course was by direct entry from university, or by competitive examination from within the force. As Mark notes, Hendon offended one of the Met's integral rules that was established by Peel on the force's inception. 'It was really a quite open attempt to attract men of good educational and social background to a service which had always been thought, even by Peel himself, to be inappropriate for those of gentle birth or upbringing' (Mark 1978, p. 83).

Hendon's brief existence was marked by uproar and dissent both in and out of the service. In the Commons Aneurin Bevan had labelled Hendon as 'an entirely fascist development designed to make the police force more amenable to the orders of the Carlton Club and Downing Street'; while the *Police Review* claimed: 'It is "class" legislation with a vengeance. In practice the plan will mean that the higher ranks of the Force will be filled in the main by young men who enter college directly from public schools and university' (*Police Review* May 1933, quoted in Ascoli 1979, p. 234).

This hostility produced a powerful sense of solidarity among those who graduated from Hendon (Mark 1978, p. 84). When Mark joined the Met in 1967 the Commissioner, Sir Joseph Simpson, himself an ex-Hendon man, had surrounded himself with other Hendon graduates as his immediate subordinates. For example, Mark had made a potent enemy in the form of the Chief Constable of Birmingham, Sir Edward Dodd. While commanding neighbouring Midland forces Mark and Dodd, an ex-Hendon man, had clashed over the allocation of resources. Mark claims that Simpson, on learning of Mark's appointment to the Met, had counselled Dodd (by now Chief Inspector of Constabulary) as to Mark's suitability (Mark 1978, pp. 84–6).

Mark arrived at Scotland Yard as a non-Hendon provincial with a reputation for dogmatism and self-publicity. He received a predictably icy reception. At the end of his first week Simpson encouraged Mark to apply for the post as Chief Constable of Lancashire (Mark 1978, p. 80). Mark declined and set about an appraisal of what his new post entailed. Beneath the Commissioner there was a Deputy Commissioner and four Assistant Commissioners. The Deputy stood in, where necessary, for the Commissioner and was responsible for disciplinary matters that did not involve allegations of criminal behaviour. The four Assistants were responsible for the four principal police departments, A, B, C, and D. Mark's initial alienation in his new post was compounded by the reality of his appointment as ACD.

D Department was concerned with recruitment, postings, training, welfare, communications, buildings, and dogs. The post was a rag-bag of roles with several anomalies, the primary one being the diversity of tasks involved: 'I was head of a department of which the components were scattered to the four winds of heaven, from the training centre at Hendon to the dog-training centre of Keston in Kent. From my dingy office, the complexity of my far-flung empire was difficult to comprehend' (Mark 1978, pp. 82–3).

After experiencing his own command, D Department was very much a step backwards for Mark. However, he was able to make some minor changes to police policy, mainly regarding the assessment procedure for an officer's loss of police property in the line of duty, and the allocation of married quarters. He also secured pay rises for the staffs of the police Friendly Society and the police Convalescent Home. In his year in D Department, Mark doubled female recruitment into the force primarily, so he claims, by employing Norman Hartnell to design new WPC uniforms (Mark 1978, p. 90). However, it is worth noting that Mark, despite being responsible for Hendon, did not introduce any major innovations to the training of police officers.

In 1968 Mark moved to B Department (Traffic); this was a brief move as, in March, Sir Joseph Simpson died. The overwhelming favourite for the vacant commissionership was ACC (Crime), Peter Brodie.

Branch Conflict

Peter Brodie was ex-Hendon and very much a Met man. As the head of C Department, Brodie was in charge of over 3,000 detectives, including Special Branch, and was one of the UK representatives on the executive of Interpol. Brodie and Mark were antagonistic to each other yet the former's omnipotence in the Met forced Mark into a distinctly subservient position. C Department had its own promotion boards and organized its own disciplinary procedures. Early in 1968 Brodie was probably the most powerful man in the Met.

It came as some surprise to Mark, therefore, that the new Home Secretary, James Callaghan, offered the Commissioner's post to him. Although there is no firm evidence for such a claim, it does appear that both Jenkins and Callaghan were making a conscious effort to impose the will of the Home Office upon the self-perpetuating hierarchy of the Met. Otherwise Brodie would have succeeded Simpson and the dynasty of the Met would have been assured. Mark declined the promotion:

I explained that I knew very little about the Met, had not a single friend or ally among its police members, that my appointment would be bitterly resented by the very people I would need to make a success of the job and that I had no doubt that some of them would lend all their endeavours to ensure the opposite (Mark 1978, p. 94).

Callaghan acknowledged the threat of a mutiny at Scotland Yard and asked Mark for his advice. Mark suggested the Deputy Commissioner, John Waldron. Callaghan took heed of Mark's advice and Waldron was appointed for a temporary period of two years. Mark was appointed Deputy for what he describes as 'four of the most unpleasant years of my life' (Mark 1978, p. 95).

As Deputy Commissioner, Mark's frustrations were multiplied considerably. He had no authority over the four Assistant Commissioners and, as previously mentioned, his responsibility for force discipline did not extend to allegations against police that amounted to criminal misconduct. Since 1879 the absolute authority under the Commissioner for dealing with criminal misconduct rested in the hands of the CID.[3] Apart from the restrictions of his new post Mark was still the target for resentment by the four ex-Hendon ACs. (Mark 1978, p. 96).

However, Mark had sought out a target of his own. Since his Leicester days he had been suspicious of the Met CID. The antagonism of Brodie and 'the department's' immunity from the disciplinary procedures applicable to the rest of the Met served only to compound Mark's feelings of helplessness. He set out to take his disciplinary powers to the limit. After some research Mark found that any policeman convicted of a criminal offence was suspended on full pay until his appeal was heard. Mark ended this and conviction was met with immediate dismissal. Mark also analysed cases brought against policemen that were acquitted in court and cases that the DPP had decided not to follow up with a prosecution. Mark found that these cases provided a stage for the flexing of his disciplinary muscle: 'In most of these we had little difficulty in formulating disciplinary charges involving suspension from duty and eventual dismissal or a lesser penalty' (Mark 1978, p. 96).

The most potent by far of the measures he introduced in his initial period as Deputy was the return to uniform of any CID man deemed unfit to continue to work unsupervised: 'It soon became plain that of the increasing number of officers being suspended, the majority were from the CID and that the uniform branch were only too pleased to see someone deal with a department which had long brought the force as a whole into disgrace' (Mark 1978, p. 97). Through these actions Mark clearly drew up the battle-lines and, in doing so, gathered around him a tight-knit group of uniformed officers who

[3] One case that highlights the state of play between the two factions in the Met involves the arrest by CID officers of two men on charges of burglary outside London. The men were charged and the provincial force involved were notified. When two provincial officers arrived at the London court next day they found that the charges had been withdrawn and the accused men were set free. Withdrawal of a charge for an indictable offence requires the consent of the DPP and in this case he had not been consulted. The provincial Chief Constable brought the matter to the notice of the Commissioner and the Met CID instituted an inquiry into their own actions. Mark claims that the Met Police solicitor, when sent the resultant report (by Mark) described it as 'so partisan as to be virtually worthless'. The investigating officer was promoted from Chief Inspector to Chief Superintendent (see Mark 1978, pp. 113–14).

were impressed with the strength of Mark's will, and sufficiently ambitious to carry out his commands to the full.

The CID were cast as villains, not for the first time. However, in implementing the transfer back to uniform of offending CID men, Mark merely confirmed their élite status. But what Mark did achieve was a rift in what he describes as 'the Hendon old guard' (Mark 1978, p. 99). When the chips were down loyalty to the uniform branch took precedence over *alma mater* and Brodie found himself increasingly isolated.

Several television appearances in defence of the police further enhanced Mark's reputation with the uniform branch (Mark 1978, pp. 99–102), and the student unrest of 1968 climaxing in the 'October Revolution' served to enhance the morale and solidarity of the uniformed officer. In 1969 Mark paid a brief visit to Northern Ireland and was later to serve on the Advisory Committee for Northern Ireland. On his return to the Met Mark found that tension between the uniform branch and CID was high due to the activities of Mark's cohorts in instituting disciplinary proceedings against as many CID men as possible. The CID was now fair game. The difference now, however, was that something could be gained from a campaign against the detective branch by treating what were to the CID routine practices, as horrific examples of corruption and/or malpractice. The final preamble to 'The battle for control of the CID' commenced at the end of November 1969 when *The Times* newspaper published allegations against a Detective Inspector and two Detective Constables (Cox *et al.* 1977). The allegations included taking bribes, giving false evidence in exchange for money, and allowing a criminal to pursue his activities. *The Times* claimed to have no faith in the Met's integrity and so published the allegations rather than handing over the evidence privately. The 1964 Police Act was not implemented, that is, no senior officer from outside the Met was brought in to investigate. Instead, an internal investigation was set up under Detective Chief Superintendent Lambert.

Incredibly, another investigation was put into operation in tandem with Lambert's. This was headed by Frank Williamson, an HM Inspector of Constabulary. Williamson was no longer a policeman and therefore held no police power (Cox *et al.* 1977, p. 69). He was given Nipper Reed's old headquarters at Tintagel House and appeared to be forming a fruitful relationship with Lambert. In 1970 Waldron's service was extended so that he might benefit from the enhanced pension that would result from rapidly improving police pay, and this afforded Mark valuable time.

In May 1970 Detective Chief Superintendent William Moody, Head of the Obscene Publications Squad, took over from Detective Chief Superintendent Lambert. Pressure on the CID continued to mount and various officers were suspended. Yet the CID continued to run its own investigations which rarely resulted in prosecution. Mark's impotence in dealing with the CID led him to demand executive action by Waldron. Waldron declined to take action against the CID and the situation deteriorated. Mark's sole weapon was the ability of the Deputy to suspend officers from duty; the consequent increasing number of suspensions and extensive publicity of CID wrongdoing in the national press resulted in pressure on Waldron to act. The final conflict between the Deputy and the ACC was postponed in 1971 when the Tory government extended Waldron's term of office for a further year.

In the autumn of 1971 Brodie left the country for an Interpol conference and holiday. At a routine meeting of senior officers, Waldron, without the imposing presence of Brodie, acknowledged the growing number of suspensions and appeared exasperated as to the reason for what apparently was a serious decline in police behaviour. Mark struck: 'The answer lies in the thoroughly unsatisfactory way in which the CID investigates allegations of crime against its own members' (Mark 1978, p. 116). In Brodie's absence Mark received resolute support from the other uniformed officers present and Waldron had no option but to respond. He ordered Mark, as the force's disciplinary authority, to act. Mark immediately set up A.10, a group of specially selected men culled from both the detective and uniform branches, working directly under the Deputy Commissioner and dealing with all allegations against Met police officers whether these allegations were of a criminal nature or not.

Before A.10 was operational, Mark left London for a lecture tour of North America. Suddenly, on 1 November, he was summoned to return to London. The press were mounting a concerted campaign for a Royal Commission, not into the CID alone but the police service as a whole. Home Secretary Maudling was aware of the wealth of evidence being compiled by a number of newspapers, notably the *People* and *The Times* (*Police Review*, 11 March 1977, p. 312) and, given Mark's growing reputation as a CID 'basher', Maudling decided to accelerate Waldron's retirement and appoint

Mark as Commissioner in the hope that the press campaign would be called off. Mark was appointed Commissioner Designate until April when Waldron retired officially. Meanwhile, Frank Williamson retired: 'He was thoroughly disillusioned and depressed by continual disagreement with and obstruction by policemen who did not share his very high standard of personal and professional integrity' (Mark 1978, p. 119; see *New Statesman* 20 May 1977).

Internal Hygiene and Major Surgery

In February 1972 the *Sunday People* published allegations that the head of the Flying Squad, Commander Ken Drury had holidayed in Cyprus with Soho pornographer James Humphries. Mark forced Brodie to suspend Drury and, nine days later, the CID chief entered hospital suffering from 'excessive strain'. Mark comments:

He never returned to duty, though we were all relieved to hear there was nothing fundamentally wrong with him. The trouble was that he believed too many of his subordinates to be untainted by corruption or other wrongdoing. He was incapable of seeing or believing the failings of many of those on whom he relied for advice. He was, too, the inheritor of a tradition of solidarity which had been fostered by C Department and some of the press for their own ends (Mark 1978, p. 121).

Had Brodie not retired when he did, an interesting situation would have come about on Mark's appointment as Commissioner, for as a condition of his appointment Mark secured from Maudling permission to make interchangeable the four Assistant Commissioners' posts. Although one can only surmise, it seems certain that Mark would have replaced Brodie, possibly switching him to Mark's old post as ACD.

Mark's preferential treatment of the uniform branch was allowed full rein. The fact that he was able to confront and defeat Brodie while still Commissioner Designate was an ominous victory in the view of the CID. Mark, on his appointment set about not only purging the CID, but also presenting the uniform branch as the instigators of 'real policing'.

The uniformed policeman in London bears the brunt of violence, whether political, industrial, criminal or from hooliganism and he had long resented the airs and graces of the CID, generally known as 'the department'. The CID regarded itself as an élite body, higher paid by way of allowances and factually, fictionally and journalistically more glamorous (Mark 1978, p. 122).

Mark set out to cut out 'a major cancer without killing the patient' (Mark 1978, p. 124). On 24 April, just seven days after taking up the Commissioner's post, Mark announced the five measures that would constitute surgical incision:

1. All detectives serving on divisions, 2,300 of the total CID complement of 3,200 officers, were to come under the command of the twenty-three uniformed Divisional Commanders.

2. The four Area Detective Commanders at the Yard were deployed to the officers of the four uniformed Deputy Assistant Commissioners who comprised the inspectorate, thereby depriving the CID of Divisional Command.

3. A.10 was set up and firmly established. The department was to have a uniformed head and be comprised of hand-picked officers from both the uniform and detective branches. Each officer would serve for two years in A.10 before returning to his respective branch to 'spread the gospel' (Mark 1978, p. 128).

4. Responsibility for dealing with pornography was switched from C Department to A Department, i.e. from CID to uniform (*Punch* 1985, p. 34).

5. Plans were drawn up for a greater measure of CID–uniform interchange. This measure eventually resulted (1977) in every DC and DS who was successful in passing their respective exams for promotion, returning to uniform duties for a minimum of two years.

Within two weeks Mark had summoned the representatives of the CID to see him. 'I told them simply that they represented what had long been the most routinely corrupt organisation in London, that nothing and no one would prevent me from putting an end to it and that if necessary I would put the whole of the CID back into uniform and make a fresh start' (Mark 1978, p. 130; see Chibnall 1977). The CID were stunned by Mark's aggression and 'the department' bore the brunt of the many resignations that followed, the most notable of which was that of Commander Drury. Brodie's successor was Colin Woods who was transferred from AC (traffic) and had no previous detective experience. 'An experienced uniformed officer of outstanding managerial skill, great determination and the moral courage to do the job without any previous detective experience, he proved quickly and not surprisingly to be the most efficient and effective head of C Department in living memory' (Mark 1978, p. 129).

The CID was in turmoil. A spate of serious, armed bank robberies provided Mark with another weapon which was partly to backfire on him. In the 1960s and early 1970s armed robbery was a particularly profitable occupation and North London in particular proved a happy hunting-ground for 'blaggers'. By the summer of 1972 armed bank robberies were occurring at the rate of one every five days. Since 1969 over three million pounds had been stolen (Ball *et al.* 1978, p. 18). The failure of the local CID to solve the robberies led to a suggestion by a local officer that a specialist Robbery Squad might be set up. One of the main problems had been traditional rivalries and the North London robberies produced a situation whereby D.11 (Criminal Intelligence) and various divisional offices were in competition. Eventually the Robbery Squad had some success and, with the assistance of 'supergrass', Bertie Smalls, and Jack Slipper's Flying Squad, more than twenty people were convicted and sentenced to a total of 308 years. However, Detective Inspector Vic Wilding and his superior at Wembley, Chief Superintendent Cecil Saxby, were prominent figures in A.10's subsequent investigations. Saxby was accused of stealing £25,000 from one of the robbers with whom he had a relationship that had lasted a number of years (Ball *et al.* 1978, pp. 162–6). Despite some intriguing tape-recorded telephone conversations between Saxby's wife and the wife of the robber concerned, A.10 cleared Saxby, who then retired from the force.

The second A.10 inquiry involving DI Wilding highlights a CID work practice that is open to exploitation by entrepreneurial detectives. Woman Detective Constable Joan Angell, a member of the Flying Squad, alleged that DI Wilding had 'behaved unethically in his relationship with police informants on the bank robbery case' (Ball *et al.* 1978, p. 166). Angell claimed that a well-established informant of hers 'Mary Fraser', had named two major participants in a raid on Barclays Bank, Wembley, in August 1972 that had netted over £138,000. Angell claimed that the information was received just three days after the raid and led to the arrest of the two robbers. Angell passed on this information verbally to her superiors and formally claimed a reward for Fraser after the men had been charged.

Fraser's claim disappeared and the entry of Angell's made in the Flying Squad's informants' register was deleted. The subsequent A.10 inquiry established that the reward money was paid to 'William Wise'. The officers who claimed the money on his behalf were DCS Saxby and DCI Wilding. 'Wise' received £2,175 in payments from the Met and Barclays Bank. Despite several anomalies in the claims made on behalf of 'Wise', A.10 cleared Wilding and Saxby. Angell resigned and, in 1976, 'Fraser' was offered £1,000 reward for her information on the Wembley raid (Ball *et al.* 1978, pp. 166–73).

By 1973 two officers a week were leaving the Met prematurely as a result of Mark's purge (Mark 1978, p. 138). The number of bank robberies within the jurisdiction of the Met fell from sixty-five in 1972 to twenty-six in 1973. The Serious Crime Squad moved into the Soho area of London's West End and began to investigate the pornography business. James Humphries, Commander Drury's holiday companion, was arrested in Holland and eventually sentenced to eight years, strangely enough for committing grievous bodily harm against his wife's lover. His diary yielded a crop of information regarding police corruption in the Obscene Publications Squad.

The new uniform-dominated squad had a pristine image and, to keep it that way, Mark instigated an inquiry into the corruption implied by Humphries' diary. The man in charge of this three-year investigation was Gilbert Kelland. Then a Deputy Assistant Commissioner, Kelland's men were all hand-picked from the uniform branch. In March 1977, six officers including ex-Commander Virgo and the same DCS Moody who had 'collaborated' with Frank Williamson in 1970, plus four other officers, were accused on twenty-seven counts of accepting bribes, totalling £87,485. All the officers were convicted and received a total of forty-eight years' imprisonment (Cox *et al.* 1977). In June 1977 three Flying Squad officers, including Ken Drury, faced fourteen charges of corruption. One man was acquitted and one sentenced to four years, later reduced to three years. Drury received eight years, later reduced to five. In 1978 Virgo's appeal was quashed by the Appeal Court.

During Mark's period in office, 487 officers were either dismissed or required to resign. Mark retired in 1977 and his era will be remembered for his attempts to bring the CID firmly under the control of the uniform branch, using 'corruption' as his most potent weapon.

Making a Mark

Mark's upbringing was middle class. He was educated at a grammar school and his entire childhood appears to have been steeped in notions of service, a belief in the Empire, and a general sense of one's place. The dominance of upper-class, public-school-inspired social mores served as a supportive pillar throughout Mark's police career.

His army service, his previously mentioned reverence for the ideals of Sandhurst, and his continual service as a police representative on many joint police/army consultative bodies, build an image of a man to whom traditional values of patriotic service, particularly through the utilization of a specifically martial ideology and reverence to familial and professional respectability, are paramount.

Mark's career, and his campaign against the CID in particular, can be seen as the result of two complementary ideologies merging at a crucial point in police history—conservatism and militarism. Mark exhibited traits of classical conservatism particularly in his rigid opposition to societal change, and his loyalty to the police. His attitude to the National Council for Civil Liberties (Mark 1978, pp. 131-3) displays a firm aversion to the recognition of conflict, and a complete and utter denial of legitimation to any group seeking to usurp long-established institutions. 'Conservatism prefers the status quo, looking to traditional regimes for its models. It is frequently patrician, discouraging activism and radicalism and the mobilisation of the masses' (Bennet *et al.* 1977, p. 9). Cleavage and ambivalence are treated as illegitimate by Mark. The death of a student at Red Lion Square in 1974 is regarded by him as the product of left-wing extremism, as opposed to police action—the result of an attempt to change an integral part of British social life, in this case the right of the National Front to demonstrate. The left-wing counter-demonstration was made up of individuals 'not a whit less odious than the National Front' (Mark 1978, p. 167). Both sides represented rapid, sudden change and, as such, were a threat. For the conservative, change should be slow 'without any of the inconveniences of mutation' (Burke 1906, pp. 206–7).

For Mark, the Labour Party appears to have represented the most unworthy mutation of all. Regardless of his avowed political neutrality[4] and despite his admiration for various Labour Home Secretaries, Mark makes no secret of his disdain for the governments in which they served. For example, of the departure of Roy Jenkins to the EEC he writes: 'I suspect he was glad to go. His stature, both intellectual and otherwise, must have made him an unpopular member of the mediocre crew in which he had served' (Mark 1978, p. 231). Likewise, the Labour minority government of 1974 is described as 'weak', 'hanging on to office by its eyelashes unable to run the risk

---

[4] 'He has not voted since the war for either the Labour or Conservative Party' (*Police Review*, 11 Mar. 1977). See also Mark (1978, p. 221).

of offending its extreme left in case it should bring it down' (Mark 1978, p. 167). Mark is not reacting to the Labour Party as such, but to his association, perhaps naïvely, of change with the Labour Party. For conservatives like Mark, change must be in accordance with natural growth and the development of institutions, customs, and practices. If change requires the utilization of a common stock of reason, and that individuals should attempt to use this stock in a positive way for the mutual benefit of all, then the inherent pessimism of the conservative is put into play: 'We are afraid to put men to live and trade each on his own private stock of reason; because we suspect that this stock in each man is small, and that the individuals would do better to avail themselves of the general bank and capital of nations and of ages' (Burke 1968, pp. 266–7).

For Mark, as with all conservatives, there are severe limitations as to what society can achieve. On attempts, or suggested attempts to improve police accountability, Mark is adamant that such measures are motivated not so much by a sense of justice as by political expediency: 'When socialists in the Commons and the Lords speak of a police force accountable to Parliament, or a national police force, they are not thinking of justice. They are thinking of police as a tool of government' (Mark 1978, p. 282). The conservative ideal, as typified by Mark, regards change as being a natural process, thereby limiting what the state can achieve, and any departure from this natural process is a perilous exercise. Crime for Mark is little more than a 'costly nuisance'; the two great problems for the next generation of policemen are 'resistance to political encroachment on their operational freedom and exposure to the brunt of social change' (Mark 1978, p. 290). Change to the existing order constitutes for Mark a serious threat, yet he was sufficiently politically astute to acknowledge slight changes if they were tempered by extreme caution: 'I should follow the example of our ancestors. I would make the reparation as nearly as possible in the style of the building' (Burke 1968, pp. 266–7).

In his campaign against the CID, the Met, in Mark's eyes, was not being subjected to change so much as reparation to its pre-1879 state. By returning the absolute authority to deal with criminal investigation to the uniform branch, the power balance was tipped further in favour of prevention, and the status quo as established by Peel was maintained. Mark's regard for the preventative principle has been stressed, I hope, earlier in this chapter. However, his loyalty to the uniform branch is also an intrinsically conservative trait, serving to construct a resolute buffer between the state and the individual that is not ambiguous in its appearance or function.

The 'good' boys are 'good' in the clean-living Englishman tradition—they keep in hard training, wash behind their ears, never hit below the belt, etc. etc.—and by way of contrast there is a series of 'bad' boys, Racke, Crooke, Loder and others, whose badness consists in betting, smoking cigarettes and frequenting public houses. All these boys are constantly on the verge of expulsion (Orwell 1971, p. 509).

Or, perhaps in a more sympathetically chauvinistic manner, 'to love the little platoon we belong to in society, is the first principle . . . of public affections' (Burke 1968, p. 44).

The second identifiable trait of Robert Mark is that of militarism. The predominance of the military ideal in British society has been a direct result of both the need to maintain an empire and participation in two world wars. Those who served in the armed forces and survived returned to civilian life as carriers of an ideology propagating military ideals, and with an inclination to imitate military demeanour. As a consequence, warlike behaviour and attitudes are usually regarded as worthy, and institutionalized violence, along with the organizational and cultural foundations of the armed services, is rated highly in most popular hierarchies of human endeavour: 'War is honorable, warlike prowess is honorific' (Veblen 1924, p. 247). Andreski (1961, p. 60) has noted that, at the end of a war 'the balance of power between the military and the civilian authorities finds itself strongly tilted in favour of the former.'

The prestige afforded to the military in the 'afterglow' of war must affect the style of control that the civil power adopts, whether consciously or otherwise. Ex-servicemen have tended to choose the police as a career as opposed to a non-uniformed occupation.

When I first joined [1966] the older, experienced men were ex-services. Because of this they were hard and disciplined—self-disciplined I mean—they found ways of doing the job right with no fuss. We used to march out of the station and they were immaculate, but they got the job done with no poncing about. I learnt from them; they taught me the rules, the real rules (Detective Constable).

Military service provides a central ethos of masculinity, a series of clues for acceptable behaviour. The police, owing to the visual imagery the job creates and the suitability of martial rhetoric to its related tasks, provides what appears to be a basic cultural requirement, an outlet for 'uniformed service'. The desire by certain individuals to provide this service is a particularly potent motive in police recruitment and is quite a separate issue from other motives such as service to the community and the variety of police work. 'It specifically addressed the satisfaction these applicants experience in being part of a disciplined body' (Fielding, forthcoming).

Additionally, the uniform branch in particular is frequently involved in quasi-military action, requiring a controlled force to act in a strictly regimented manner. For instance, in crowd control (Reiner 1978, p. 188; Waddington 1987), the police are required to act as a cohesive whole and not as individuals. Patrol work, however, is a largely unobserved and autonomous activity carried out by the individual officer. Despite the lack of direct supervision, the patrolman is required to obey rules and instructions that are imposed, often implicitly, by drill and a rigid disciplinary code. 'The police are to be organised in a strict hierarchy of authority in which subordinate ranks are expected to execute dutifully and unquestioningly the decisions and instructions of their superiors' (Reiner 1978, p. 6). The police, and in particular the uniform branch, provide what Reiner calls an example for the rest of society, an ideal type of social organization with aims, goals, and general morality in tune with those that hold power: 'Internal organisation and general demeanour reflect the desired pattern for society as a whole, a smoothly operating, hierarchically structured system of operating units.' As with the armed services, there is an established chain of command and officers 'subordinate their own interests and inclinations to the demands and decisions of their superiors' (Reiner 1978, p. 6).

The Thin Khaki Line

The 'disciplined body syndrome' (Reiner 1978, p. 161), is a powerful and pervasive theme in British society, providing a touchstone for masculinity. Its source is to be found in our society's military heritage and stems from an ideology that reflects classical conservatism: 'it tends to emphasise order, hierarchy and the stabilising institutions of society (church, family, private property). It maintains a pessimistic image of human nature and is dubious of the prospects of eliminating war' (Abrahamsson 1971, p. 71). If 'war' is deleted and 'crime' inserted we have a quote that succinctly outlines the militaristic, essentially conservative ideology that Robert Mark sought to impose on the Met. However, given the initial hostility that the CID so openly showed to Mark's regime, and the remarkable conflict that took place between the two branches throughout the 1970s, it is important to consider the essentially ideological nature of the 'war against the CID' and the origins of the ideology of the detective as well as the uniform branch.

The central focus of the Metropolitan Police has always been upon its preventative function and the CID's emphasis upon detection had been regarded as something of an anomaly for some time. However, Mark brought to the Met more than military rhetoric for although, as I have already suggested, the uniform branch is based on a militaristic model, Mark heralded the beginning of an era that would introduce militarist, technological, and tactical innovations which would make the war against the CID an inevitability. Mark's close contact with the military, and particularly his involvement in Northern Ireland and with the Working Party set up to review the army's policies in respect of aid to the civil power in 1970, suggests that the Home Office required him to gain as much experience as possible of the utilization of military force in conjunction with police operations. A crucial part of the militarization of the Met under Mark was the expansion of the role of the Special Patrol Group. The SPG was formed in 1965 as an élite, specially trained body of 100 men.

They are all volunteers drawn from London's police and receive special training in riot control and gun and C.S. gas handling. Each unit consists of twenty eight constables, one female constable, three sergeants and an inspector, and each unit has three transits. A transit can carry twelve officers including the driver and the radio operator. The radio operator monitors two channels, one for the S.P.G. unit and one for the normal London police channel (Bunyan 1977, p. 95).

The SPG did not come to the fore until the large-scale political demonstrations and industrial disputes of the late 1960s and early 1970s created a demand for their specialist skills. The ordinary, traditional, uniformed policeman was found to be ill-equipped in every way to cope with what was an undoubted increase in militant action, notably by members of the working class. Given the state's reflexive obligation to react to any perceived threat it was inevitable that the police responded accordingly.[5] The SPG was expanded and was used, comparatively discreetly, in suppressing the student disorders of 1968, including the Grosvenor Square demonstration that constituted the 'October Revolution' and, in 1969, was sent to Anguilla as part of a police/army contingent whose task was to police a movement for independence. In the early 1970s there was severe industrial unrest. Miners, building workers, engineers, and the Upper Clyde ship-builders were all involved in major disputes. The Conservative government declared a state of emergency five times in the first two years of the decade and there were many police actions that resulted in direct confrontation. The success of 'flying pickets' in 1972 in getting the Saltly Coke Works closed, despite 180 arrests, led to the setting-up of several short-lived vigilante groups such as GB75, to take over vital installations in times of unrest (see Rollo 1980, pp. 169–73).

Following their defeat in 1974 the Tories campaigned for the formation of a volunteer force to be formed as an aid to the civil force. As early as 1961 a Home Office Working Party had been set up to investigate the need for a third force in times of crisis and in 1971 the committee concluded that the British public would not support the formation of such a paramilitary force. By the time Mark was appointed Commissioner in 1972, the SPG had begun to adopt many of the tactics of the RUC and the army, notably snatch-squads and 'wedges'.[6] The ever-expanding SPG was present at all the major disputes of the era, including the dock-workers' and building workers' strikes. However, it was not until 1973 that public and media attention was drawn to the existence of the SPG. The incident that attracted this attention was the fatal shooting of two men at India House by two armed SPG constables. The initial outrage caused by

[5] Stuart Hall (1980, pp. 11–17) appears to regard the police response to the perceived threats of the 1960s and 1970s as somehow retrograde. Hain (1979, p. 19) also offers some fond nostalgia for the days when George Dixon ruled. It appears that the predecessors of our contemporary 'paramilitary wing of the police' were of a very different breed: 'The SPG's activities give special cause for concern since they are confirming the established tendency of such élite groups to extend their role and be called into situations with which a strictly civilian police force has coped adequately for 150 years.' The benign presence of the police at Cable Street in 1936, the combined police, army, and navy operation in Liverpool in 1919, and the police and army co-operation of 1926 (Morgan 1987, pp. 111–47), amongst numerous other incidents, would appear to have been aberrations not worthy of consideration.

[6] This latter tactic is attributed widely among senior policemen to Sir Kenneth Newman and was the result of his experiences as a young police officer in Palestine at the time of Israel's 'war' of independence.

the fact that the deceased were carrying only imitation and not real firearms, soon subsided and parliamentary indignation was focused upon the retailing of toy and 'replica' pistols. The fact that an élite squad of policemen was proved to be routinely carrying firearms was, however, firmly established:

The claim that the British police remains substantially an unarmed force, the only one in the world, is largely a semantic quibble. The fact that the accessibility to arms and similar equipment is still limited does not undermine the substantive fact that, for good or ill, in all those cases where it matters, the British police are now in effect an armed and fully equipped technical force (Hall 1980, p. 14).

Mark's reign marked an era of expansion not only for the SPG but for the idea of both the involvement of the military in civil policing and the adoption of military methodologies by the police. For their part, the SPG has attended every major strike, demonstration, and terrorist incident since 1972, including Balcombe Street, Red Lion Square, Grunwicks, Lewisham, Southall, and Brixton. Twice the SPG has been accused of being responsible for deaths that occurred on those occasions. What Bunyan (1977, p. 270) describes as 'increasing paranoia', allowed the militaristic ideology of Robert Mark to be fully expressed. Mark received considerable ideological support, notably from the military hierarchy.

Subversion, then, will be held to mean all measures short of the use of armed force taken by one section of the people of a country to overthrow those governing the country at the time or to force them to do things that they do not want to do. It can involve the use of political and economic pressure, strikes, protest marches and propaganda, and can also include the use of small-scale violence for the purpose of coercing recalcitrant members of the population into giving support (Kitson 1971, p. 3).

Mark was able to home in on this paranoia[7] and pronounced that 'the worst of all crimes is the furtherance of political or industrial aims by violence' (Mark 1977, pp. 74–85). In January 1974, on being informed of an imminent terrorist attack on London Airport, Mark put into action a joint police and army operation that involved the occupation of Heathrow (Kettle 1979, pp. 33–5). By the end of the year the airport had been occupied a further three times and, as Bunyan (1977, pp. 272–4) notes, by this time the occupation had

[7] Bunyan (1977, p. 268) notes that in 1970 Prime Minister Heath had reported to the United Nations that internal rather than external forces constituted the 'real' threat to democratic states.

acquired 'normal' status for both the participants and the public. Mark's consistent affiliation with the military soon became a pre-occupation of the Met. The Special Air Service was deployed at Stansted Airport in January 1975 to deal with a hijacker and the Balcombe Street siege of 1975 again saw Mark use the SAS as a last resort and the 'four seedy, cowardly degenerates' (Mark 1978, p. 184) surrendered on learning of the élite soldiers' presence. Troops of an unspecified regiment were also on hand to deal with the Spaghetti House siege of that same year. In this case, three armed robbers were caught in the act and, for five days, held eight hostages in the base-ment of a restaurant in Knightsbridge. The robbers surrendered without any violence yet Mark was able to describe the incident as 'the most dramatic and difficult siege since Sidney Street' (Mark 1978, p. 191). He was able to exploit to the full the public relations potential of the siege and stress again his high regard for military values: 'The soldier, in contrast to the policeman, is the embodiment of the ultimate sanction of force which is necessary to every govern-ment, even the most democratic, for protection from external attack or for dealing with revolutionary activities for which the machinery of government by contrast is inadequate' (Mark 1977, pp. 25–6).

Mark's militaristic attitude and use of the army in the field of civil policing were complemented by a perceived crisis that led to an over-reaction to any possible threat to capitalism, order, democracy, or decency. Consequently Mark was able to establish a military model of policing based firmly on traditional notions of prevention that are inherent in the uniform branch, and reinforced this traditional image by bonding the police and the military and exploiting the siege mentality that responded so vehemently to 'the threat from within': 'Both police and army are inspired by the same ideals of service to the people from whom we are drawn and whose wellbeing is our mutual objective' (Mark 1977, p. 33).

Given the primacy of militarism for Mark and its domination of policing in London during Mark's term as Commissioner, 'the cleaning up of the Augean stable' (Hall 1980, p. 13) was a predictable exercise. For in its organization, demeanour, and discipline and in its situationally justified and bureaucratically defined roles, the CID represents the antithesis of the military model of policing. If the uniformed officer is, by definition in both symbolic and ideological terms, militaristic, then the detective should be described as entre-preneurial.

5

The History of East London: A Stroll down Felony Lane

No more dreary spectacle can be found on this earth than the whole of the 'awful east'.

Jack London, *The People of the Abyss*

I have attended in the course of the last three chapters to the historical development of the CID and the subsequent organizational and ideological context in which the contemporary CID officer operates. However, it is my intention to argue that the idiosyncratic nature of CID work, while isolated from the dominant uniform branch, is influenced by its occupational environment to the extent of adopting crucial characteristics of the culture generated by that environment. As Niederhoffer (1969, p. 52) has noted, writing of policemen in general: 'Gradually he learns to neglect the formal rules and norms and turns elsewhere for direction.' I will later argue that the detective, particularly the detective working in London, will turn to the culture in which he polices.

This chapter is concerned with the development of an area, and the evolution of its culture, for this culture appears to encapsulate many essential features that invite comparisons with the CID. Notable among these are the emphasis placed upon independence, tough masculinity, a traditional deviant identity, and, most importantly, entrepreneurial ability.

1. Defining and Locating the East End of London

Most writers who have concerned themselves with East London are motivated by ethnic or familial connections, by a spirit of adventure, or by political zeal. As a consequence each writer's definition of the area is subjective and prone to a myriad of boundary variables (Bush 1984, p. xvii). The resulting demarcation disputes reveal much about the motivation of certain individuals who, in acquiring the necessary clout to put their views into print, reveal little more than subjective criteria in their choice of subject-matter and focal points of analysis.

Academic and non-academic East End Jews have tended to focus their attention upon the 'old' East End—Whitechapel and Stepney. This is a reflection of the importance of these two adjacent boroughs as primary bases of settlement for Jewish immigrants over several centuries. Fishman's 1979 work points out that by the 1880s a long-term presence had been established in Whitechapel, and the same author defines the East End in respect of Whitechapel alone. Kops (1969), Alin and Wesker (1974), and others define the East End according to similarly subjective criteria, that is, in terms of Jewish settlement and parental home.

East London, particularly during the final quarter of the last century, attracted more than its fair share of well-meaning gentlefolk who sought, through good deeds or the distribution of alms, drastically to alter the social character of the area. It is to these people, motivated by religious or political ideals, that we owe such a great debt for the documentation, in various forms, of the living conditions of the population of East London. Charles Booth acknowledged the unique economy as being crucial in defining the area, and Stepney, Bethnal Green, Poplar, Shoreditch, Wapping, and Limehouse are included in his overall analysis. Booth explains that Bow, Bromley, the outermost parts of Bethnal Green, and Hackney in its entirety were of a 'different character' to the aforementioned areas. His criteria for omitting these localities can be found by perusing the street maps of the era. 'Not only are there some large spaces open to the public . . . but the map begins everywhere to show more ground than buildings. The streets are wider; the houses have gardens of some sort; and in the houses themselves fewer people are packed' (Booth 1889, vol. i, p. 30).

However, Booth appears to have travelled from the City outwards along the Mile End Road where some of the larger houses that he refers to still stand as offices or multi-occupancy residences. A similar journey eastwards along the parallel Commercial–West India Dock–Barking Road, would have taken Booth in 1889 along a considerable section of London's twenty-six-mile waterfront, and much of his journey would have been spent looking at the massive dock wall that marks the boundary of the docks, and the many houses built to house dock-workers and their families. As Sir Walter Besant notes, with uncharacteristic precision, the building of the Victoria and Albert Docks in 1855 and 1880 respectively, led to an overflow of East Londoners settling in East and West Ham, resulting in these two hamlets by 1901 boasting a population of 360,000 (Besant 1901, pp.

213–14). Besant includes Hackney and Stratford in his definition noting that by 1903 their suburban status was inappropriate.

Sidney and Beatrice Webb (1927) documented the 'inner East End', as did numerous other political and philanthropic activists, notably William Booth (1890), Barnardo (Barnardo and Merchant 1907), and Barnett (1918). The long-term and institutional nature of these individuals' activities is reflected in their writings which could hardly keep up with the rapid expansion of East London and its changing definition.

Millicent Rose, writing as recently as 1951, restricted her analysis to Stepney, Poplar, Bethnal Green, and Hackney. Her criteria are vague, for by the 1950s Stepney and Whitechapel eastwards to West and East Ham and well into Barking and Dagenham had long since been established as a single-class district. Llewellyn Smith (1939) is equally vague about including West Ham but not East Ham, and while lengthy references to the area's pre-industrial past are made (including tribal opposition to the Roman invasion), direct reference to the heritage of West Ham is omitted.

Journalists have also attempted to define the area and, of this group, by far the most valuable contribution was made by Henry Mayhew. His descriptive journeys through London included many forays east, notably when documenting poverty, crime, and depravity. Mayhew's East End was the 'old East End'—Whitechapel, Bethnal Green, and Stepney. In the middle of the nineteenth century these were rational choices as dock buildings had not yet extended beyond these areas. However, James Greenwood (1874) is irritatingly vague as to the precise location of his sometimes bizarre 'Wilds of London', although Ratcliffe (Stepney) is predictably mentioned in a chapter concerning prostitution. Jack London also concerned himself with the 'old East End' and, in doing so, highlighted the problem of defining the boundaries of such a huge area. On arriving in the capital from California, London could find no one with knowledge of the area, nor a cab-driver able to take him there (London 1903, pp. 2–6).

A Subjective Definition: the One-Class City

> He's OK. He's one of us, not a guv'nor. You know, an East-Ender.
>
> Terry

East London's boundaries are not directly aligned to any specific coagulation of concrete, steel, or tarmac. They are defined by the inhabitants as an alignment of commonly held strategies. This arsenal of options is manifested daily in the form of a culturally structured process of selection, whereby strategies are graded and selected according to their suitability.

This store of knowledge, and the cueing and selection process described, is common to all cultures, in particular to working-class cultures that rely upon unofficial data banks of orally transferred knowledge. East London, however, unlike most other identifiable British working-class areas, constitutes a huge land mass inside the capital with a culture built around several unique and contradictory factors. Unlike, for instance, the distinctive cultures of a mill-town or pit village, created by the social isolation of single occupational residence, East London's economic heritage is so diffuse, and its industrial base so precariously transitory, that to discuss the physical boundaries of the area without attempting to define its culture is a mere exercise in cartography. I will argue that East London is a distinctive region with its own culture that has formed over several centuries. As Weightman and Humphries (1983, p. 11) have noted, London was 'designed not on the drawing-board but in the market place'.

This is notably true of the area east of the city wall that first developed as a servant of the City. As the capital expanded certain trades and crafts became indigenous to East London, and the area began to attract a work-force of an identifiable social type. The gradual onset of capitalism and the polarization of the population led to a parallel segregation of the work-force and, as the East End expanded industrially and rolled further eastwards, the middle class were kept in a state of constant transition by an ever-impending working-class deluge. Despite the odd outpost of bourgeois settlement in Wapping and Hackney and bizarre shrines to gentility in Spital-fields, the East End has evolved as an exclusively working-class society inhabited by over half a million people. Not a street, borough, or town, East London is a disparate community bonded by a culture rather than by any single institution or governmental agency. This one-class society locates its own boundaries in terms of subjective class definition, and east of the City of London you are either an East-Ender, a middle-class interloper, or you can afford to move sufficiently far east to join the middle classes of suburban Essex (see London 1903, p. 27).

This type of definition also accommodates buffer zones, where the two classes reside if not in harmony, then in the same borough. In these areas conflict is easily observed, notably among the 'escapees' who no longer reside in a working-class neighbourhood yet retain their working-class life-style. The 'escapees' experience threats from middle-class culture when residing in a buffer zone that are absent in a single-class community such as East London.[1]

Inside East London the culture remains intact yet essentially flexible and the central issue of economic survival functions as a perennial stimulant to the continued use of inherited problem-solving devices. The boundaries of the area are to be identified by observing the indigenous culture, and by noting at what point the problem-solving devices are no longer appropriate to East London, one may say 'there stands the fence'.

The Social Ecology of East London

East London is a 'natural area' (Zorbaugh 1929) only in part. Indeed it has distinctive economic and topographical features, its western border indisputedly lying at the boundary of the City of London, its southern extremity and primary *raison d'être*, the Thames. The problem lies in defining its eastern and northern boundaries, neither of which can claim any distinctive physical barriers. To complicate the issue further, East London's twenty-six mile waterfront, from St Katharine's Dock in Tilbury, adds a physical dimension to the issue of defining a natural area. As Morris (1958, p. 9) has noted McKenzie defined a natural area in terms of 'the characteristics of its populations, race, language, income and occupation: that is as a cultural rather than physical isolate'. Burgess (1929), however, highlighted the importance of physical considerations in the forma- tion of social relationships. For Burgess these physical considerations were prime factors in the formation of an 'ecological community'. When a social system emerges which is characteristic of a locality, Burgess claims that it is legitimate to refer to a 'cultural community'.

Locational and geographical features in the form of locationally specific economic and occupational opportunities have produced a culture that is characteristic of East London, justifying the definition

[1] Wirth (1964, p. 253), writing of Jewish immigrants to Chicago, notes that the real threat to the culture of immigrants is experienced during the process of secondary settlement. 'Families tend to disintegrate under the stress of behaviour patterns which result from the importation of extraneous cultural influences into the home by the children of the immigrants'.

of 'cultural community' and the ensuing cultural heritage is transmitted largely unopposed. In the east private housing and public
transport provision combined to ensure that the hegemony of East
London's exclusively working-class culture phases out in Waltham-
stow, Redbridge, Barking, and Dagenham. Varying degrees of
marginality exist in these areas, all of which should be regarded as
buffer zones where the distinctive culture of the East End rubs
against middle-class settlement. Piecemeal housing projects that have
transplanted entire streets from Canning Town, Poplar, or Bethnal
Green to remote areas of Essex beyond the underground railway
network have produced spores of East End culture in such areas as
Avely, Basildon, and Stanford-le-Hope, where second-generation
escapees often take advantage of cheap housing to buy their way into
marginal status. In the east, then, the definite boundaries of the
culture are located in the buffer zones, while satellite East End
communities have firmly established themselves in large areas of the
flat Essex countryside.

To the north, Hackney has suffered some middle-class infiltration
along its border with schizophrenic Islington, yet remains for the
most part an essential segment of the working-class cultural community of East London (see Chapter 9). A buffer zone is encountered
in Stamford Hill, roughly marked out by Finsbury Park in the west,
along Seven Sisters Road, Amhurst Park, and Clapton Common.
Defining cultural frontiers in Hackney is undoubtedly fraught with
problems, for apart from middle-class infiltration, the influences of
North London's working-class culture are brought to bear. For
example, East London has only one soccer team commanding mass
support from East London and Essex. Yet in North London, Arsenal
and Spurs compete for support. North London's working-class
heritage is different, and part of Hackney increasingly reflects this
heritage as one moves northwards. This is manifested in the school
playgrounds of the borough where the white shirts of Spurs and the
red of Arsenal vie with the claret and blue of West Ham for play-
ground supremacy. In the south, along the river, a mixture of
exclusive housing projects and gentrification from St Katharine's
Dock to Wapping feature most prominently. This fact of 1980s East
End life has served to reinforce the community's boundary at the old
dock-gates, a place that, ironically, for several centuries marked an
entrance to the East End's very soul, the river Thames.

The boundary that I am suggesting is a class frontier encasing a vast working-class city of three Inner London boroughs, which also influences a large part of the county of Essex. It is bounded and identified in terms of its unique culture, which in turn has developed as 'a set of ready-made definitions of the situation that each individual only slightly re-tailors in his own idiomatic way' (Downes 1966, p. 4).

The question that must be asked is how these definitions emerge and in response to what problems. The answer to both these questions is to be found in the unique history of the area, an analysis of which will illustrate the potency of its culture, and its later seductive influence upon both the contemporary population of East London, and those who seek to control that population.

2. Pre-industrial History and Development

The City of London had by the twelfth century established itself as a haven for those wishing to escape the oppressions of serfdom and become freemen. A steady flow of those wishing to achieve this status led to an expansion of the population, and conditions inside the City walls deteriorated. The agricultural hamlet of Stepney just outside the City's eastern boundaries became established as a place where the overflow of refugees from feudalism could be accommodated. In the fourteenth century Stepney received the accolade of being the first area in Britain outside the City where men were officially 'free'.

At this time in the City of London every trade and craft was strictly controlled by the guilds. However, Stepney was outside the jurisdiction of the City and soon became recognized as a place where artisans, craftsmen, and small merchants could ply their trades without the restraints imposed by the City's guilds. As a consequence of being unshackled by the restrictive tariffs and work practices of the guilds, Stepney tradesmen were able to compete with and undercut their City competitors. Accordingly Stepney rapidly acquired a reputation for shoddy goods and poor workmanship. As Stow (1755, p. 33) explained: 'They practised deceits having none appointed to oversee them and their works. For they belonged to none of the companies of London and so were under no control or restraint.'

Initially, agricultural Stepney had sold its produce to the City and by the thirteenth century had established market stalls in Chepe. In the fourteenth century the Black Death had an unusual effect on

Stepney: in wiping out half the population, it increased the value of the survivors in Stepney, an area by now firmly established as essential to the continued growth and prosperity of the City. The survivors of the plague were able to achieve large increases in pay and a tradition of negotiation was established. (See Chambliss (1971) for an alternative view of the plague's effects on the labouring classes.)

The expansion of the City and its establishment as a centre of commerce increased pressure on available space, and its inhabitants began to regard certain essential trades as being out of character with the City's image as the commercial centre of the nation. Consequently 'noxious trades' were banished from the City walls, the first of which were the City abattoirs: 'all oxen, sheep, swine or other large animals for the sustenance of our City aforesaid to be slaughtered, should be taken to the village of Stretford on the one side, and the village of Knytterbrigge on the other side of the said city and there be slaughtered' (Smith 1939, p. 211 quoting City Ordinance of 1371). As Bermant (1975, p. 11) has noted: 'Knightsbridge was later to become part of fashionable London. Stratford as part of the East End, continued to be a depository of nuisances.'

As industries developed to serve the needs of the City, so the East End became established as an area far enough from the City walls to contain the more distasteful and unpleasant trades without offending the senses of the powerful. Yet the area was close enough to the City to deliver the goods on time. One of the many noxious trades that technology of the period was able to develop was the extraction of alum from human excrement. This industry was founded, like many other odorous processes, on the banks of the river Lea. However the beer-drinking monarch of the day, Charles I, issued an order that human excrement should not be discharged 'whereof beer is made for His Majesty's Service' (Bermant 1975, p. 42).

East London was already developing a distinctive character of its own by the fourteenth century. With a reputation for shoddy workmanship, adept at negotiating and sharp trading, the East-Ender lived in poor housing in a congested area whose water supply, air, and highways were polluted with the flotsam and jetsam of the largest city in the world. For the rich and powerful the East End was an unsightly and unhealthy sore on the periphery of the capital: 'no small blemish to so famous a city to have so unseemly and unsavoury a passage thereunto' (Stow 1755, p. 44).

The Docks

By the end of the fourteenth century the overseas adventures of Henry VIII and Elizabeth I, and the subsequent expansion of the navy, led to increased production in the small shipyards of the City of London. The increase in noise emanating from the yards led to ship-building moving east along the river to Ratcliffe and Blackwall, and south-east to Rotherhithe and Deptford. East London's trades by now were baking, brewing, the slaughter of animals, and shipbuilding. Its inhabitants were those involved in these trades along with street-traders and stallholders.

International trade blossomed during the reign of the Tudors, and the City wharfs were inadequate to deal with the deluge of goods that resulted from state-funded foreign adventurism. Ships were constantly queueing several miles east waiting to approach the City where they would be unloaded into small boats and barges. Ships were also getting bigger and eventually began stopping further east at Ratcliffe (Stepney). The sacking of Antwerp by the Spanish in 1576 resulted in European trade switching to London, and the small riverside hamlets of Ratcliffe, Wapping, Shadwell, Limehouse, and Poplar merged gradually into one community whose livelihood was almost exclusively gained from the river and its associated trades.

As the river trade moved east and dockland became established, the associated trades of ship-repairing, shipbuilding, and ship supplies followed, as did the concomitant industries of the production of glue, turpentine, vitriol, varnish, and naphtha. The expanding waterfront, still reliant on a series of small wharfs, rapidly became the habitat of shipwrights, seamen, and watermen. The growth of the Port of London was accelerated by the establishment in 1512 of the head-quarters of the East India Dock Company at Blackwall, and by 1580 the population of Stepney had grown to 14,000 and was expanding at an unprecedented rate.

Finishing and Consumer Trades

London represented the largest consumer market in Britain, and as a consequence many trades developed that required imported raw materials, which passed through the docks to small handicraft workshops. The East End's proximity to both the docks and an affluent consumer market was crucial in the development of the clothing, silk, and furniture trades (Stedman-Jones 1971, p. 20).

The finishing trades tended to be centred in the 'old' East End—Stepney, Whitechapel, and south Hackney—while the steady development of the waterfront following the building of the West India Docks in 1801 gave industrial development an easterly momentum. While the docks and 'noxious trades' established themselves ever further eastwards, the craft and finishing trades stayed close to their markets hardly participating in the area's geographical expansion.

By 1763 the *Annual Register* described Ratcliffe Highway in Stepney as a place 'of dissolute sailors, blackmailing watermen, rowdy fishermen, stock fish hawkers, quarrelsome chairmen, audacious highwaymen, sneak thieves and professional cheats ... footpads, deserters, prisoners of war on parole, bravos, bullies and river vultures' (Bermant 1975, p. 25).

The imagery and mythology of East End street-life was firmly established before the Industrial Revolution. The expansion of the docks, development of workshop trades, and entrenchment of the noxious trades that were brought about by the Industrial Revolution, merely translated dirty, deprived, poor, and criminal into 'working class'. The development of an industrial working class from an agricultural population that took place during the eighteenth and nineteenth centuries was a phenomenon that did not manifest itself in East London. From medieval times the populace had dealt with the City, negotiating both status and pecuniary reward. It had developed traditions of dealing and street-trading, and established itself as an area specializing in the production of sub-standard goods, and as an area that had distanced itself from the exclusivity of the City, while maintaining the profit motive.

3. Immigration

Of the three principal immigrant groups that settled in East London in the years preceding this century, the Huguenots were by far the most easily assimilated. In attempting to evade religous persecution in their native France, the Protestant Huguenots fled to Britain in the seventeenth century (Gwynn 1985). Many were attracted by the prosperity of the capital, and were drawn to East London where the craft and finishing trades were well established. The Huguenots brought with them cutlers, watchmakers, instrument makers, jewellers, opticians, hatters, glovers, and most importantly silk-weavers. The silk-weavers established themselves in Spitalfields, on the very border of the City, in workshops consisting of a master, two or three weavers, and one or two apprentices (Bermant 1975, p. 32).

Unlike later arrivals, the Huguenots were not hindered by colour, religion, or culture and were easily assimilated and many weavers became masters of their own workshops. However, changes in trade and manufacturing technology led to a rapid deterioration in pay and conditions. So much so in fact that in 1763, 1765, 1766, and 1769 the weavers regularly rioted in protest. An unruly mob of foreigners at the gates of the City required prompt governmental action, and in 1763 the Spitalfields Act was passed to regulate prices and wages. As a consequence of this legislation, manufacturers moved away from the East End and set up workshops in areas outside the jurisdiction of the Act. The trade was already dying when in 1860 the Cobden Act restored free trade, which in turn prompted an influx of cheap silk imports from France. Unable to compete, the silk trade in East London all but disappeared and poverty returned to Spitalfields.

The rapid rise and fall of Huguenot culture left little impression upon the overall inheritance of East London. All that physically remains are a handful of streets in Spitalfields with names like Fleur-de-Lis Street and Blossom Street to commemorate the Huguenots' passion for flowers. However, it is significant to note that the Huguenots were the first of several ethnic groups who settled in the area to adopt an entrepreneurial style.

The Irish

> We shall find the social condition of nearly one-half of London to be nearly as low and degraded as that of Ireland in its worst days.
>
> J. Hollingshead, *Ragged London in 1861.*

There had been an Irish presence in East London for many years before the onset of the Industrial Revolution. Economic blight and religious persecution were the prime motives for immigration, and anti-Catholic riots occurred in the East End in 1736, 1768, and 1786. The Irish were attracted to the area by cheap housing and by the opportunities for manual work that the East End could provide. The first major influx of Irish to the area came with the demobilization of Wellington's predominantly Irish army after the defeat of Napoleon. They soon 'formed the core of the floating armies of labourers who built the canals, the docks, the railways and transformed the face of England' (Bermant 1975, p. 43). Many were drawn by dock construction and waterfront trades to East London, but the labouring culture of the Irish imposed itself in a more significant manner after the potato famine of 1846. Half a million Irish flocked to England and a significant number were attracted to the housing and employment structure of East London. The arrival of the Irish depressed wages, particularly in the docks where many of the immigrants joined the surplus of casual labour competing for work.

Culturally the Irish were well suited to the developing casual employment market of East London, with no liking for the monotony of regular employment and showing a penchant for making money in short spasms in the markets, the docks, or in chance occupations such as street-trading (Bermant 1975, p. 69; Mayhew 1861). Seventy per cent of East London's Irish population were descendants of the famine influx, and for them there had been no gradual change from peasantry to industrial proletariat. They had left a futile life of subsistence farming for a new life in a society that offered a realistic chance of a wage, and if necessary poor relief. This rapid improvement in life chances and social conditions owed nothing either to class consciousness or solidarity, for the Irish immigrant was individualistic and independent of organized support.

The casual attitude of the Irish cockney to earning a living was based on a long-standing labouring culture that, in turn, was informed by the experiences of generations of peasants. England was a last resort for the Irish peasant. Those who were fortunate enough to afford the passage emigrated to America or Canada; only the destitute settled in England (Thompson 1974, p. 472), and the dreadful condition in which the Irish arrived has been vividly drawn by Engels (1969, pp. 104–7). However, what is relevant to this discussion is the conditions to which the Irish landworker was accustomed before his departure. The peasant participated in a sub-subsistence economy and his plight is vividly described in an 1836 report on Irish poverty as one of abject destitution and demoralization: 'Their habitations are wretched hovels ... a family sleep together upon straw or upon the bare ground ... their food ... dry potatoes ... one spare meal on the day ... they never get meat except at Christmas, Easter and Shrovetide' (cited in Thompson 1974, p. 472).

But the Irish imported with them much more than a culture of poverty; they were imbued with the culture of pre-industrial land-workers and consequently were unfettered by industrial work discipline. The new English working class had received from their landworking ancestors an inheritance that had been seriously affected by land reform, the mechanization of agriculture, and finally a shift to the cities in search of work. These factors produced an unconscious growth in tolerance, over several generations, to the work disciplines of the emerging capitalist structure, of which the factory system performed a central disciplining function.

In the industrial north of England, displaced Irish landworkers rapidly established themselves as a supplementary labour force utilized at the very base of industry in heavy manual occupations that did not require 'steady methodological application, inner motivations of sobriety, forethought, and punctilious observation of contracts' (Thompson 1974, p. 473).

The Irish community in England emerged as a lumpen subclass engaged in unpleasant manual occupations to which the English worker, successfully moulded by industrial work discipline, was no longer suited, either physically or temperamentally. Capitalism created a market for heavy manual labour at the very rump of numerous industries, and after the feudal conditions of Ireland, the remuneration and relative freedom of contract offered by these occupations were relished. Consequently, by the middle of the century entire occupations had been colonized by the Irish, and as Thompson (1974, p. 473) has noted employers could benefit by exploiting the best of a labour supply from both pre-industrial and industrial societies. The English either refused the unpleasant menial work, or could not keep pace with the Irishman's phenomenal work-rate. Skilled and semi-skilled occupations remained the prerogative of the English, while the Irish would take any job requiring brute strength. The 1836 Report emphasized the emergence of the Irish as a substratum of society and, in the industrial north of England in particular, where the working-class were subdivided by the hier-archical structure of a factory-based occupational structure, navvies and labourers would indeed have constituted a substratum or underclass (see Roberts 1973, p. 22). However, the Irish who settled in London, and particularly in East London, were confronted by an economy that owed nothing to the factory system of production, and consequently was not policed by the proletarian hierarchy that in northern England relegated the Irish to the lowliest occupations.

With few exceptions the only occupations open to East Londoners were (a) heavy manual work paid at piece- or gang-rate, such as dock-work; (b) street-trading; or (c) a craft trade that required no apprenticeship, was subject to workshop discipline, and amenable to self-employed status. As a consequence of the economic milieu in which the Irish immigrant found himself in East London, he was not merely complementing the indigenous work-force, but competing with it. Anti-Irish feeling lingered in the capital long after inter-marriage and occupational demarcation had become the norm elsewhere. The settlement of so many Irish in the East End com-pounded the essentially deviant image of the area. They gained near monopoly of such trades as coal-heaving, where exhaustion and coal-dust resulted in heavy drinking, and their subsequent drunken behaviour, abetted by the fact that they were often paid out in pubs, was an additional factor in defining the area as deviant.

The 'moral economy of the factory system' (Ure 1835) barely affected East London: the central cultural ethos was determined by the dominant pre-industrial mode of production. The Irish immi-grants' status was determined by their ability to compete with the indigenous population in the area's traditional occupations rather than take up unpopular jobs that the natives were unwilling or unable to do. The transformation of the Irish immigrant to East London from pre-industrial rural poor to pre-industrial urban poor was a relatively smooth process in that no traumatic alteration to their religion or language was necessary, the similarities in culture were considerable. East Londoners, like the Irish, were untainted by the Puritan virtues of thrift and sobriety that had combined with the factory system of production to impose discipline on the working classes of northern England. Methodism and capitalism grew together, and mutually complemented each other in the North, the former gaining its flock almost exclusively from the new industrial working class, extolling discipline and order, providing the 'inner compulsion' when wages and piece-rates might fail (Thompson 1974, pp. 385–440). It was not until the 1880s that factory production became anything like a feature of the East End, and in Canning Town and Silvertown in particular the work remained largely seasonal for many years (Hugill 1978).

Economically, culturally, and socially the Irish dovetailed into the East End, dominating certain occupations and reinforcing the area's emerging deviant image. Uprooted from a poor, rural society, the

Irish were as untainted by industrialism as the indigenous East-Ender, and their presence contributed greatly to the composition of the area's cultural heritage.

Jews

Like the Irish, a Jewish presence had been established in London long before the Industrial Revolution. Their expulsion from Britain in 1290 and readmission in 1656 is indicative of the varying fortunes of the Jewish people throughout the world and in Europe in particular. By the time Jewish immigration to East London started to peak in the 1880s as a result of Tsar Alexander II's pogroms, a middle-class Jewish base was well established. Wealthy Jews expelled from Spain and Portugal who had settled in England were aware of the tradition of anti-Semitism and the derogatory image of Jews that had persevered for many centuries. Sensitive to the prejudices of the host nation's indigenous population, and using their own experience as refugees as a reference point, the middle-class Jewish Community in Britain set up numerous organizations designed to reduce the pariah or scrounger image so often attached throughout the centuries to the Jewish immigrant. This move towards improving the image of the Jew established a tradition of self-help, and spawned organizations such as the Jewish Bread, Meat and Coal Society in 1779, the Norwood Jewish Orphanage in 1795, the Jewish Blind Society in 1819, the Society for Relieving the Aged Needy of the Jewish Faith in 1829, and the Spitalfields Soup Kitchen in 1834. These organizations were designed to reduce reliance upon poor relief, yet the most powerful (and distinctively bourgeois) organization set up by the Anglo-Jews was the Jewish Board of Guardians, formed in 1859 (White 1980, p. 133).

As White (1980, p. 250) notes, in eastern Europe under feudalism 90 per cent of Jews were engaged in trade, representing an inter-mediate class between the aristocracy and the peasantry. Most of the remaining 10 per cent were independent artisans involved in clothing manufacture. The growth of capitalism created an indigenous bourgeoisie that displaced the Jewish trader class. The subsequent emancipation of the peasantry via the capitalization of agriculture created a large market for consumer goods among the newly created proletariat. The ensuing growth in output led to changes in production methods, especially in clothing, footwear, and furniture, the traditional Jewish trades. Displaced peasants formed a large, cheap, unskilled work-force, which, combined with mechanization, served to oust the Jewish artisan.

The pogroms of 1881 triggered an influx of poor displaced east European Jews into the major cities of western Europe. These refugees were not only displaced, but within the space of two generations had experienced, by way of the Industrial Revolution, a severe loss of economic and social status. The East End of London as a finishing-centre for consumer goods was an ideal haven of pre-industrial production, where the trades in which the Jews had once prospered were well established. The Jews moved into these trades and made them their own, and while the social, family, and religious life of east European Jewry began to replicate itself in East London, the pre-industrial mode of production that, by the 1880s, was unique to the area offered an opportunity for the Jews to 're-establish the economic independence and security which they and their parents had lost in the past' (White 1980, p. 252).

The trading inheritance of the immigrants, fostering both competition and individualism, made them ideally suited to the economic climate of East London. The structure of the workshop trades was essentially small scale, often in premises adjacent to or within the family home. These businesses required very little capital and employed few workers. In a survey carried out in 1888, of 900 East End tailoring shops, 76 per cent employed less than ten workers, while the boot-and-shoe trade and cabinet-making involved similarly small work-forces. The opportunities and temptations to escape from the drudgery of waged employment were considerable; to become a master required little capital and was always a legitimate option. Centred around Whitechapel and Spitalfields, Jewish immigrants built up around the tailoring, shoe-making, and furniture trades a community based on tiny workshops and sweated labour. If one did not aspire to become a master, then it was viable to turn to contracting, obtaining a contract with a wholesale or retail outlet, and employing individuals to manufacture the goods in their own homes or at piece-work rates. The localized structure of these trades allowed individual contractors to establish for themselves what White (1980, p. 256) calls 'semi-proletarian' status. The contractor or small master resided in the same housing as those he employed, reflecting the pluralism of their ghetto inheritance, employer and employee sharing both religion and social habits. The preoccupation of the culture was, while restoring and maintaining the pre-industrial pluralism of the Pale, to avoid proletarianism.

The well-established Jewish middle class that manifested itself in the form of the Jewish Board of Guardians endeavoured to socialize the immigrants by collaborating with the synagogue to assimilate the East End Jew into bourgeois English society. Small craft workshops and informal retailing were traditional ways of acquiring the economic independence of pre-industrial eastern Europe. The Jewish Board of Guardians interpreted this desire for independence as work-ethic-inspired upward mobility, and set about making it financially possible for the immigrant to join the middle class by awarding interest-free loans to those wishing to become a master or independent trader. For example, from 1900 to 1910, 26,479 loans of an average of £7 were awarded for this purpose. These loans were made as a direct attempt to improve the image of British Jews, and the small amount of capital required and subsequent profusion of small businesses are indicative of the peculiar economic climate of East London.

The geographical consequences of mass Jewish immigration were not limited to the unconscious replication of the ghettos of the Pale. Settlement to the east of Whitechapel into Stepney was halted at Wapping by the long-established Irish community who had settled close to the docks. West was the City, which by the 1880s was an almost exclusively commercial zone. South lay the river, so northwards was the only way out. Those Jews who gradually had adopted the culture of bourgeois Anglo-Jewry, shrugging off the traditions of pluralism and self-help that were prerequisites of ghetto survival, tended to move into the private housing market in Stamford Hill and later Golders Green. However, many comparatively wealthy Jews stayed in Whitechapel and the ghetto was bonded by their non-involvement in the 1914–18 war. The castigation of the East End Jewish community for their unwillingness to fight (for a nation to which they felt little allegiance) alongside Russia (the nation from which many of them had fled persecution) served to heighten anti-Jewish feeling, as many tailors in particular benefited from the war effort. The East End Jew owed allegiance to the Whitechapel ghetto, rather than Whitehall or Minsk.

The Jewish immigrant introduced elements of individualism and entrepreneurial endeavour to East London based on an economic heritage founded in the pre-industrial ghettos of eastern Europe. The established middle-class Anglo-Jewry attempted to inculcate a bourgeois belief in mobility, and financed the ghetto trades in an effort to embourgeoisize a pre-industrial community that had not experienced proletarianization. Consequently initial attempts at embourgeoisement failed and the Whitechapel ghetto mirrored the hierarchical internal structure of the Pale. The entrepreneurial ethic was reinforced by the Church, and competition and economic independence flourished. The inheritance of ghettoization served to strengthen the internal economic structure as monopolies over certain markets were established.

Summary

The Huguenot craftsmen did much to establish East London as a centre for finishing and precision trades, yet their rapid assimilation into the indigenous population, and the rapid decline in their trades, left only a limited impression upon the cultural heritage of East London. The Irish influx of cheap manual labour and their essentially pre-industrial culture had massive implications for the development of the area. A preference for short-term heavy manual work was coupled with a culture untainted by Methodism and factory discipline, and in East London they discovered an emerging culture based on manual labour and short-contract casual employment. Essentially independent, the Irish labourer made the East End his home, reinforcing the economic and cultural norms of the area. Thrift and sobriety were never established characteristics of East London, and the Irish culture based on sub-subsistence land-labouring, served to reinforce the pre-industrial culture of East London and compound that culture's predominant characteristics, notably a predilection for casual labour, a deviant self-image, and independence. The beleaguered Jews infused skills and crafts along with entrepreneurship and self-reliance.

The cultural inheritance of East London has been formed by a fusion of communities; independence, internal solidarity, and pre-industrial cultural characteristics combining to form a community that does not conform to either proletarian or bourgeois cultural stereotypes. The vital contradiction of this cultural inheritance is that it is essentially working-class, favouring an entrepreneurial style that is rooted in pre-industrial forms of bargaining and exchange.

4. A Deviant Area

Before a more thorough analysis of the local economy of East London is attempted, I will briefly turn my attention to some of the factors that have combined to define the area as deviant or criminal. As Pearson has noted, the emerging Victorian middle class were not slow in associating the physical conditions of the working class with their moral condition (Pearson 1975, p. 161). The most obvious physical manifestation of what was regarded as 'the problem' of the East End was found in the almost negligible sewer system of the chronically overcrowded area, yet the resultant poor insanitary condition of the populace was not a phenomenon peculiar to East London. However, the area's close proximity to the increasingly affluent and prosperous City, coupled with the constant housing crisis that resulted from the poor of the City and West End seeking refuge in the already overcrowded areas in the East End, helped create an unparalleled image of filth and depravity.

The sanitary and moral conditions of the poor were regarded as one and the same problem—both emanated from the harsh reality of man at his worst. 'The coincidence of pestilence and moral disorder' (Chadwick 1842, p. 132) became crucial in the restructuring of the City and the realignment of those habits of the working class that threatened to stifle capitalist progress. Attempts at public health reform marked more than an effort to improve the sanitary conditions of the poor; what was at issue was 'the regimentation of disciplined work habits and reasonable political habits among labouring men, and not just a regimentation of their bowels' (Pearson 1975, p. 171).

Indeed, regimentation of any sort was, in East London in particular, an impractical objective. East London was reliant upon the Thames for its livelihood, and the opportunities for theft and pilferage were numerous. As Bermant (1975, p. 122) has noted: 'They lived on the river, and the river meant plunder.' For centuries before the docks were built, East-Enders had plundered ships, barges, wharfs, warehouses, and even the mud of the river itself (Mayhew 1861, Vol. 4, pp. 291–304). Theft was normal, and the theft and sale of items identifiable as corporate and not private property, was essential to the formation of contemporary attitudes to property in East London today. Theft and its encumbent opportunity structure was one of the few benefits of living in the area, and this approach to property and to crime permeated all those occupations concerned with waterside work (Colquhoun 1979, p. 220).

Thieving, and the buying and selling of stolen goods became integral to East End culture, everybody was 'at it' and as a consequence, 'Everything was vendible, and everyone was on the look-out for something to vend. It made for a certain keenness and vivacity, and if there was poverty in the riverside parishes, it was poverty tempered by loot' (Bermant 1975, p. 23). The normality of property crime and the characteristics of 'keenness' and 'vivacity' that resulted were only part of East London's deviant heritage. Throughout the nineteenth century, housing conditions in East London deteriorated, and as poor housing was often associated with crime and disorder, the East End stood out as a significant example. Lord Shaftesbury highlighted this connection between disorder and housing conditions most cogently: 'If the working man has his own house I have no fear of revolution' (cited in Weightman and Humphries 1983, p. 163).

Market forces were solely responsible for the worsening overcrowding as the century progressed. The building of the London Dock from 1800 to 1805 resulted in 1,300 houses being destroyed, while the building of the St Katharine's Dock in 1828 led to the demolition of 1,033 homes. Yet as Stedman-Jones (1971, p. 164) has noted, the population of these areas continued to increase, putting extra pressure on the existing housing stock. As commercial prosperity blossomed, the areas on the eastern fringe of the City were gradually colonized by offices and warehouses. The rise of the West End of London as a centre of bourgeois residence, shopping, and entertainment led to the destruction of the area's poorer housing, notably the notorious 'rookery' of St Giles (Chesney 1968, pp. 122–34; Rock 1983, p. 208). Between the years 1830 and 1880, West End urban improvement displaced some 100,000 persons, and railway-building displaced further tens of thousands between the years 1853 and 1909 (Stedman-Jones 1971, pp. 162, 171).

Residential areas were cleared in order that docks, railways, and warehouses could be constructed on the capital's cheapest land, and as central London developed as a commercial centre huge populations were forced east. As the housing stock of East London declined in both quality and quantity, the population of London doubled between 1821 and 1851, and doubled again by 1900. Workers could not move far from the City or the docks, as these were the centres of employment. For instance, women workers traditionally employed in laundering, office-cleaning, charring, and the sweated trades were obliged to reside close to their place of employment for, as in the case of dock and market workers, they began work early in the morning without any system of public transport at their disposal. Costers not only needed to reside close to the markets but required sheds for their barrows and somewhere to stable their donkeys. As Stedman-Jones (1971, p. 172) notes, this often led to a decline in housing conditions: 'The choice nearly always confined itself to decaying slum courts, where rubbish could be thrown out of the windows and the donkeys could sleep in disused privies.'

Early morning call for casual workers at the dock-gates meant that queues began forming in the early hours, again necessitating near residence for the docker to have a realistic chance of gaining employment. Central London and the dock-gates developed as the central focus of the casual labour market, not only as centres of employment but, just as crucial, as places where information concerning work and work-related issues were formally and informally exchanged. East London consolidated itself as an area of working-class residence, and was constantly supplemented by influxes of casual and poorly paid workers from central London, Ireland, and eastern Europe. Meanwhile the single-class nature of the area was reinforced by an exodus of middle-class residents who could afford to use the new railway system and commute to and from the City.

As the East End became more crowded housing deteriorated. As Stedman-Jones (1971, p. 176) shows increases in persons per house were rapid, and the worst overcrowding occurred in those areas immediately adjacent to the City. The vague and largely impotent structure of local government negated any hope of controlled rehousing until the 1877 Street Act was brought to bear. The Act decreed that not more than fifteen houses could be demolished without alternative housing being found for the displaced residents. Unofficially, however, it would appear that the majority of displaced residents preferred to take a compensatory payment and find their own housing in the same locality, thereby further increasing overcrowding and squalor. In an analysis of one specific redevelopment on the very perimeter of the City, it was found that of 150 families, 72 settled within half a mile of their previous home, 49 settled half to one and a half miles from their previous residence, and only 14 settled over one and a half miles away (Stedman-Jones 1971, p. 182).

As the century progressed London's economy became increasingly dominated by non-industrial capital, such as banking and commerce. Very few East-Enders were employed in these fields, and there developed an absence of direct economic links between East London and the rest of the capital. A vast pool of casual labour, living in overcrowded insanitary conditions had been moulded by market forces from the emerging working class. They were no longer of any lasting economic value to the City, being unable to adapt to alterations in the economic structure of London, their culture based solidly upon pre-industrial patterns of employment. When this culture was no longer of strategic utility to the forces of capital, they were discarded and regarded as a problem—a vast, dirty, impoverished, criminal problem.

One answer to the problem of the East End was to improve the lot of its population via charity. The flood of charitable funds that followed the publication of Mearns's *The Bitter Cry of Outcast London* in 1883 and the indiscriminate distribution of these funds, led to more unemployment and destitute men and women flocking to the area, adding to the general deprivation and overcrowding. It became an area of dark, foggy alleys, and seething rancid tenements, a place where the cast-offs from foreign shipping established their habits and vices. Due to housing conditions, spasmodic heavy manual work, and poor diet, the area even developed its own physically inferior type. The East End established itself as an area where an insidious deterioration of the British race had apparently begun, and recruitment of East Londoners into the army was widely blamed for British defeats during the Boer War: 'the first stage of decay had already been reached when the stolid, God-fearing puritan of two and a half centuries ago has given place to the shallow, hysterical cockney of today' (Anon. in Whitehouse 1912). Wheeling and dealing, fighting and stealing for work, property, a home, a contract, or a loaf of bread, required a social personality that was voluble and aggressive (London 1903, p. 137).

The fear of the East End that the physical, economic, and moral deprivation of the area provoked can be best illustrated by concentrating briefly upon two separate moral panics:

(i) 'King Mob'—the threat from the east In February 1886, 20,000 demonstrators consisting of dockers, building-workers, and others demanding employment gathered in Trafalgar Square. They were

addressed by Ben Tillet and John Burns after which a small break-away group overturned carriages, looted shops, and after some provocation broke windows at the Reform and Carlton Clubs. The response was hysterical—'King Mob' had emerged from the east to wreak havoc. Rumours of a vast army of East-Enders gathering to attack the West End quickly spread, yet the marchers went home singing 'Rule Britannia' and although elaborate precautions were taken on the days immediately following, the threat never material-ized (Weightman and Humphries 1983, p. 152). However, the 'East End mob' was fully established as a folk devil *par excellence* whose image was to be periodically regurgitated at times of social crisis and economic blight (Chibnall 1977, pp. 127–31). The mob as Robert Park has noted is an urban symbol: 'the situation they represent is always critical that is to say the tensions are such that a slight cause may precipitate an enormous effect' (Park *et al.*, quoted in Stedman-Jones 1971).

East London emerged as 'the mob', a huge population of uniformly destitute, hungry, casual, or unemployed workers, residing on the periphery of the Empire's epicentre. Every form of deviation was to be found in the area, and its physically deprived state was merely a manifestation of the inhabitants' inherent criminality. The City and West End required this threat within to reinforce and strengthen its own identity and affirm its alignment with the emerging capitalist state. The East-Enders in their periodic excursions 'up west' threatened not only the livelihoods of shopkeepers, but also imperil-led 'the riches and civilization of London and the Empire' (Stedman-Jones 1971, p. 13).

(ii) Jack the Ripper, sex, murder and aliens—the embodiment of evil During four months of 1888 there was a number of murders in Whitechapel that served to compound those essential elements that together have formulated the East End's deviant image. Between August and November a series of murders were committed, and the victims were, with one possible exception, all prostitute women with an addiction to alcohol. The details of the killings are vague to the extent that the exact number of victims remains unclear, but there were probably five or six. Violent death was commonplace in and around Whitechapel, and the first two throat-cuttings followed by disembowelment warranted little more than casual interest. However,

the third murder in September provoked the Gentile population of the East End to the verge of a mini-pogrom: 'it was repeatedly asserted that no Englishman could have perpetrated such a horrible crime as that of Hanbury Street and that it must have been done by a Jew' (*East London Observer*, 15 September 1888, quoted in Fishman 1979, pp. 84–5).

Various rumours concerning the sexual, moral, and religious habits of Jewish men rapidly began to accumulate, the most damaging probably emanating from the east European correspondent of *The Times*, who, reporting upon the ritual murder of a Christian woman in Vienna, claimed that in parts of Germany Jews fashioned candles for the uterus, candles which in turn gave off fumes which rendered people unconscious and were used by criminals to incapacitate victims (Bermant 1975, pp. 112–13).

Adjacent to the third corpse was found a leather apron, a fact that pointed the finger at a craftsman, and as the crafts of the East End were by this time dominated by Jews the ethnicity of the murderer seemed even more certain, and a Jewish bookbinder was taken into custody, only be be released later on the establishment of his innocence (Bermant 1975, p. 114). The next craft to come under suspicion was that of the Jewish slaughterman. There were many kosher slaughterhouses in the area, and those that worked in these establishments possessed a knowledge of anatomy, access to and a dexterity with a variety of knives, and most importantly would be religious scholars. As Odell (1965, p. 153) has noted: 'A ritual slaughterman steeped in Old Testament law might have felt some religious justification for killing prostitutes. Talmudic law was harsh where harlotry was concerned and in certain cases whores could be punished by strangulation or stoning.'

As the killings continued the descriptions of 'Leather Apron' culled from various sources, began to merge into one. A dark, bearded figure dressed in black, as Camps and Barber (1966, p. 30) indicate, is almost a description of the 'stage villain'. The official description was less theatrical and more pragmatic: 'Age 37, height 5 ft. 8 in. Rather dark beard and moustache; dress, dark jacket, dark vest and trousers, back scarf and black felt hat. Speaks with a foreign accent' (McCormick 1970, p. 33). This was a description of a Jew in a Jewish ghetto.

After the fourth murder, some graffiti containing bizarre spelling was discovered on a wall in Goulston Street (Bermant 1975, pp. 116–17). The message 'The Jewes are not the men to be blamed for nothing' was inconclusive, yet the spelling suggested a strong Hebrew influence, and prompted a tentative correspondence between the Commissioner of Police and the Chief Rabbi (Knight 1976). When no arrests were forthcoming, anti-Semitic feeling increased and the murders focused attention upon the East End in a manner that confirmed the reputation of its occupants and reinforced the image of the area as a dangerous and parasitical 'no-go' area, inhabited by individuals ill-equipped for productive enterprise within the normative order.

Summary: A Deviant Area

The increasingly unpalatable extremes of urban life could be located in East London, and the area became a metaphor for crime and depravity. As I have suggested, specific types of crime are normal in East London as a result of the area's peculiar economy, creating enhanced opportunity for property-related offences. If we accept that crime marks out certain moral boundaries in any given society (Durkheim 1964, p. 68), we can see the crucial importance of East London in defining the essentially 'good' qualities inherent in the City and West End, blending the parallel interests of the emerging middle class, capitalism, and the state. The East End served as a writhing symbol of respectable fears and anxieties, the population was dehumanized and classified as deviant by definers whose power-base was in the City. The social distance between the City and East London was maintained by the structure of the latter's economy, which in turn created a physical boundary to a deviant world which was only breached by deliberate adventurism. As Rock has noted: 'Physical boundaries also restrict access to deviant worlds. When deviancy is stabilised and concentrated in certain areas (such as Soho, Harlem, The Tenderloin or earlier on, the Ratcliffe Highway and Five Points) possiblities of random and unintended confrontation with deviants are considerably reduced' (Rock 1973, p. 30). Societal reaction to the East End served to define the area as deviant, thereby stigmatizing successive generations of East Londoners. Market forces created the East End, and its culture is a cumulative response to the problems created by those forces. Crime was crucial in the primary formation of that culture, and like the coercive power of capital remains an enduring feature of East End life.

5. Ducking and Diving: Casual Work and the Small Master

By the middle of the nineteenth century London had established itself as Europe's major port, the nation's largest consumer market, the centre of government and the royal court, and the focal point of conspicuous consumption and its related luxury trades (Stedman-Jones 1971, p. 19). The Industrial Revolution relied on coal and steam-driven power, and London's distance from the centres of coal production, and an excessive tax imposed on imported coal by the City, coupled with the high cost of land, resulted in few factories being built in the London area. As Stedman-Jones (1971, p. 358, Table 1) using data derived from the 1861 census indicates, the population of London was employed largely in distributive and finishing trades. The disciplinary aspect of factory production missed London in general, but East London developed as a finishing-centre based on small workshops, and as a docking community based on casual manual labour. As capitalism progressed, the casual labour market expanded into other industries, market forces thereby supplementing a poverty-stricken population with further insecurity, low wages, and overcrowding.

The Docks

The West India Docks were opened in 1802, and initially a permanent labouring work-force was appointed of 200 men, who were also recruited into a special regiment to protect the docks and its warehouses from plunder (Stedman-Jones 1971, p. 111). Casual work was, on the foundation of the dock, kept to a minimum. Likewise with the opening of the London Dock in 1805, 100 regular workers were employed and casual work scarce. By the end of the Napoleonic Wars however, the vast pool of surplus labour resulting from the demobilization of Wellington's armies led to a decrease in wages, and the seasonality of dock-work led to a gradual transference to the utilization of cheap casual labour. By mid-century, changes in patterns of trade, and the intense competition caused by the opening of the Victoria Dock in 1853 led to the dock companies taking full advantage of the casual pool. Dividends had been high for the dock companies in the first half of the century and in order to maintain these dividends wage-levels were slashed, and it became commonly acknowledged that casuals would work harder than permanent

workers in the hope that they might be employed full time themselves.[2]

Technological innovations, such as the telegraph and steamboats,
led to the regulation of world trade, and the seasonality of much dock
trade reduced the need to utilize the massive warehouses upon which
both the dock companies and much of the population relied for
dividends and as a source of rich thieving opportunities. Steam and
the switch from wooden to iron shipping required bigger docks; in
1880 the Albert Dock was built, and in 1886 a dock was completed at
Tilbury. Although overall tonnage increased, the upper-pool docks
declined. Competition was fierce, and the introduction of steam
involved massive capital investment. Without the sailing-ship's
reliance upon tide and wind, the steamship was more reliable and
punctual, and precise timetables evolved that allowed shipping to
take advantage of seasonality of production and varying harvests
around the world. This meant a further reduction in warehouse
utility that eroded profits and cut wages. Rapid turn-around was no
longer a matter for tide and wind but for manual labour, and on
reduced wages the casual docker was pressurized to work harder.
Payment was now made by the hour, and the decentralization and
increased competition among the dock companies led to dockers
working intensely, sometimes all night at hourly rates, to achieve
turn-around, knowing that the gaps between ships were growing.

The inner East End suffered from its proximity to the upper-pool
docks as shipping tonnage moved ever eastwards. By the 1880s
London, having created a huge pool of casual labour was overdocked
with its twenty-six-mile waterfront extending from St Katharine's to
Tilbury.[3] Mayhew (1861 Vol. 3, pp. 300–12) highlights the problem by
stating that 12,000 men depended on the docks for work, competing
for some 4,000 jobs. While Booth's 1892 figures show that despite an
expansion in dock-work the pool consisting of those competing for
work had also expanded. Booth shows that 21,353 competed for work
which only gave a maximum of 17,994 and a minimum of 11,967
men daily employment. This pool of casual labour was continually

---

[2] Stedman-Jones (1971, p. 116) notes that tonnage in the Victoria Dock increased
from 410,463 tons in 1856 to 850,337 tons in 1860. Dividends increased correspondingly from 5 to 5.25%, while in the same period London Dock dividends declined from
5% to 2.25%, and St Katharine's from 4.50 to 3.25%.
[3] Stedman-Jones (1971, p. 118) describes the calamitous effect of overdocking in
some detail.

being supplemented by the collapse of some industries and the casualization of others.

Silk-weaving

Silk-weaving in East London had in 1824 employed 50,000 but by 1830 this figure was reduced to 20,000. The trade was finally killed off by the Cobden Free Trade Treaty with France in 1860 which opened up the country to cheap imports (Hollingshead 1861, pp. 75–6). By 1880 there were 3,300 weavers in East London and according to a Poor Law Report of 1837 it became traditional for unemployed weavers to seek work in the docks.

Shipbuilding

Another traditional East End trade, shipbuilding at its peak in 1865 employed 27,000. When the building of iron ships took over this coincided with the end of the railway and building booms, and according to *The Times* (17 January 1867) there were 30,000 out of work in Poplar alone. A harsh winter, a slump in trade, and a poor harvest made the year 1866–7 particularly hard and shipbuilding never recovered. By 1871 only 9,000 were employed in the trade. Shipbuilding moved north, close to the centres of raw material production, and the East London trade shifted almost exclusively to repair work, the spasmodic nature of which led to the casualization of the trade by the 1880s (Booth 1902, Vol. 1, pp. 269–86).[4]

Entire trades such as coppersmiths and boilermakers became casualized and, as a consequence: 'The rhythm of work, and consequently the habits of the men, were closely analogous to those of dock labourers' (Stedman-Jones 1971, p. 57). Transport, building, decorating (Stedman-Jones 1971, pp. 58, 60) and a vast catalogue of other trades developed individual pools of labour to deal with the peculiar fluctuations of their specific industries.

The enormous size of the casual labour pool was a reflection of 'the importance of London as a port, as the largest concentration of population in the world, and as a capital city, a centre of the rich and thus a magnet for beggars and "loafers" and a universal provider of casual jobs' (Stedman-Jones 1971, p. 65). As a tradition of casualization developed, employers, by now flocking to the area, had different motives for maintaining the casual system. In the docks, as I have

---

[4] Stedman-Jones also notes that repair work was more plentiful in the winter months due to the increase of collisions on the river.

mentioned above, many factors came into play including over-docking, technological innovation, the maximization of profit, and seasonality. Ship repairs became casualized due to technological change and seasonality. Employers in the transport industry utilized the casual system as a way of maintaining discipline, while even the noxious trades and other factory-based industries (the few that existed in the East End) employed workers on a casual basis (Booth 1889, Vol. 2, p. 103).

Small Masters—Clothing, Footwear, and Furniture

These workshop-based trades produced for the wholesale, ready-made market, competing with provincial factory-produced goods in an effort to cater for an expanding mass market. In direct contrast to many nineteenth-century industries, technological innovation served to preserve an essentially pre-industrial mode of manufacture. In particular, the invention of the sewing-machine in 1846, the band-saw in 1858, and the ingenious adaption of the sewing-machine to shoe manufacture in 1857, allowed the small East End workshop to compete economically with provincial factories by reducing staff to a minimum and distributing specific tasks to homeworkers. Thereby expensive capital equipment was substituted in favour of cheap unskilled labour (Hall 1962, pp. 92–3). The effect was a further deskilling of the work-force.

Employers were able to cater to fluctuating fashions and season-able demands by avoiding the stockpiling and machine resetting that was characteristic of factory production. The workshop entrepreneur enjoyed a measure of flexibility by employing outworkers who, despite self-employed status, found their meagre wages depleting as the second half of the century progressed, and a steady flow of cheap unskilled or displaced skilled labour put pressure on workers in the sweated trades. For instance, an East End needlewoman in 1848 was paid 5s. 0d. per week while by 1860 the wages had reduced to 3s. 2d. per week. As Jewish immigration to the area increased, indigenous casual labour was undercut further, and the sweated system reinforced. Unemployed indigenous sweated workers traditionally sought employment in the docks, while unemployed dock-workers and their wives often sought employment in the workshop (Booth's evidence to the House of Lords Select Committee on Sweating 1888).

Apart from contributing to the expansion of the casual system, the proliferation of small workshops in East London meant that the ownership of the means of production was widely dispersed throughout the area. The survival of small-scale industries bolstered by a huge pool of casual labour, and the small amounts of capital needed to establish or maintain production, meant that not only East London's economic structure, but also its socio-political character and emergent culture were totally distinct from any other nineteenth-century industrial region.

Street-trading

The last resort of the unemployed casual worker was to take to the streets. The costermongers aroused in the emergent middle-class of the mid-nineteenth century unparalleled consternation. They were with their 'flash' clothes, coded language, and unruly behaviour the physical manifestation of an underclass whose economy was increasingly contrary to emergent capitalism, the success of which rested upon order and social stability.[5] The costers were street-traders dealing in the 'green market', buying green vegetables at the wholesale markets of London and selling the goods on the streets. They were unruly and violent, constantly clashing with the 'New Police' who in the years immediately following their formation gained favour with the middle classes by harassing street-traders and stifling traditional working-class recreations and pastimes (Cohen 1979, pp. 116–33; Mayhew 1861, p. 22). More than any other group in East London, the costers were untouched by the puritanism that paved the way for the factory system in the North. Often choosing not to marry partners, the male coster frowned upon thrift, and spent his profits on leisurely pursuits, notably drinking and gambling. Their deviant life-style and unwillingness to conform to a subservient working-class role, epitomized to the middle classes the tripartite threat of mob, unruly worker, and godless fiend.

The green trade was largely hereditary, but the scope for making a living on the streets of London was considerable, and consequently attracted many to street-trading of whom the costers were the most successful practitioners. Mayhew (1861) has provided the most illuminating record of nineteenth-century London street-life, and I do not intend to expound upon its overall qualities. However, the desperate plight of many casual workers driven to street-selling honed a fine edge of cutthroat competition to their enterprises.

[5] For elaborations upon the unique nature of the costers' culture, see Chesney (1968, pp. 43–56) and Mayhew (1952, pp. 28–98).

Jewish immigrants and displaced Irish peasants undercut one another as vast numbers of dockers and their families alternating between the docks and the markets attempted to survive against competition from unemployed craftsmen.[6] While many failed, those who were successful in obtaining a living from the streets embodied an independence and a sharpness of wit that served to entrench their economic and social foundations firmly in the working-class city of East London.

Seasonality

The outstanding factor in defining a trade as casual was seasonality. Constant respites in production or the provision of a service affected all the major industries of East London, and while the weather predictably played its part, other elements affecting seasonality contributed to create the economic climate for casualization.

A fashionable season developed in the West End of London during the nineteenth century. Originating as an off-shoot of the social activities of the royal court, the aristocracy who had benefited from their landholdings during the housing and railway-building booms, left their country homes for the spring and summer to indulge in the social events of the London 'season'. Over a million people were employed on a casual basis for these four months ranging from tailors, dressmakers, furniture-makers, and milliners, to servants, cooks, coach-builders, saddlers, and builders. By July they were out of work and forced to ply their trade in some other manner or to encroach on some other overcrowded profession (Weightman and Humphries 1983, pp. 42–69).

During the summer months demand for gas and coal was negligible and this affected lightermen, coal-heavers, and sweeps among others. During the winter months these workers usually found employment, whilst most other casually employed East-Enders suffered during inclement weather, with the notable exception of undertakers who took on additional labour in November to cope with the anticipated influx of winter corpses. Dockers and other water-front workers were especially susceptible in times of poor weather, but skilled workers could turn to other trades in times of hardship, and flexibility became a valued characteristic of many trades. Bad harvests, frozen conditions, and a contrary wind that made it

---

[6] Mayhew (1952) notes that the Irish orange-seller was able to undercut his Jewish rival by being willing to live rough.

impossible for ships to sail up river, led to poverty among dockers and outdoor workers and those in skilled trades who relied upon imports for their raw materials. Workers were constantly looking to other trades, and seasonal slumps resulted in many setting up their own businesses. Stedman-Jones (1971, p. 52) notes that Mayhew traced the proliferation of small masters in the East-End furniture trade to the slump of 1847, and Booth noted a similar response in the furniture, bootmaking, and clothing trade of the 1880s. Consequently competition thrived and a downbidding of contract tenders served to intensify the poverty of those employed in a trade as master or worker. Small-scale production exacerbated the problems of seasonal oscillations in trade and compounded the need to maintain a pool of casual labour in order that the peaks of seasonal demand could be met.

As nineteenth-century British society moulded itself in the image of the 'workshop of the world', East London retraced the footsteps of capitalism, and as the century progressed, market forces reinforced the area's pre-industrial economy. Casualization increased as a result of technological innovation, deskilling, seasonality, and international trade agreements, and consequently small-scale producers increasingly employed casual and self-employed labour to compete with factory-produced goods. Yet above all it was the existence of a vast pool of unskilled labour that made it possible for employers to exploit East London's geographical and commercial advantages to the full.

Conclusion

The area of East London is defined by its population's subjective experience as members of a single-class society. In turn, the parameters of East London were created by the area's relationship with the City, and by unique economic and employment structures the origins of which are located along the banks of the Thames. Specific topographical features then can be observed in retrospect to have made a considerable contribution to the emergence of the region's cultural community. In both the casual labour market and the small workshops of the finishing-trades, individuals developed and displayed a sharp entrepreneurial style as a crucial tool of economic survival. Casual workers developed skills in seeking out informal contacts from whom information concerning employment might be obtained. Rates of pay and bonus payments were negotiated by workers, and elements of autonomy and independence became firmly established as essential characteristics of the local populace. Workshop and sweated workers were able to acquire independence by establishing businesses that required small premises and minimal capital. Likewise street-traders required little capital, and in common with the workshop trades enjoyed a huge market, catering for a wide range of consumer goods, from cauliflowers to china cabinets. Responsiveness to the demands of the market encouraged an ability to see the opportunity to make a profit from anything: a 'commodification' of reality.

The object is a product of the individual's disposition to act instead of being an antecedent stimulus which evokes the act. Instead of the individual being surrounded by an environment of pre-existing objects which play upon him and call forth his behaviour the proper picture is that he constructs his objects on the basis of his on-going activity (Blumer 1969, p. 80).

The East-Ender's commodification of reality involves the realignment of objects that are manifested in the market-place initially as constraining influences. Yet, by commodification, East-Enders are engaging in a form of *bricolage*, their response to the strictures of capitalism as they are manifested in the market-place consisting of 'ad hoc responses to an environment [that] serve to establish homologies and analogies between the ordering of nature and that of society, and so satisfactorily "explain" the world and make it able to be lived in' (Hawkes 1977).

By engaging in commercial activity, and adopting a predominantly commercial form of discourse, the core elements of capitalism are stretched to breaking-point, and a unique meaning for, for instance, the word 'business' is generated. What Hawkes has termed a 'science of the concrete' (*bricolage*) is a rational response to the market-place that contains elements of resistance in its sharp impertinence, yet retains an essentially pre-industrial proletarian reaction to a very intimate yet ambiguous relationship with capitalism. Commercial discourse is appropriated by East-Enders only partly as a weapon in 'semiotic guerrilla warfare' (Eco 1972), for bereft of the limited but sturdy cultural props of a conventional industrial proletariat, they must comprehend and articulate their unique universe using whatever means are at their disposal. The adoption of commercial discourse does not mark the embourgeoisement of East-Enders, rather the reaffirmation of their status, via *bricolage*, as unique agents of entrepreneurial proletarianism.

The population of East London experience in both physical and symbolic terms a close proximity to the epicentre of capitalism, and the language and ethics of conventional business enterprise have been appropriated and realigned to assist in the interpretation of everyday life. Imbued with the argot of the commercial world, East-Enders are able to justify legal behaviour and neutralize illegal action by utilizing the rhetoric of capitalism. 'Doing the business' may sound like a quaint colloquialism, an elaboration of the essentially mundane. However, its usage, along with other references to commercial activity are in context with the East-Ender's intimate relationship with capitalism. This relationship continues to be a stormy one. Entrepreneurial and labouring cultures of successive waves of immigrants, and the contradiction between the area's essentially pre-industrial economy and the manner in which market forces continually re-emphasized those pre-industrial characteristics, created poverty, disease, and crime on an enormous scale. This served to encircle East London in a moral barbed-wire that the City and West End erected and became entangled with at will. The forces of capital utilized the East End of London as a gamekeeper might string up dead birds and vermin. The East End was a land of the living dead, a symbol to all of the consequences that befell those unable to partake in the normal activities of capitalism.

Despite such taboo status, survival for an East Londoner depended on his or her ability to adapt to structural changes and fluctuations in the market. Unhindered by the proletarian hierarchical social structures so common in the northern industrial heartlands, East-Enders entered into short-term contracts, extracting wages as an employer extracts a surplus. The distinction between wages and profits became blurred as the status of workers continually fluctuated between unemployed, employee, self-employed, and employer. The emergent culture was shaped by business ethics and commercial language as workers adopted the practices of business and within the structural confines of capitalism moulded these practices to the requirements of an urban proletariat adapting capitalism to an essentially pre-industrial mode of production.

The resultant culture is essentially entrepreneurial in that the peculiar economic structure of East London has required generation upon generation of individuals to acquire and internalize the essential characteristics of the business entrepreneur, while continuing to operate at the very rump of capitalism. The East End entrepreneur deals and trades in commodities and services within the parameters of a localized version of legitimate business practice. Therefore, despite the East-Ender's status as an essentially unskilled manual worker, clashes with the forces of capital have been evaded by developing a long-standing relationship with the City that is based upon repartee as opposed to conflict. In turn the repartee functions by utilizing innuendo in the form of quasi-commercial language and activity. 'Doing the business' can mean doing somebody else's.

The ambiguity of the area's economic heritage manifests itself in the sharp, cunning, manipulative persona of successive generations of East-Enders. Trading and dealing are an integral feature of a culture strengthened by a lack of middle-class influence, yet stereotyped working-class solidarity is tempered with a powerful independence forged by centuries of individualistic endeavour, both in and out of work.

Consequently any individual or organization seeking to survive and prosper in this environment must adopt the distinctive style of the locals. In a trading culture potency in the market place is determined by the commodity in which one deals, and the dexterity with which one is able to extract profit from business transactions. Anyone entering this arena requires access to saleable commodities, and/or legitimate currency. Those who seek to trade must also be able to inject a lump sum of legitimate currency as security and as a sign of faith. Historical precedent, by infusing the qualities of business practice into the everyday experiences of an exclusively working-class community, requires the entrepreneur to deposit cultural collateral into a common community fund. Trade can then commence, and the business is done.

6

The Adolescent Entrepreneur: Youth, Style, and Cultural Inheritance

Working doesn't seem to be the perfect thing for me so I continue to
play, and if I'm so bad why don't they take me away?

Popular song of summer 1968.

This chapter is concerned with the continuity of the East End's
entrepreneurial inheritance, for it would be an error to switch from
Victorian London to the contemporary East End without referring to
the process by which culture is transmitted from generation to
generation. In order that this process might be comprehended, I have
focused upon youth or, more specifically, working-class youth's
subcultural style. It is my argument that a close and sympathetic
analysis of this phenomenon provides an opportunity to fill a gap in
the area's modern history, and, more importantly, to locate youth as
the crucial stage in an individual's adoption of class-specific
responses to the market-place.

The culture of East London has altered in an adaptive response to
changes in the 'economic ecology' of the area. This response
manifests itself in specific linguistic and stylistic forms that allow for
change while meeting the immediate requirements or impositions of
the market. The culture is not then a static phenomenon of Victorian
urban life, for as the environment changes the responses of
individuals will modify accordingly within the boundaries set by
precedent. As Rose (1962, p. 14) has noted, the individual can 'within
the limits permitted by the culture define for himself somewhat new
patterns suggested by the variation among the old ones'.

History can be seen to function as a mediating factor in the
development of East End culture. The economic ecology of the area
provides the dynamic for an ever-expanding environment, and the
culturally defined characteristics of autonomy, independence, and

entrepreneurship provide necessary sensitizing instruments for the development of a breadth of perspective that defines situations and forms a frame of reference, which in turn structures possibilities for action (Warshay 1962, p. 51; Mead 1934, p. 245).

Delinquency and Dressing Up

Youth can be viewed as probably the most crucial sensitizing phase in the evolution of a culture. The reason for this is best addressed by considering recent empirical work on youth and culture. During the last twenty years there have been attempts to link the study of youth to a broader analysis of culture. For example, Downes (1966) established crucial connections between delinquency and the local job market, and Parker (1974) found that working-class youths tended to take over traditional adult practices, which is hardly surprising as the adolescents and adults of the 'Roundhouse Estate' shared most of the basic cultural constraints and social inequalities of everyday life. Paul Willis (1977) established adolescence as a period when young men learn in their daily conflicts with middle-class culture via the school, of their inherited position on the labour market.

However, it was Phil Cohen's (1972) brief paper that provided the most illuminating and far-reaching analysis of youthful style, a style that evolves in the form of a sensitizing device as a response to inherited restraint within a changing environment. Cohen identified three factors that underpin all traditional working-class communities and East London in particular, namely the extended kinship structure, the local economy, and the ecology of the neighbourhood. For Cohen, the post-war breakdown in those three interdependent elements produced a weakening of historical and cultural continuity leading to internal conflict within the newly isolated nuclear family, conflict that was decanted into generational conflict. The emergence of youthful stylistic innovations functioned as attempts at solving contradictions within the parent culture that persisted at two levels. At an ideological level the contradiction was between what Cohen calls the 'new hedonism of consumption' and traditional working-class puritanism; and at an economic level the contradiction lay between the socially mobile élite and the 'new lumpen'. Therefore, the 'respectable' working class are unable to join the trend towards upward suburban mobility as practised by the élite, and yet naturally resist sliding downward into the lumpen group.

For Cohen, and those of the Birmingham School who were influenced by his analysis, post-war British youth subcultures represent attempts to resolve these contradictions, and these attempts lead to explorations of the options facing the respectable working class, i.e. up or down. The upward option was explored symbolically by the 'Mods' while the 'skinhead' explored the downward option. However, the difficulty with these subtle interpretive schemes often lies in locating plausible empirical evidence for them.

None of my respondents was apparently aware of facing contradictions, and the initial tentative adoption of a specific style appears to have stemmed from a subsequent interest in their own appearance rather than an attempt at solving contradictions within the parent culture.

Mick. I suppose I started getting interested in clothes and that when I was 11 or 12. There was a couple of kids older like who had scooters, and I suppose we looked up to them. I wouldn't say they were heroes or nothing; it was mainly the way they dressed.

While certain aspects of the style did mark an exploration of upward mobility, the central issues remained unchanged, and a specific style is only unique in terms of the clothing worn by subcultural members, and the settings in which the clothes are worn. The Mod, for example, possessed a well-defined sense of place and occasion and a line was firmly drawn between 'casual' and 'formal' social settings.

Ken. But if you was going out you would wear a smart suit, maybe a tie, or I suppose it was a little bit later, a short-sleeved Fred Perry. Nice trousers like Yorkers and a decent pair of shoes. But we all used to like dressing up didn't we? I used to love wearing a suit.

These rigid formal rules regarding appearance were largely due to the unique nature of the tailoring trade in the 1960s, a trade that still fostered the small one-man business and was consequently able to produce original high-quality clothing. The Mods did not 'redefine' the suit as Hebdige (1979, pp. 52–3) has claimed; they merely redesigned it according to the fashion of the day. Hebdige ignores the fact that most men in East London regardless of occupation had their suits 'made to measure'. In the pre-boutique days of the early to mid-1960s 'off-the-peg' clothing was of inferior quality, and the suit was a regular, normally Christmas-time purchase for males of all ages. The suit was a standard item of male attire to be worn outside working hours, while at work old suits were worn by dockers and men in a wide range of jobs. Specialist working clothes were rare and labouring men wearing old lounge suits at work would appear to represent the redefinition of a commodity, or a relocation of meaning far more bizarre than the ageless pursuit of fashion by youth.

Changes in youthful style can be observed as running parallel with alterations in the local socio-economic structure, and in the 1960s the sharp style of the Mods was, along with other influences, directly linked to employment opportunities. As a docker's son Mick, who left school in 1966, would have followed his father's profession, yet chose instead what Phil Cohen has termed the upward option; he became an office boy:

Mick. Me old man had me name down to go in the dock when I was 18, but I never fancied it. It was good money and that but, well I never fancied labouring, 'cos that's what it is, labouring. When I left school I fancied a bit of office work. I used to fancy myself in a suit. That's all it was really, just showing out.

Also important in the formation of style was the cultural overlap of the East and West Ends of London that occurred in the 1960s as a result of alterations in gambling laws, the resultant indiscreet manifestations of East End villains in West End clubs, and the fashionable 1960s notion of classlessness. Conversely show-business personalities and members of the aristocracy flirted with East End pubs and drinking-clubs, and a cockney accent became *de rigueur* for acceptance into bourgeois society as pop stars, hairdressers, and photographers rediscovered their humble roots. For young East-Enders, this opened up a privileged and exotic domain, and they emulated their elders, taking a short trip on the Central Line to spend their wages on a Friday night. 'Going up West' was a traditional adventure for East End kids, but now with an economic base established by their elders, they were no longer tourists.

Bill. I used to like Friday night the best. We'd be nicely dressed—suits—and go up West, do some of the clubs. They were good clubs, nice music, never any trouble.

The suits, music, and West End clubs represented the exploration of a successful, and very visible, masculine type, the tough, stylish, resourceful, and leisured East End male. John McVicar has cogently described this phenomenon.

I graduated to the Billiards Hall and Public House, and as I established myself on the fringe of this kind of world, I became both fascinated and challenged by it ... their rakishness, their flamboyant clothes, their tough, self-reliant manners, their rejection of conventional attitudes to sex and money—such things forced me and mesmerized me into conquering the mysteries of the world they lived in. I unconsciously modelled myself on the more successful representatives of this new society (McVicar 1979, p. 158).

Down Market

By the late 1960s, the office boy came to realize that it took more than smart clothes to become a managing director:

Mick. It was all right at first going on the train and that, but I got bored. I never really got on with people. They came from all over London. Some of them were well off and the way I talk, well I just never felt comfortable. I could do the work standing on me prick, but it was boring so I left.

The decline of dock-work brought about further changes in style, which in turn allowed Mick to explore and reaffirm one of the key central characteristics of East End culture: autonomy. Mick left clerical work after just eighteen months and, in Cohen's terms, proceeded to explore the 'lumpen option', working first as a plasterer's mate and then as a plasterer. As a plasterer in the early 1970s he earned up to £150 per week, but:

Mick. I never liked being told what to do. I started having rucks with the guv'nors. They started checking when we started and finished and that .... So I thought bollocks .... I left.

At this point the tentative explorations of youth are abandoned in favour of admission to the adult world. 'Magical' solutions are made redundant in favour of conscious instrumental efforts to chisel a niche for oneself within capitalism by way of exploiting the entrepreneurial ability that is the inheritance of all East Londoners. This inheritance has been structured by market forces over many centuries, and is manifested in an exclusively working-class population largely untouched by the regimented discipline of the factory system, and forged in an environment of casual labour and small workshops that nurture independence and autonomy.

For Mick at the age of 23, certain realities became apparent. With both the 'upward' and 'lumpen' options occupationally and stylistically explored he was jobless; office work offered low wages and illusory status and the brief ascendancy of the manual worker had waned. He is now the manager of a small hardware shop, receiving a wage of £70 per week. However, he also receives a tax-free lump sum of £200 per week, thanks to negotiations between the shopowner, his accountant, and Mick. Various agreements with lorry-drivers, lucrative arrangements with customers involving VAT fraud, and his involvement in the buying and selling of stolen paint provide regular additional sums. Mick, after the explorations of youth, has cashed in his legacy.

The strategies, rules, and rituals that are first encountered in youth often become so ingrained that there is little trauma experienced when entering the adult world, for it is as malevolent, violent, and seemingly irrational as that of the teenage mugger, disco thug, or football hooligan.

Rucking and Stirring

The metamorphosis of violent youth into violent adult is made apparent by the willingness of many adults to resort to violence. When Paul was 24 he was involved in a pub fight:

Paul. I got me back to the bar lashing out and the landlord punches me in the back, well I thought he punched me, then he comes round the bar and has a go at the front. . . . I was throwing and hitting out with bottles, glasses, anything. I got one geezer, a black bloke, with a glass and I see the blood spurt out of his forehead . . . I got outside and me back was hurting, so puts me hand there and it's soaked with blood . . . Turns up it just missed me kidney by the width of a hair.

Violence is a fact of working-class life and is not restricted to youth. The rules, strategies, and codes of violence are inherited, passed on from generation to generation. Despite Paul's close escape he reacts to violence in a similar manner some twelve years on, never slow in responding to threats with violence of his own. His understanding of the realities of East End life have led Paul to ensure that his seven-year-old son is well equipped to cope:

Paul. He will just steam in and fight anybody. He was having a go with a kid with an iron bar, just standing there saying 'come on then, you want a fight', and this kid's swinging a fucking iron bar. I shouted 'oi', and then I bollocked him, and he just said 'I'm not scared of him', so I told him, 'if someone's got an iron bar, you fucking run', 'cos I teach 'im a few tricks, Dick, you know, don't fuck about, kick 'em in the bollocks [*laugh*].

While strategies are symbiotically modified, violence and the expression of tough masculinity remain resilient, ever-present features of the youth and parent cultures. Terry, at 35, is a famous local street-fighter. His head and body are covered in scars, and he has an awesome reputation for fighting which stretches back to his teens. After being involved in one affray that left him with six stitches in a scalp wound, he reflected 'and the thing is, we ain't kids. We ain't just some yobs down the road hitting each other, we're grown men, 32 and 35, and we're still fucking trying to kill each other. I mean the yobs do it and so do we'.

Fathers and Sons: the Inheritance of Delinquent Style

Stan Cohen's (1980, p. 15) emphasis on the metaphysical anomalies, particularly in the work of Hebdige, has served to shift attention away from Phil Cohen's original analysis of East London community that produced the tripartite model of traditional culture, the basis upon which the new theories are totally dependent. It is my belief that a closer examination of the concepts of kinship, ecology, and economy as they are applicable to East London will prove to be fruitful in terms of an analysis of subcultural evolution and stylistic innovation. In doing so I must question the accuracy of the historical frame within which Phil Cohen originally located delinquent sub-cultures. The accuracy of the ecological structure that Cohen refers to is not questioned here, nor would I query the description of East London's extended kinship networks. However, the third factor in Phil Cohen's tripartite model, the local economy, is problematic, and warrants a more detailed examination than has been given to it up to now. Cohen identifies the economy of East London as being reliant upon the docks, their accompanying distributive and service trades, and craft industries, notably tailoring and furniture-making.[1]

Furniture-making and its allied trades were traditional East End crafts and had been for many years. Hall, using 1861 census material reports that 'The biggest branch of the industry was in the inner East London boroughs of Shoreditch, Bethnal Green and Stepney' (Hall

---

[1] Cohen (1972). Cohen also mentions 'the markets', but he fails to elaborate on what is meant by the term 'markets'. Whether this refers to the street-markets that proliferate in the area, or to specialized wholesale institutions such as Billingsgate and Spitalfields, is not made clear. Consequently I shall avoid speculative analysis and concentrate on the docks and craft trades.

1962, p. 72). Indeed, 31 per cent of the furniture trade's work-force were centred in the area.[2] The next ninety years saw a considerable growth in the trade[3] and the corresponding expansion of the work-force. However, with this expansion came the establishment of large factories outside East London and despite the expansion of the trade, the diffusion of manufacturing plants meant that by 1951 East London had only 17 per cent of the work-force (Hall 1962, p. 72). The 1960s witnessed actual decline in the labour force; between 1961 and 1971, 26,390 jobs were lost in London's timber and furniture industries, with traditional crafts such as french polishing all but disappearing.

In the same decade, 1961–71, the clothing and footwear industries also suffered (Hall 1962, pp. 37–70 and Table 4). The net effect of cheap imports, automation, and economies of scale resulted in 40,000 jobs being lost in London's clothing and footwear industries, which were centred in and around East London (Hall 1962, pp. 44–5).

Phil Cohen accurately noted this deterioration in the principal craft industries of East London, and their demise would appear to be consistent with the polarization of the work-force and the subsequent emergence of economically-specific subcultural styles. However, I feel that understating the importance of the docks in East London, and distinguishing what Cohen calls 'Dockland' is akin to separating coal-pits from mining-villages. In order that I might stress adequately the historical primacy of the docks in East London, it is necessary first to look rather more closely at events in and around the Port of London, with particular emphasis on the 1960s. The decline of London's docks began in the early 1960s due to: 'Changing patterns of trade in British ports and improvements in handling techniques which reduced labour requirements, but it only became a subject of public concern towards the end of that decade' (Hill 1976, p. 1).

Bigger ships' holds, increased use of fork-lift trucks, containerization, and palletization all contributed to this decline, particularly containerization as this enabled the man-handling involved in the

---

[2] Samuel (1981 p. 97). Arthur Harding notes that the furniture trade was a family affair: 'You brought up your family to do it.'

[3] Harding also indicates the expansion in the furniture trade: 'A bedroom suite was the first furniture I bought when I got married in 1924, to keep the clothes clean of bugs.' He also notes that: 'Wardrobes were practically unknown when I was a child. You put the same things on the next day. It was a question of sticking them on a chair when you went to bed of a night. If you had any best clothes you kept them in the pawnshop' (Samuel 1981, p. 199).

preparation of loads which used to be done in the docks to be carried out elsewhere. Consequently: 'The new methods greatly reduced the demand for labour by removing the labour intensive part of dock work outside the industry altogether' (Hill 1976, p. 4). Parallel to this technological shift, capital was employed to enforce changes in labour usage. For instance, the Port of London Authority invested £30 million in the modernization of Tilbury docks, which constituted the only location in the London system deep enough for the new containerships, while having sufficient land adjacent for the storage of container units.

Meanwhile, the employers were aware that apart from a decrease in their labour requirements, they also required fundamental changes in the day-to-day practices that had suited them admirably for the previous 100 years. However, it is doubtful if anyone could have foreseen the revolution in industrial relations that would take place as a result of those changes.

The docks had always revolved around a system of casual labour. How the system worked and the indignities it generated is vividly described by Bloomberg:

At seven forty-five a.m. the foreman came out and stood in the road eyeing the men up and down. The registered men stood with their registration cards in their hands. All the registered men had to go to work first and any tickets left over allowed the 'nonners' as they were called, to go to work. After all the registered men had been called, everything became a shambles. Men were calling the foremen by their names: 'here John', 'over here Jack', pushing and shoving till it was impossible for the foreman to give the tickets out. Some of the foremen seemed to get pleasure from throwing the tickets on the ground and watching the men scramble and fight to pick a ticket up. Such was the system of calling men on. Is there anything more degrading? (Bloomberg 1979, pp. 16–17).

Although this process described by Bloomberg had improved somewhat by the early 1960s, with the advent of the National Dock Corporation and the 'Bomping Box' (Bloomberg 1979), the ability to hire and fire and day-to-day control over labour allocation lay firmly with the shipowner. As early as April 1963 the carrot of decasualization was being dangled in front of the dockers, against a background of falling dock registers due to 'natural wastage and retirement, not by redundancy' (Lloyd 1963).

Against this background of a declining dock register, changing patterns of trade, and alterations in handling techniques, the Devlin

Report was implemented in 1967. Devlin introduced the National Dock Labour Board which administered the registered work-force. The employers paid a levy to the board and this levy paid for holidays and sick pay, and a daily wage was to be paid (44s. 4d.) instead of mere attendance money (18s. 0d). A guaranteed weekly gross wage of £15 was agreed although, 'average earnings, uniess volume of work in the docks diminishes, should be about £25 per week' (Devlin 1966, p. 18).

The avowed intention of the report was that 'the casual system should be ended, that there should be regular employment of all dock workers, and that all restrictive practices which were essentially a feature of the casual method of employment should be abolished' (Devlin 1966, p. 3). What was actually achieved was the removal of the right to hire and fire from the employer, with the effect that the employer failed to maintain power over labour allocation and disciplinary procedures.

For a brief period in the late 1960s, the docker enjoyed a measure of autonomy rare in industrial society. Those dock-workers who could resist the ever-increasing severance payments were enjoying the kind of élite position normally afforded to craftsmen. The prominent, successful masculine model for adolescents to adhere to was no longer the craftsman, white-collar worker, or to a lesser extent the successful local criminal,[4] but the docker, with money, material possessions, and an occupation that adhered to the criteria of tough masculinity that is intrinsic to all post-war youth subcultures.[5]

What I am suggesting is that rather than symbolic resistance via a magical solution, the kids were in fact performing the mudane adolescent ritual of copying their elders 'that they consider culturally unremarkable' (Corrigan 1979, p. 141). Dock reform (largely

[4] Throughout the 1960s, Reggie and Ronnie Kray and their associates were rich, successful, respected, and most importantly, conspicuous manifestations of private enterprise, certainly more approachable and immitable than other local doyens of capitalism of that era such as Lord Vestey, or the chairman of Tate and Lyle. However, since most of the 'firm' were arrested in May 1968, local villains have tended to specialize and maintain low profiles and, on becoming successful, move out of the area, usually to suburban Essex.

[5] Brake (1980, pp. 148–54) has pointed out that while subcultures are used to establish one's gender, the stress on masculinity makes subcultural membership essentially one-sided. Brake continues to argue that within a patriarchal society male-bonding, and the exaggeration of masculinity, are essential strategies in maintaining power over women, while distancing themselves from what are regarded as the restrictions of domesticity.

successful) increased industrial militancy,[6] and the emergence of this new industrial élite as a racist organization,[7] and the general economic decline since 1966,[8] heralded the emergence of the skinhead on the subcultural continuum. Response to contradictions in the parent culture and to the harsh facts of the labour market in a manner that confronted the state took place, not in an imaginary way, but actually on the street, at school, and at work. The skinhead style was aggressive, communal, and non-magical, rooted firmly in confronting the day-to-day problems of the manual labourer in an increasingly hostile world; just like Dad. Indeed, the lumpen option was explored by youth as a rational response to the brief cultural hegemony that manual labour enjoyed in the East London of the late 1960s.[9]

In terms of youth culture theories, a major part of the work of the 'new theorists' is to present specific subcultural styles as forms of

[6] The militant attitudes of dock-workers, and London dockers in particular, are noted by Hill (1976, pp. 103–8). The disputes of the late 1960s, however, were of a particularly aggressive and occasionally spectacular nature, a case in point being the attempts by dockers to impose 'scheme' conditions of work to Chobham Farm container depot. A full blow-by-blow account of these disputes can be found in *The Dockworker*, 1968–70.

[7] In April 1968, Enoch Powell gave a speech on race relations that prophesized racial warfare and called for repatriation. Powell was sacked from the Tory Shadow Cabinet and the first demonstration of support from the electorate came in the form of a march by London dockers to stake the claim of 'Enoch for PM'. While only a small proportion of the work-force took part, the dockers were one of the few groups with the self-confidence and motivation to demonstrate a point of view that, according to Schoen (1970, p. 37) was shared by between two-thirds and three-quarters of the electorate.

[8] Employment figures indicate that unemployment remained steady from 1961 to 1966, and, 'With two brief intermissions have gone up every year since then'. David Donnison ex-director of the Supplementary Benefits Commission, in *New Society*, 22 Jan. 1981, p. 153. See also *Social Trends 1981*, Table 5.16 (Unemployment).

[9] The benefits reaped by decasualization were, however, short-lived. From 1967 to 1970, 7,085 jobs were lost, and considerable sums were being paid in severance payments as inducements to those wishing to leave the industry. Those dockers whose length of service did not warrant an acceptable severance payment transferred to Tilbury; as a consequence East London lost almost an entire generation of dockers and their attendant skills and traditional work-practices. This occupational inheritance had fostered a tangible and pervasive historical perspective among dock-workers, as was noted by a pre-Devlin Official Report which stated, 'few industries are so burdened with the legacy of the past. We have been struck by the extent to which many facets have to be understood against the background of history. Practices and attitudes can often be traced back a long way; old traditions die hard' (Report of a Committee of Inquiry into the Major Ports of Great Britain (1962)).

There was massive investment in the 'super scab ports' (*The Dockworker* 1973, no. 15) such as Felixstowe and Colchester. Employers had a free hand in these ports; for instance any dangerous cargoes such as asbestos and bone-meal that would have resistance to subordination. The precise form in which this resistance is manifested is not real or actual, but symbolic or magical. Sub-cultural action is, as Stan Cohen (1980, p. 10) has commented, an 'historically informed response mediated by the class culture of the oppressed'.

In decoding a specific style via Lévi-Strauss, we are presented particularly in the case of Hebdige, with an interpretation that considers only the concepts of opposition and resistance, and 'this means that instances are sometimes missed when the style is conservative or supportive: in other words not reworked or reassembled but taken over intact from dominant commercial culture. Such instances are conceded, but then brushed aside' (Cohen 1980, p. 12). However, I am suggesting that in the case of East London and the emergence of skinheads, there was a genuine attempt to recreate traditional working-class community through mimicking the most readily available masculine stereotype which, as I have explained, within the parameters of East London was blatantly successful.

That East London was in decline in the late 1960s is not in dispute; rather the point is that one could hardly detect its decline in a community enjoying regular wages and into which hundreds of thousands of pounds of severance pay was being pumped. Clarke's (1976, p. 46) image of the skinheads as 'dispossessed inheritors' does not hold up in light of the militant communal action that typified the industrial struggle in and around the docks at that time. For instance, the skinhead quoted by Clarke who voices his frustrations concerning authority in general and the 'fucking bosses' in particular, is positively restrained compared with the action of dock-workers at this time. Examples can be found in an analysis of the regular shower of abuse aimed at Lord Vestey in *The Dockworker*,[10] and the dockers' violent confrontations with the police in industrial disputes of that era (Rollo 1980, p. 178).

provoked a flurry of wage and conditions negotiations in London, were unloaded in unregistered ports by unorganized casual labour at great personal risk.

The ability of the employers to transfer capital to the smaller unregistered ports is demonstrated by the increased tonnage, both containerized and general cargo at one port, Felixstowe. In 1967, the year that Devlin was implemented, Felixstowe's total tonnage was 1,242,678 tons and by 1970 this figure had nearly doubled to 2,259,981 tons.

[10] Lord Vestey, the chairman of Scruttons Maltby Ltd., one of the docks' major employers was a particularly unpopular individual with London's dockers. His regular clashes with unions and individual dockers led to his private telephone number being published in *The Dockworker* and an obscene picture of him being circulated among his employees.

A Yank Goes to Stepney

The 'new' theorists, following Phil Cohen, have accepted the skinhead style as being that of the 'model worker' (Cohen 1972) and I have gone to some lengths to confirm that the communal model of masculine behaviour exemplified by skinheads had its roots in manual labour. However, the notion that skinheads were copying the appearance of an imaginary (in Phil Cohen's thesis) or an actual (as I have suggested) working man is only part of the story. Workers in East London or anywhere else in Britain tended not to have their hair cropped. For work they would certainly have not worn US Army surplus flight-jackets at three times the cost of a donkey-jacket. The trousers were, for the 'hard cases', green US Army surplus. In surplus stores around the Royal Docks these were sold as 'docker's jeans' and dockers did indeed wear these, while elsewhere they were sold as 'jungle greens'.

The most significant and ambiguous item of clothing was the 'Doctor Martens' boots. These were not at the time 'industrial boots' (Brake 1980) in the sense of being common footwear for manual workers. They were too expensive[11] and the soft, light-weight leather and calf-length of the boot did not make them the most practical boot for heavy work. At this time a traditional army-style boot could be bought for less than £2. These were cheaper, heavier, and consequently a more potent weapon in a fight than the light-weight 'DMs'.

Skinheads, while inheriting the remnants of traditional behaviour from the parent culture, lacked the industrial muscle that made the dockers a potent force. Given that the community was under siege at the time—'with all this lot against us, we've still got the yids, pakis, wogs, 'ippies on our backs' (Daniel and McGuire 1972, p. 68)—and the traditional culture to which the kids clung was changing,[12] a style of aggressive masculinity with a more visually intimidating image than donkey-jacket, monkey-boots, and sandwich-box was required. Every night on the TV news throughout the period US Marines in high-legged jungle-boots, cropped hair, and decked out in jungle fatigues leapt out of helicopters and into battle. If those concerned with symbolism can attribute special significance, for instance, to the wearing of braces, then surely the 'intellectual pyrotechnics' (Cohen

---

[11] In the late 1960s 'Dr Martens' cost about £5 a pair.

[12] Phil Cohen's model of a declining social structure, despite my misgivings concerning his treatment of the docks, is an invaluable study.

1980, p. 20) involved in the appropriation and utilization of a militaristic style to which youth had been subjected over a period of up to a decade are not beyond serious consideration.[13] In decoding style, greater attention should be paid to 'the spell cast on the young by the borrowed cultural imperialism' (Cohen 1980, p. 20) instead of 'affording exaggerated status to the internal circuit of English working-class history' (Cohen 1980, p. 12).

The Teddy Boys' 'slick city gambler' style (Jefferson 1976, p. 86), their adoption of American cars, and their use of the Confederate flag were all built around a solid wall of white American rock and roll. The Mods' utilization of black American music, and the smooth, Ivy League casual style that emerged towards the end of the Mod era, dominated British pubs, clubs, and dance-halls during this era. As Hebdige (1979, p. 81) has noted the appropriation of American 'types' was nothing new: 'the Brooklyn sharp kid had been emulated by the wartime black marketeer, the wide boy and the post-war spiv, and the style was familiar, readily accessible and could be easily worked up'. It is fair to deduce therefore that the evolution of post-war British working-class subcultures owes much to George Raft, Arthur English, and Max Miller.

Stan Cohen has criticized the 'new' theorists, and Hebdige in particular, on a theoretical level, but my main complaint is empirical—that in so many cases working-class subcultures are totally misread and distorted so as to make the working-class community of less than two decades ago unrecognizable, and its culture further detached from the reality of its participants than any writings of the 'old' school.[14] Hebdige continually confuses middle-class and working-class subcultures; the confusion is exemplified by his statement that 'Punk reproduced the entire sartorial history of post-war working-class youth cultures in cut up form' (Hebdige 1979, p. 124). Punk's origins are firmly rooted in New York via the Kings Road. Glue-sniffing, untutored rock bands, (Hebdige 1979, p. 25), and the tradition of acned rebellion passed down by James Dean and Marlon Brando, were imported wholesale, purchased, and appropriated by middle-class kids, who had left the Home Counties

[13] Two publications that feature pictures of American servicemen looking like Canning Town skinheads are: *G.I.s Speak out Against the War* by Fred Halstead (New York: Merit 1970, pp. 2 and 10) and *War*, ed. by A. Leventhal (London: Hamlyn 1973, pp. 224–51).

[14] S. Cohen (1980, p. 30) notes that the key texts remain A. K. Cohen (1955); R. Cloward and L. Ohlin (1960); and D. M. Downes (1966).

for West London's tried and tested version of Bohemia. This bourgeois experiment with decadence is now in its umpteenth generation[15] and has little connection with any attempt to solve problems instigated by contradictions within a deteriorating working-class community whose traditional culture is faced with extinction.

This misreading of style, while shrouded in the jargon of conflict, resistance, and change, constitutes a familiar language of contempt and patronage that the middle class, regardless of political persuasion, tend to utilize when dealing with working-class phenomena. An example is Hebdige's assertion that Punk magazines were 'determinedly working class' because they were 'liberally peppered with swear words' (Hebdige 1979, p. 111). So much for the richness of working-class culture. I find this attitude typical of a specific type of analysis that, while attempting to glamorize and romanticize working-class children as noble savages, succeeds merely in opening up Gouldner's Zoo (Gouldner 1968) to accommodate not only deviants, but the entire working-class population. It is less than surprising to find, pro rata, more punks at the LSE than in any East London comprehensive.

Finally, it is Hebdige's own misreading of the black influence on subcultural style that provides the most irritating attempt to comprehend the natives: 'the history of post-war British youth culture must be re-interpreted as a succession of differential responses to black immigrant presence in Britain from the 1950s onwards' (Hebdige 1979, p. 29).

The black influence on the Teds, for whom the Confederate flag was a symbol of their whiteness, is difficult to find. It was not until Haley's and Presley's whining versions of black Blues records were marketed that black music in its prostituted form was consumed in quantity by white youth.

Graham. Tamla, down to anything Tamla. Martha and the Vandellas, Supremes, Stevie Wonder, Smokey Robinson, then it was Otis and Wilson Picket. Soul and Tamla. Four Tops, Marvin Gaye, that was the thing.

Their appreciation of these entertainers had nothing to do with the indigenous black population. These black American acts were smooth, cultured artists, spectacular dancers, and expensive dressers. The Mods incorporated these elements into the style of the upwardly

---

[15] J. Young in Cohen (1971, p. 32) notes the self-instigatory nature of the middle-class Bohemian's existence.

mobile office-worker, the local villain, and the suddenly prosperous professional footballer,[16] all overtly successful, visible masculine types. Indeed ex-Mods and skinheads appear to share remarkably uniform views on blacks.

Mick. But the coons made it worse. Pakis never 'ave council places do they. They buy places; a bit shrewd. But the coons I could never stand them. When I was at school there weren't any at our school. Now there's no whites. My sister-in-law still lives there, and it's like a fucking jungle, the muggings and that.

The pop-art-inspired art-school graduates may well have been inspired by black culture, although Melly's comment that 'for us the whole coloured race was sacred', which is quoted by Hebdige (1979, p. 44), tells us much about the ability of the entertainment industry to exploit black culture and little about working-class subcultures.

Indigenous black culture had little effect on working-class subcultures until the skinhead emerged. Hebdige's comments on the fusion of black and white youth cultures have more credence today, where white emulation of black style and argot are increasingly attractive to whites, who for the first time lack successful, accessible models of masculinity within their parent culture.

The 'rapport' that Hebdige (1979, pp. 53–4) refers to between black immigrant culture and white youth was negligible in the early to mid-1960s and while he quotes a Mod as claiming to 'hero worship the spades', the 'spades' were American, and Phil Cohen's upward option was not to be found in Wolfe's mystical 'noonday underground', but in the pubs along the Mile End Road where 'the chaps', the successful and not-so-successful villains, immaculately attired, could flaunt the work-ethic by boozing lunch-time, or anytime. Indeed, some of the pubs most popular with young people in the early to mid-1960s had close connections with the thriving East London underworld of that era.

Mick. Mostly Black Boys, Green Gate, Bethnal Green, Globe, all them . . . we used to do all the usual pubs with a bit of music.

As style is inherited, so a specific youthful adaptation of working-class culture should be viewed as an exploration of the masculine options that are made available by the parent culture. Stylistically, youthful manifestations of working-class male culture survive the

---

[16] I. Taylor in Cohen (1971, pp. 134–64) notes the change in status within the working-class community for professional footballers that came with the abolition of the maximum wage in 1961.

individual's adaptation to the labour market. The crucial point is reached when the consumer pressure of the youth market is relocated and a realistic accommodation to the labour market is made.

While Mick's various occupations can be seen to parallel Cohen's theoretical frame, the move from youth to adult life is not geared in all cases to conventional occupational choice. For many, the move out of youth marks a reaffirmation of a deviant identity that had been established in their teenage years. Bill had been involved in theft and serious violence throughout his youth. Shop-breaking, razor-fighting, and taking and driving away were regular occurrences. After he received a razor wound to his face his status among his peers was increased.

Bill. Course then I do fancy myself with a nice stripe an' all. People used to look at me and think I was fucking Al Capone. If we was anywhere and there was a ruck I had to be upfront. (See Patrick 1973, pp. 46–7.)

Yet there was no real tension between Bill at his peak, and his parents. Bill was safe in the knowledge that 'the old man had been a bit of an evil bastard when he was young'. Bill's behaviour was 'normal', never contradictory to the parents' culture. Both youth and adult cultures informed and reinforced each other.

Bill. I suppose he just thought I was feeling me way, . . . I used to go down the Peacock of a Sunday dinner, and he'd be in there with his brothers. They'd be talking about the good old days, and what he got up to in the army.

One of his brothers was a real hound, got in with the Krays, shooters the lot. I remember once I was working on site, and this geezer, brickie, comes up and says 'you Johnnie Smith's boy?' So I says 'Yeah, what of it?' Well he's about 40 and a bit tasty. So he says, 'Well your uncle Tom give me this', and he's got this stripe up his arm from here to here.

The essential continuity between the youthful Bill and the parent culture finally resulted in a fusion at the appropriate age of 21. While working as a builder's labourer, he was part of a 'team' that stole a quantity of sheepskin coats. The rest of the team were older and more experienced and he was paid £100 while the goods were 'put down' for a while. Bill was still owed £1000.

Bill. After a couple of months me and two pals went in their drinker by Crisp Street, and I fronted them . . . and one of them says 'well if that's how you feel pal you'd better take it out of that'—you know points to his chin. So I stabbed 'im in the face ... we managed to get out and Plod pulls us as we tried to get a cab.

Bill served three years' imprisonment. His move into adult theft and violence is of no more significance than Mick's move from plasterer to entrepreneurial shop-work. It is an adaptation to the realities of the market, an exploitative attempt at creating some measure of autonomy and achieving a lucrative reward for their endeavours. The extent of this element of autonomy, and the size of the reward, is not always made apparent by adopting a purely structural notion of class that regards the job-market as one-dimensional and static. Crime for Bill was a logical extension of his activities as a youth, and these activities were rational options that emerged from his inheritance as it was manifested in the tough macho world of the parent culture (see Patrick 1973, pp. 144–54). Mick's fiddles and fencing were entered into as extensions of the activities that the parent culture had informed him were normal. After exploring several options in his youth, he was able to express culturally defined, highly valued characteristics of autonomy and entrepreneurship.

Entrance to the East End's adult entrepreneurial world represents maturity. No longer 'magical', the adults' actions are firmly grounded in the problems that emerge from an individual's 'real' position on the labour market. The temporary appropriation of a style whose meaning is to be found by analysing youth-specific responses to the parent culture, gives way to the adoption of an entrepreneurial style that incorporates an assimilation of the entire stock of knowledge that represents the cultural precedence of working-class heritage. In East London this results in a rational and imaginative response to capitalism.

Early Dealing

All respondents appeared to have shown considerable entrepreneurial promise at any early age. Mick in particular showed early indications of possessing the type of business acumen that was later to make him one of the most successful and discreet fences of stolen paint in East London. At the age of 14 Mick sold newspapers for three hours, four nights a week after school, while one night and all day Saturday he worked on a market stall selling seafood. Sundays were not wasted, as he toured the streets, pushing a hand cart.

Mick. Crabs, prawns, whelks, roll-mops, everything. We'd go round ringing a bell and shouting our fucking heads off.

Much of his income, then as now, was 'fiddled'.

Mick. For Friday and Saturday I used to get £2 for the market job. Sunday we'd get £3 each, which was good money. Plus we used to eat loads of prawns as we was going round, and we always had ten bob and a crab, and a couple of pints of prawns each. So Friday and Saturday I got, including fiddles, say £5. 10*s*.

This process of inheritance which informs individuals of the availability and viability of such practices, takes place via the oral culture generated by the immediate environment. This knowledge is transmitted by word of mouth and is highly valued as it is passed on.

Mick. But the papers were the best, 'cos the fiddles I used to work with the van-boys. The bloke who did it before me told me about it and I sort of handed it down to the next kid when I left. I used to get £3 off the bloke whose pitch it was, and I was getting £5 out of the fiddle. (See Ditton 1977, p. 42.)

Mick's total income while still at school was over £5 more than his weekly wage when he entered full-time employment. This solid grounding in entrepreneurial activity is common to all generations of East Londoners. In Mick's case the uniqueness of his inheritance can, on an obvious level, be attributed to the East End's geographical location in relation to the print industry where his fiddle with the 'van-boys' originated, and from the local demand for seafood without which there would have been no market for him to exploit. However, on a wider level, the unique diversity of the area's economic base has created a precedent for individualistic action in pursuit of pecuniary reward outside the conventional contract implied by an employer–employee relationship.

Sixty-six-year-old Charlie was born into a family of costers. However, a family argument resulted in his father entering the clothing trade, but he did work on the stalls at the weekend.

Charlie. It was like someone lifted a cloud off him ... The weekend kept him going.

Charlie had done part-time jobs since he was very young.

Charlie. Us kids, we always earnt money. We was always out after anyway of earning ... I used to help the toffee-apples man ... then when the carters came back we'd take the 'orses back to the stables. Then there was the tobacco company. It was when the big strike was on. I was only a tot, and they would throw out the big barrels ... we'd smash-em up bundle-em up, and sell-em for firewood. If you got a shilling, well a shilling was worth pounds.

Charlie's childhood endeavours also helped formulate his adult entrepreneurial career. He went on to inherit a body of knowledge in the form of both legal and illegal practices that earned him a reasonable living throughout his working life. He was able to achieve a high degree of autonomy in his working day that can be regarded as directly attributable to his cultural inheritance and the explorations of his youth.

I am not suggesting that subcultural membership forms a basis for long-term solutions to class-specific problems. Rather it is argued that the adult and youth cultures have a symbiotic relationship, each informing the other, transmitting, receiving, and interpreting information, before modifying the content and transmitting back. It is through this process of symbiosis that capitalism, in essence an exploitative and oppressive regime, might be negotiated.

Youth prepares individuals for the labour market, and youth is constantly informed about appropriate behaviour by the parent culture. Upon maturation and establishment on the labour market, the experimentations of youth are sifted and sorted, and specific central issues located in youth are brought to bear and utilized in adult life (Becker 1964, p. 52). In this way men can be seen to be both carriers and creators of culture. The culture changes, but alterations are carried out by individuals with a powerful sense of history, insulated from intrusive middle-class cultural influences, but vulnerable to the whims of the market and the mobility of capital.

The entrepreneurial model offers the East-Ender a way of maintaining the vitality of youthful experimentation, while constructing a strategy that does not threaten the existence of capitalism but makes it considerably more bearable. The essence of this strategy is to be found 'in the subtle manipulation of everyday life rather than in the dramatic or revolutionary gesture' (Cohen and Taylor 1976).

The symbiotic relationship between the youthful and adult world is a crucial stage in a continual adaptive response to alterations in the economic ecology of an area, and the stylistic forms that are readily observable within the relationship represent sensitizing devices that function to explore possibilities for action within an expanding environment. These stylistic formats explore past experiences as well as present interactions, and as a consequence tease out both those possibilities for action set by cultural precedent and those set by current and prospective interactions.

The common characteristics that structure possibilities for communal action in East London are autonomy, independence, and entrepreneurship—tried and tested adaptive responses to the marketplace.

7

East End Entrepreneurship

Physically, culturally, and metaphorically the East End of London stands on the very periphery of British capitalism. Informed by historical precedent, East-Enders exist on the brink of the City of London's legitimate commercial enterprise and legality. Bourgeois cultural hegemony may define, via the coercive force of the market-place, the parameters of the area but it rarely impinges upon the day-to-day dynamics of East End culture. As Zorbaugh (1929, p. 152) has noted: 'The life of the slum is lived almost entirely without the conventional world.'

Like Chicago's 'Little Hell', East London has functioned as an area of first settlement for generations of immigrants. Like its American counterpart the East End's isolation and reliance upon the whims of the market-place take over from more traditional social forces, such as religion and the family, and by absorbing those characteristics appropriate to the market, a culture has been created that is a hybrid of various ethnic groups, yet still retains an essential identity that is not Jewish, Irish, West Indian, or Asian but is that of the East End.

I have already described this culture as entrepreneurial, that is the dominant core characteristic of East London's culture is entrepreneurial ability. However, individuals living in the area are not equally equipped to operate competently within the entrepreneurial framework. Some are more competent than others, utilizing their cultural heritage in collaboration with knowledge that is appropriate to their specific position on the labour market. Within the culture there exists a whole range of individuals whose abilities to utilize entrepreneurial culture varies from the incompetent to the highly skilled. Some of their activities are illegal, others are legal or most commonly what Henry (1978) has called 'borderline activities', occupying the grey area between theft and the consumption of goods either stolen or acquired outside of the normative retailer–consumer relationship.

In attempting to present the full richness, texture, and variation of possibilities available in this culture I have constructed an entrepreneurial scale, featuring a typology of seven sections supported by

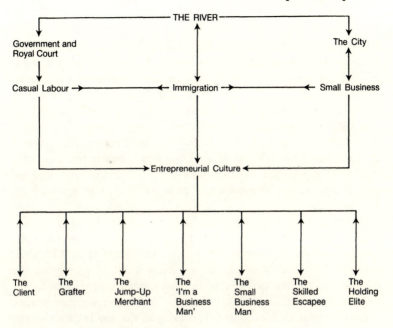

Fig. 1 An Entrepreneurial Scale

case studies. These categories are not exhaustive; the typology represents an attempt to focus upon typical behaviour 'approaching the phenomenon principally through the actors' shared abstractions' (Irwin 1970, p. 6). The types I describe can be justified on the grounds that their specific characteristics were generic, and in several cases the types were identifiable to members of the culture thus becoming what Lofland (1976) has termed 'member-identified categories'. These seven types are an attempt at analytic description of the underlying properties of the East End's culture.

In my presentation of these case studies it will become apparent that it was necessary that I should be involved in certain illegal activities. To avoid any legal action against myself I appear in the text on various occasions under a pseudonym, as do all other participants. All names and locations have been altered to protect the guilty. The ethical and methodological implications of this are discussed in Chapter 1.

Framing the Scale: Bar Business

It is in the pub that deals are struck, and information regarding cheap goods, stolen commodities, and exchanges of skills are relayed and it is in the pub that businesslike behaviour is presented for display (Hutt 1976). While these entrepreneurial fronts are not necessarily façades, the imagery or image management involved is so total, so complete, that discriminating fact from fiction becomes an impossible and irrelevant task. The essential cultural characteristic that informs the East Londoner is entrepreneurial ability, whether this manifests itself in a commercial transaction or as an attitude or pose, and the central dynamic of the culture is provided by the imagery of the entrepreneur.

In the pub, individuals congregate to perform specifically 'dialogistic interpersonal rituals' (Goffman 1971, p. 63). For example, when Barry was approached by Vince and offered several hundred yards of high-quality stolen carpet, Barry was not interested, yet promised to attempt to find a buyer. Barry could have refused to buy the goods and left it at that; however it was important that Vince's entrepreneurial abilities were acknowledged, thereby reaffirming the mechanisms and language of exchange as a core organizational device of the indigenous order.

This 'supportive interchange' (Goffman 1971) offers a more detailed analysis of informal or hidden economy currency than Henry's 'favours' (1978, pp. 98–102), yet hardly requires further elaboration. In the cited example both parties have provided mutual support in the course of an interchange that acknowledges the entrepreneurial qualities of each man, and an element of bonding by essential elements of discretion and trust is infused into the relationship, a relationship that was previously based simply on assumptions born of a common cultural inheritance.

The member of this entrepreneurial culture will attempt to cultivate a specific style, a front that will single him out as someone with something to sell, as a dealer. The City Arms is a local pub that provided an ideal arena for the locals to do the business, numbering more than its share of villains, 'corner-men', 'jump-up merchants', 'dabblers', 'ex-boxers', and assorted 'clients'. Keith was a client.

The City Arms is a rigidly stratified institution. Section 1 is reserved for hard-men, full-time villains, and CID officers. From a position at the bar in the shaded area the entire clientele can be

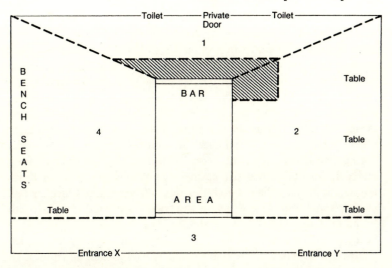

Fig. 2 The City Arms

observed and both entrances watched. Those in the shaded area will
be drinking with the 'guv'nor' or with guests of the 'guv'nor'.
Drinkers in section 1 enter through entrance Y, and walk through
section 2 acknowledging friends and acquaintances, but ignoring the
corner-men and car-dealers. The closer to the overlapping shaded
area and the further from the entrance an individual manages to
establish himself, the higher his status. Section 3 is no man's land, a
void into which you step from the street. Only itinerants and
strangers drink in this area, maintaining a buffer zone, an archi-
tecturally inspired vacuum, between the élite social space of sections
1 and 2, and the also-rans of section 4.

1. The Client: Keith

Keith drinks in section 4 along with the other 'clients'. They all 'do a
bit of business' (even if they are only dialling the talking clock),
assume nonchalant stances at the bar, and pose in their 'everpress'
slacks while fingering the gold 'belcher' chains round their necks and
the Victorian full-sovereign rings on their forefingers. It's mean looks
all around from the chaps in section 4 as they try hard to emulate the
formidable sense of conspiracy of the chaps in sections 1 and 2. Keith

was on no more than nodding terms with the con-men and 'business men' of section 2, and knew by name the two villains who were the most regular inhabitants of section 1's shaded area. However, until his common-law wife's death Keith stayed firmly in his place, going through the ritual motions of buying and selling, conspiring to set up vacuous schemes that could never come to fruition. The farce continued night after night, grown men mimicking the wheeler-dealer world of 'business', the plots, plans, and deals restricted to others who shared a total lack of cultural collateral. The strict segregation in the City Arms served to isolate their absurd posturing and delusions of 'doing the business'. Problems began when Keith altered his drinking habits. Keith's wife died, and it was a local as well as a personal tragedy and family and friends gathered to help. Keith found the City to be a far more welcoming pub than it had previously been, and drinks and words of sympathy came in from all angles. Even those sections of the pub's clientele who looked down with an almost tangible contempt on 'clients' like Keith, were sympathetic, and his drunken, crying jags were quietly tolerated before he was carried home and put to bed by one of the regulars from section 2. He was often included in conversations that had previously been closed to him, and gradually Keith was able to move across the pub. However, the racy tales and wheeler-dealer 'blag speak' of the 'chaps' proved to be heady, and instead of merely soaking up the feeling of privilege and well-being that was being nurtured, Keith tried to become part of the proceedings.

He told one group that he had earned money in the past as an enforcer. On another occasion he informed dumbstruck drinkers in section 2 that he was an ex-captain of the British Junior Boxing team and another time that he had a part-time job coaching squash at a local sports complex. When others were discussing 'business' whether legal or otherwise Keith felt qualified to lend a hand. His tough talk, ridiculous boasts, and unwanted advice were tolerated solely because of sympathy for his recent loss. It must be stressed that Keith had nothing to trade, he was still a punter, and as such could not participate in the core activities of the élite sections. Three separate episodes were to put Keith back in section 4, but first some issues should be discussed.

Throughout the six months immediately after his wife's death Keith had continued to work as a bricklayer, earning a fair wage. However, he was missing more and more work due initially to hangovers from the night before. His routine was increasingly to rise at 10.30 a.m., go into the City, leave at 4.00 p.m., sleep, eat, and return at 7.00 p.m. until chucking out time or until 'afters' had been served, which in my experience could be 1.00 a.m. His average weekly wage declined steadily and he borrowed money from many people to finance his drinking. His lunch-time sessions brought him into contact with an élite who had no need of even a front of 'kosher' employment. Lunch-time drinking is an important component of working-class leisure aspiration. While the majority of workers can only graft and look forward to a couple of hours' drinking in the evenings, the lunch-time boozer can treat the pub as a private club. The comparative lack of trade during the day enables the customer to attain a level of intimacy with the landlord that is then carried on to the evening. 'Afters', free drinks, use of the phone etc., follow. Keith came into contact with individuals who were skilled in their manipu- lation of social security and welfare agencies, dividing their attention between drinking and negotiating for money or access to state- supplied goods or services. Keith resolved to 'go professional'. He was a mug to work, and had to find a way of entering the twilight world of the City full-time. He decided to go mad.

He climbed over the wall of the cemetery and tried to go to sleep by his wife's grave and a guard-dog disturbed his slumber and tore his jacket sleeve before the police were called. He sat down on the floor of section 2 and conducted a conversation with a beer mat. He complained of migraines and allowed his home to deteriorate physi- cally. Eventually he was at home more often than at work and his debts mounted. When the Gas Board broke into his home and removed the meter it proved too much. He returned from work a week later announcing that he kept thinking of committing suicide while climbing scaffolding, and that he was not going to work any more. He became officially unfit to work, and started a new career in the City.

Keith's 'illness' and his status as a full-time man of leisure were the two enabling factors which led to him being involved in three episodes, the cumulative consequences of which re-established Keith back in section 4.

1. Three very accomplished local thieves paid Keith for the use of his lock-up garage to store stolen goods. Keith told anyone who would listen what was being stored and one month later someone cleaned out the entire stock. This led to several of the original thieves touring

the area and visiting local pubs often armed, 'advising' prospective punters not to buy from thieves who steal from thieves.

2. Keith was asked to steal some scaffolding by the two most prominent denizens of the shaded area of section 1. Keith, the budding business man, employed two young men to assist him. The police intercepted the trio *en route* to the drop-off point, but due to the unique 'community policing' connections within the City Arms the scaffolding was re-erected under intermittent police supervision.

3. Finally Keith was offered a regular 'cash-in-hand' job. Billy D, another small builder, owned two white Daimler limousines which were hired out with a driver for weddings. A stalwart of section 2, Bill was banned from driving a couple of years ago and Keith chauffeured him until the ban was up. Eventually Keith started driving wedding-cars every Saturday for Bill, and their relationship began to thrive. However, within one month Keith was referring to their arrangement as 'our business', but Bill like many others still treated the man with sympathy due to his bereavement and shrugged off the continued references to 'our partnership'. Eventually this became 'my business', and he began to treat Bill as an employee. One day Bill went to get a haircut and while the barber snipped away he told him that Keith's business must be doing well and praised him for being such a straight, honest person.

Bill left the barber's and went to the City for a lunch-time drink. Still fuming, he asked the new barmaid if Keith had put in an appearance. She replied: 'No, but he'll definitely be in later 'cos he's taking me for a driving-lesson.' Cautiously Bill asked what car they were intending to drive. 'Oh,' said the barmaid, 'he let's me drive his big Daimler. He's a lovely man. He's got a good business, doing very well.'

Bill threatened to kill Keith, but on arrival at Keith's house, his 12-year-old daughter was sent to the door to say that her father was not at home. Eventually Bill pinned Keith to the wall of section 2, told him what he thought of him, and walked into an adjacent pub where he handed the keys of the Daimler to Terry, who has now been driving for Bill for eighteen months.

Keith had not only proved himself to be incompetent and unreliable but more importantly he had failed to trade successfully. He abandoned the ethics of the market-place, and discussed the where-abouts of stolen goods, ruined a lucrative deal in stolen scaffolding, and finally deluded himself into believing that he owned a business to the detriment of the real owner. Keith had no cultural collateral, nothing to trade, yet his unique situation won him acceptance within an elevated social grouping. However, his willingness to involve himself whole-heartedly in these various entrepreneurial schemes verifies the powerful cultural dynamic that drives the everyday world of East London.

To be a 'business man' is to be quick, intelligent, perceptive, tough, and forceful. It is also to be in control of one's own working day, without the restrictions imposed by an oppressive boss, yet with a profit that stems from the autonomy earned by a 'man to be respected' (see Horowitz 1983, pp. 231–4).

Keith returned to section 4, ceased to drink at lunch-time, and was taken to court for non-payment of debts. But the 'chaps' had not finished with him yet. A rumour circulated the neighbourhood that Keith was sleeping with his daughter and he was cornered in the City by two residents of section 2 and openly and loudly accused. Keith broke down in tears. It was Billy D who had spread the rumour.

Ditton (1977, p. 176) has cogently identified 'fiddling' or the hidden economy as 'a cultural interpretation of business'. Keith interpreted incorrectly, returned to work, and can be found most evenings adrift in section 4 along with the other clients.

2. Grafters: Nob and George

This section deals with unskilled and semi-skilled individuals who, despite their lowly position in the labour market, are able, by implementing skills and strategies derived from their cultural inheritance, to carve out an autonomous space based upon entrepreneurial ability; a space that cushions and insulates the 'grafter' from some of the more insidious effects of low-status employment.

There was a thirty-year age-gap between Nob and George and, until recently when George died, they had worked together as warehousemen in an old-established firm in East London. The company paid exceptionally low wages and there was a tradition amongst the labourers and warehousemen of generating additions to their incomes by involving themselves in a variety of 'fiddles', semi-legal activities, and thefts.

George

George had worked for the company for over fifty years, right up to his death. His knowledge of the trade was awesome and individuals of all ranks would consult him in an effort to tap his vast stock of wisdom. Indeed the secret of George's power within the company lay in the fact that only those willing to approach him as junior partners in a potential business arrangement would receive the benefit of his experience. George was a wiry yet physically powerful man, with a loud voice and quick temper. Any labourer working under his jurisdiction who made a mistake was a 'silly bastard' at least. Yet in the warehouse's pervading atmosphere of sullen, lumpen machismo, such reprimands echoed like praise.

He would blatantly confront management, and many times I witnessed George violently oppose a member of the office staff. He always approached these confrontations at least as an equal, one whose opinion should not be ignored. Indeed his value to management was reflected in his negotiating clout. He arranged to begin work at seven in the morning, one hour early, in order that he might leave for home an hour earlier in the evening, thereby missing the rush hour. After unlocking the warehouse at 7 a.m. George would retire to the café (no one actually saw him pay his bill) where he would conduct some business, before returning to work at 7.50. When he moved some forty miles out of London several years ago, he persuaded the company to provide an interest-free loan to pay for his rail season-ticket, a tactic unsuccessfully mimicked by several members of management.

All day long George received his own personal 'customers', many of whom were long-standing acquaintances whose business had blossomed with George's assistance. Often arriving in large expensive cars, formal business courtesies were thrown to the wind, as George was sought out and dealing commenced. George regarded himself on a par with these men, and their attitude was always respectful, their mutual transactions carried out with decorum and discretion. While I cannot be certain, it would appear that George did not become involved in direct theft. Instead he utilized his knowledge of the trade, the company, and its employees to contrive alternative strategies to thieving such as arranging special discounts, reserving damaged or obsolete stock, or other similar methods within the parameters of the twilight zone of 'good business' (Ditton 1977, pp. 173–84).

In return for this preferential treatment George usually received 'favours' as opposed to cash. The exchange of favours within the entrepreneurial culture should be acknowledged as more than the fulfilment of a moral obligation by one individual to another (Henry 1978, pp. 98–9). The confirmation of a specific trading network is only marginally closer to the subjective reality of this type of activity, ignoring the cultural context in which it takes place. This is especially crucial in a one-class society such as East London, where supportive interchange as it is manifested in fiddling and thieving collaborations, functions as a confirmation of relationships upon which the very existence of the culture depends. For entrepreneurship is not a secondary or peripheral characteristic of the culture, but the central element by which expanded environments might be explored and mutual support be provided to individuals who are both beneficiaries of, and contributors to, a common stock of cultural collateral. Supportive interchange is then a mutually exploitative relationship that may well utilize 'favours' as its core currency, while these favours provide both support for the culture and the provision or promise of accessibility to a stock of goods and services (Sharmer 1972, quoted in Henry 1978, p. 110).

A regular client of George's was a local garage-owner, and George's car was indeed an immaculately turned out, highly tuned machine. Every Friday lunch-time George would visit other regular clients of his, a butcher and a fruit and vegetable wholesaler, and by the afternoon his tiny 'office' was full of punnets of strawberries, trays of peaches, and every imaginable kind of produce. There would also be a large bag of choice cuts of meat, sausages etc. Sometimes his customers would deliver to him at the firm, and the labourers would unload the foodstuffs, plundering fruit despite George's watchful eye.

Most of the goods and services that George required could be obtained from a business acquaintance of his, either at cost or as a favour. When he needed some garden fencing, he brooded for some months until a suitable contact seeking a bargain visited the firm and an arrangement was reached. Likewise when some brickwork needed attention several months of market reconnaissance eventually yielded a bargain-hunting local builder.

Coming from a family of costermongers, George had worked on a market stall as a very young child. He collected and sold firewood and performed chores for anyone willing to pay, and from an early age the possibilities for exercising business acumen and accumulating wealth were abundantly apparent to him:

Some of those [market] people were rich people in their own right. My father's brother when he went to market, he was a 6 ft.-tall beanpole, and he wore a long poacher's coat lined with pockets. Well, what was in them pockets! On his fingers he had jewellery that lords and ladies didn't have. All the tearaways used to bring the stuff they had nicked, and he would buy it ... When my uncle died it was like the Jersey flower show. Bethnal Green Road was packed end to end.

When his grandfather died the business folded, and much as he loved market-life George found himself at the age of 14 looking for work.

George. I was just lucky to get a job ... there was a depression on, so my mother just put her hands together when she found out there was a wage coming in. I went up for a job and the guv'nor said, 'Are you strong?' and I said, 'yes, sir. I have been lifting 100 cwt.-sacks of spuds in the market.'

Employed for his physical strength, George rapidly gained control of certain specialized areas of the trade.

George. 'Cause I had a good tutor in Ben Byrne [foreman]. When Ben knew a traveller [salesman] was coming in he'd say, 'If the bastard don't drop [tip] he don't get the order'. Then they'd have to drop him or Ben would put his spoke in.

George's reminiscences are always couched in commercial language. Those practices that he inherited and those he invented were seen as versions of conventional business conduct, conduct that is often more blatantly illegal than George's 'favours for vegetables' sub-economy.

George. Old Archibald [a senior director] he went inside for buying black market gear during the war. The whole firm was at it, everybody knew about it, but when the police found out Archie held up his hands, and when he came out of the nick they promoted him for taking the can. They have all been at it at some time.

George considered himself to be an astute business man and was always willing to enter into the realm of management prerogatives and apply his knowledge of the trade, profit margins, and commercial etiquette.

George. If a customer moaned to me about a price and they were good customers, I would always get them some extra discount. You might lose 30 per cent but they will gain confidence, and if you do it on bread-and-butter orders then when a special order comes up you can charge them what you like and they won't question it.

The quest for profit, albeit a crude mimicry of commercial life, created for George an autonomous space, a gap nurtured by scams, fiddles, and arrangements that gave life an edge unblunted by the torturous grind of manual labour that structured his formal status on the labour market. When George died the practices and fiddles of over forty years' survival did not disappear, for they were still appropriate strategies for negotiating the 1980s, and just as George had inherited the basis for his 'business' from Ben, so Nob now carries on a tradition that could eventually reach a dynastic proportion.

Nob

When George died the onus for continuing his business lay with Nob. At 39 years of age Nob was probably the oldest apprentice in Britain, yet for fifteen years he had been George's second in command, learning about both the official and unofficial trades. He had operated a few spasmodic fiddles of his own, earning the odd £5 for loading 'extras' on to customers' vehicles, but George had retained his specialized knowledge and made the unofficial trade in particular his own exclusive realm, and as a consequence Nob was often driven to outright petty theft.

Nob. I worked with George for fifteen years and he never told me about any of his fiddles. He worked with 'the team'; he was in it. It was George, Ex, and Ray. Between them they could supply anything. But George mainly had his own customers.

Consequently, when George died there was a huge void that Nob somehow had to fill. Most of George's customers had just disappeared, Nob needed money and there was a security clamp-down at the firm. Taking advantage of the retirement of several powerful members of the warehouse staff, management had installed closed-circuit TV cameras and plain-clothes security men throughout the premises. In addition, Nob's comparative lack of knowledge, coupled with a violent reputation and a delinquent past, made him in management eyes a more obvious deviant than the dignified, authoritative cloth-capped George.

Over fifteen years Nob had picked up some of the key strategies of George's business without being actively involved in any of the transactions, and he was largely untested in the field of discrete controlled fiddling.

Nob. The easiest way was—and I learnt this myself but George did it first—was to give them the most expensive gear, and mark down in the books that it was the cheapest.

Nob quickly discovered that the company's reliance upon warehouse staff to deal with stock-taking and routine stock control was his main tool in extricating a surplus from conventional business transactions. As well as the misrepresentation of goods in stock records, Nob also inherited the practice of deliberately damaging goods as a useful fiddling strategy. For this method trusted customers would order goods and negotiate with Nob as to the best method of damaging the goods so as not to hinder their function. The goods would be damaged in this specific manner, entered in the books as damaged, and sold to Nob's customer at scrap price plus Nob's 'commission' on top (Henry 1978, pp. 30–1, 58).

However, while Nob had gleaned crucial elements of fiddling methodology from George he still had to find customers for the goods at his disposal, and it is at this stage of drumming up trade that the fundamental nature of the entrepreneurial culture is made apparent.

Nob. Usually they are a friend of a friend. They want soemthing so they see me. They say they want it and I usually say, 'Fuck me though, they're expensive'. They say, 'Are they?' So I say 'Yeah, about fifty notes'. So they say, 'Well can't you find some damaged or old stock then?' Then you know.

Nob is very careful about who he deals with and normally requires 'references' if he is propositioned by someone who is an unknown entity.

Nob. You have to be careful Dick, some people take liberties. Some geezer had me over. He'd had some gear, a good bit and he was good as gold with the dough. Then one day I put some gear on his van and he says he was coming back that afternoon to pay me. The dirty bastard hasn't been in since [laughs].

Nob was not offended by this incident, for as with George, deception is just part of 'good business'.

Nob. Sometimes I say to them you know, 'it's expensive, £50'; I sell it to them for £30 and its only worth £20. What about last week, my brother-in-law wants a . . . so I get him one and charge him £60. I said 'Now Ken, I'm not earning out of you, I wouldn't would I? But the geezer I work with wants £60.' I gave Jason £15. The wife had some shoes, the girl needed a dress and I had a nice drink, so it all goes.

While deception and misrepresentation is regarded as part of the trade and mere variations upon the theme of conventional business, outsiders—those who are neither subject to nor contributors to the entrepreneurial culture—are regarded as vulnerable and valid targets.

The Arab

Nob. This geezer turns up in a Daimler looking like a fucking Arab, fucking jewellery weren't in it, great bracelet on one hand and a watch studded with diamonds. When I see that, I thought, 'he's got a few bob'. So he wants to see some gear and eventually I got him quite a lot. He came up every day with a different bird, t'riffic looking, and I'm getting him gear and he kept on saying 'There will be a nice drink for you'. Anyway it comes to over £400, and he's still well pleased and gives me the drink. I thought about a tenner. When he's gone, I count it and there's £70.

D.H. You did well.

Nob. Yeah I just put it through the books as normal and he paid the normal price. He thought he was getting it cheap so that was that![1]

While goods go 'through the books', the scope for profit is reduced in accordance with the risk involved and to maximize profit is to increase risk. 'Going through the books' involved Nob taking few risks and he was at all times in control of any transaction. Ideally Nob likes to have a few days' notice from customers, and very precise specifications of goods required. Then he proceeds to evaluate the current security situation and the likely flow of traffic at the time of the prospective pick-up. Profit and risk are weighed up and, to date, a balance is achieved. Yet Nob is always in charge of the situation dictating to the customer *modus operandi* and, crucially, price.

Nob. If things are busy, like about 3 o'clock, when all the drivers come in, if they got a van, it goes straight on the back, and I see them round the café. Otherwise it goes straight through the books.

However, I was able to observe the elaborate but essential pantomime that accompanies what is in essence a simple case of theft. The customer is instructed exactly where to park, so as to avoid obstructing traffic and drawing undue attention, and to be as close as possible to where the goods are stored. The advantage of preplanning is that parking-spaces can be reserved, and goods collected from far-flung sections of the warehouse and temporarily stored in a convenient spot close to the place of loading. Then Nob, flaunting a fistful of documentation, diligently loads the goods, carefully packs them, and bids his customer farewell. They then meet at the next

[1] Klockars notes that Vincent, his professional fence, did nothing to discourage customers from believing legitimate goods to be stolen. In fact Vincent used the label of 'hot' goods as a lure to entice custom to his premises (Klockars 1975, p. 79).

break in a nearby café where the transaction is completed over a cup of tea.

Occasionally transactions involving direct theft are completed without this pre-planning. Then goods take time to be found, or are unavailable and substitutes negotiated. Parking-spaces adjacent to loading-bays cannot always be found and loading and packing the goods becomes an obtrusive and risky operation. For instance, on one occasion Nob and an accomplice made three trips carrying heavy, bulky goods some fifty yards along a side street to complete a hastily arranged transaction on a day when traffic was heavy and parking-spaces at a premium.

However, risk-taking behaviour such as this was rare, and both Nob and George despised those few who went too far, thereby jeopardizing the enterprises of many.

Nob. Like, the worst ones are those cunts in shipping; that's why they put the security in. They always get greedy. Somebody gets nicked and then they have a clamp-down. Spoils it for everybody.

Normally Nob would reduce to a minimum any risk of apprehension, and theft and fiddles merge together to form an autonomous space, a gap in the monotonous grind of the workplace.

Both Nob's and George's 'business' activities can be seen as attempts to structure their day, to take control of part of the workplace or trade that otherwise would constrict them. The business activities of 'grafters' serve to lubricate the daily grind, like 'being busy' when large lorries need unloading, or clearing all outstanding work before lunch with the prospect of an easy afternoon ahead. For in these autonomous alcoves within the bowels of capitalism, individuals fend off the overt oppression sponsored by the profit motive, while contributing to the persistence of the prevailing socio-economic order by picking at the debris left in the wake of the free market economy.

3. The Jump-up Merchant

Jack

Jack has a motto, 'Never turn down a pound note'. In the last five years he has been a painter and decorator, a van-driver, lorry-driver, window-cleaner, builders' labourer, roofer, handler of stolen goods, thief, and publican. In a similar manner to Zorbaugh's 'squawker', (Zorbaugh 1929, pp. 110–14) the 'jump-up' negotiates a living by partaking in any activity that proffers pecuniary reward without engaging him in the normative contractual arrangement suggested by employer–employee relationships.

Jack has for many years shunned employment possibilities that require him to be employed by someone else, preferring self-employment and casual work to 'a job on the cards'. Most mornings for Jack commence in a bright glow of anticipation, not knowing what the day will bring. An early start, a few phone calls, and an excursion in his transit van to pick up and deliver some roofing-tiles may be worth £15. Or a two-hour drive around the area 'to see what's on offer' may result in a blank, no profit, little more than an update on the opportunities on offer in his locality.

Jack is open to offers, willing to partake (with few exceptions) in any task so long as their is 'a pound note' at the end of the day. As a husband, and father of three children, Jack seldom earns sufficient to fulfil his responsibilities. Consequently he is officially separated from his wife so as to enable her to take full advantage of the social security system, although Jack would never lower himself actually to register as unemployed and claim for benefit himself. As a consequence of this fierce independence, Jack operates as a kind of buccaneer, roaming the streets day or night free to plunder and prosper without any hindrance from the Inland Revenue, DHSS, or any other branch of the state.

Flexibility and optimism are key characteristics of any successful entrepreneur and Jack is no exception. One night he attempted to rob business premises but was thwarted by security arrangements, and the one accessible article of worth was an ancient wooden ladder. The following day he became a window-cleaner, the next day he decided that he was scared of heights, and by the end of the week had sold the ladder.

Criminal activity is just one option available to the 'jump-up', and because of his fluidity across the width of the entrepreneurial spectrum, the range of criminal activity that he is likely to be involved in is far wider than, for instance, that of the 'grafter', who is restricted by his position on the labour market. The 'jump-up' does not differentiate between legal and illegal opportunities and with few exceptions will judge an opportunity according to potential profit and loss. For instance, when sounded out by a local 'firm' about his possible participation in an armed robbery:

Jack. No, for a million pounds I wouldn't risk eight or ten years;

for me it's not worth it. But if someone pulled up with a hundred grand of whisky on a lorry then you wouldn't see me for dust 'cos what's it worth if it comes on top—two years, two years maximum. For me that's worth a chance.

For Jack legal and illegal money-making devices represent parallel opportunity structures that are differentiated not by the assumptions of a moral order linked to a homogeneous code of conduct, but to a pragmatic consideration of such crucial factors as risk, chance, and the practical application of the law as opposed to the assumed philosophical and moral hegemony of statute. For example, while working as a casual builders' labourer Jack was introduced to a new branch of the hidden economy.

Jack. What I do like is to dabble. Oh, I do like a dabble. I 'ave a little mooch, and there's so much building going on round there. Well, I 'ave a look around, and the foreman on the house next door to where we're working, he's well at it. He likes to dabble; he's like me. I said to him, 'Anything going cheap? 'cos I want what you got.' So he said, 'Come back about 3 o'clock.' You know me, Dick, I'd 'ave been there at 3 o'clock in the morning. So I've 'ad bricks, wood, everything.

Jack's ability to deal successfully in relatively unfamiliar commodities and to negotiate competently in new markets is crucial in maintaining the 'jump-up's' marketability.

Jack. If I get known as a wheeler-dealer, a right grafter, then when another job comes up, they're going to say, 'We want Jacko. We want him on this. Where is he?'

Jack's knowledge of a diverse range of markets is a crucial part of his entrepreneurial imagery. When he and I bought a quantity of legitimate goods we both found that retail shops could undercut us. However, when Jack relayed the impression that the goods were stolen he sold out in two days, despite being more expensive than legitimate high-street retail outlets (Klockars 1975, p. 79). His reputation as an entrepreneur provides the corner-stone of his public *persona.* He is a man to be respected.

After a long period of casual work and several unfruitful deals and attempts at theft Jack arrived at my home one night beaming. He was immaculately dressed, his gold jewellery fresh out of the pawnshop, glinting testimony to recent success. He had a huge gold J on a chain around his neck, an elaborate gold bracelet, and a gold ring with his initials studded in diamonds. He stood in my living-room, spread his hands, and looking like some perverse thirteenth-century Pope rejoicing at the benevolent sanctity of free enterprise, pronounced:

Jack. I've had it off! It was an inside job, Easter weekend, great big warehouse, ... Bobby set it up with the manager, ex-docker, good as gold he is ... drove in ... locked the doors behind us and took our time.

The booty consisted of Italian casual clothing with a street price of over £10,000.

Jack. We loaded up, and the manager says, 'What about the hole in the wall?' I says, 'What fucking hole?' He says, 'There ain't one.' So I says, 'Out of the way, I'll give you a fucking hole in the wall.' So I jumps in the fork-lift and goes bosh: 'There's your fucking hole.' They just pulls the bricks through and make it look like we come in through the wall.

For Jack the real pleasure to be gained from this venture was to be found in the dealing that occurred in the process of disposing of the goods which consisted of shirts and sweaters displaying a distinctive designer logo.

Jack. It all went so easy 'cos it's good gear 'Bonetti'; everybody wants it don't they! Some people was having a few hundred in a parcel. I knocked most of it out myself. I went to work punting same day as we got it. The others said, You can't do that.' I said, 'You watch me.'

Jack took charge of the pricing of goods, and like George was enthusiastic in his nurturing of 'good customers' by offering them generous discounts. Jack halved the normal retail price of each item, the legitimate price being ascertained by visiting a wholesaler and posing as a prospective customer hoping to start his own business. His assessment of the 'right' price for the goods was correct as the clothing was sold quickly to eager customers some of whom then resold the goods for a small profit, thereby flexing their entre-preneurial muscle. However, as the instigator of the main enterprise as well as of the various off-shoots and spin-offs generated by the theft, Jack experienced an elevation of his previous status, and a massive boost in the esteem in which he was held, particularly amongst the community that were aware of the extent of Jack's achievement. Consequently, in the local pub where most of the deals were struck, Jack and anyone in his company were the main focus of attention, drinks arriving from all sections of the bar as a mark of respect. On one such night the extent to which the community shared in the spoils became apparent when, after being deep in conversation with Jack, I surveyed the crowded pub to find virtually every male wearing casual clothing augmented by a garish 'Bonetti' logo.

He Who Dares etc.

Crime takes its place alongside legal money-making ventures in the lottery of Jack's existence. Chance and gambling metaphors are primary features in his descriptions and re-enactments of episodes in his life, and from my own experience the daily grind of the 'jump-up' is random in the extreme. Up at dawn, Jack would often breakfast with a relative in a house opposite his home, while enjoying the spectacle of police raiding his house. Then with a beer mat as a substitute for a road-tax disc it was time to tour his 'manor'. He might clear a garden for £10, check out the lorry parks for a likely target, or decorate a flat for a fellow business man. On one occasion we stopped outside a parade of shops while Jack checked the alarm system on an electrical shop. While I waited in the van a sales rep offered me £2 to carry a heavy video-recorder into the shop, and that paid for our petrol that day.

Even the successful 'Bonetti' enterprise was a fortuitous escapade, as Jack and his partners had no idea what type of goods were being stored in the warehouse, and when the same crime was re-enacted the following Whitsun, a packed warehouse proffered no booty of marketable quality. For every successful enterprise there are dozens of failures. For instance, employed by a local business man as a minder, Jack ended up in magistrates' court after being involved in a fight with his employer's partner. However, it is crime of a semi-project nature that is the most random of the 'jump-up's' activities. The term 'jump-up' itself comes from the literal description of a person who follows delivery vans and lorries until the driver stops to make a delivery, and at an opportune moment our stalking hero 'jumps-up' and grabs whatever he can. *Ergo*, 'I am just a jump-up merchant.'

If an opportunity occurs for Jack that promises money, autonomy, and freedom from the normative employer–employee relationship, then it is an opportunity that is ripe for entrepreneurial exploitation. The merging of legal and illegal opportunities into the category of business, as well as the futility of much of this activity is shown by the following two examples.

A business acquaintance of Jack's took up the lease on a local shop.

As the previous leaseholders had left in some haste, the premises were in need of some attention before the shop could be reopened. Jack was employed by his friend to clear out the shop and after noting that the premises would make a 'nice little slaughter',[2] he then observed that a quantity of stock had been left behind. Immediately, Jack negotiated a new rate for the job, and it was agreed that no money would change hands, but that all the remaining stock was his. This appealed to his entrepreneurial spirit, and in exchange for several days' labour, he inherited a few hundred bottles of artificial sun-tan cream, several tea-chests full of assorted zips and buttons, and several hundred large reels of cotton. He also acquired four large rolls of sleeping-bag material and six pairs of men's size-twelve platform-soled 'Gary Glitter' shoes. But his real prize was two gross of pregnancy-testing kits.

Jack. Worth a fortune, Dick, if only I can find a buyer. Jimmy's gone in the Paki chemists on the bridge all covered in cement, dirt and shit; gone bosh! on the counter; 'Want to buy some of these pal?' Fucking wally. I'm going in suited and booted and do it right; they must sell. When I got 'em I phoned Davey, you know the punter, a diamond. Before I put the phone down he's in me house, the boot of his car open, and he's up my passage rubbing his hands together looking at all these cartons piled up saying, 'What have you got for me Jacko?' When I showed him I saw his face drop. He just said 'You're taking the piss' [laughs], Yeah! nice, eh! taking the piss. 'Pregnancy-kits. It's a bit *por favor* that'.

Jack even tried to interest me as an agent:

Jack. All them students, there must be a fair bit of that going on. We could clean up.

After investing several days in this venture Jack found that he had made a loss as the few pregnancy-testing kits he had managed to sell proved to be disastrously defective (my heavily pregnant wife registered a negative result) and the sun-tanning cream had actually cost Jack money to be dumped at a local refuse depot. Yet the venture was legal and its only risk was wasting time, unlike my second example which involved the risk of 'doing time'.

It was just before Christmas when Jack and two associates decided to rob a warehouse that was leased to a major delivery company.

---

[2] A 'slaughter' is a safe place where stolen goods can be unloaded and distributed.

Because of the time of the year it was realistic to assume that the premises would be packed with a variety of commercially viable goods, and after a brief period of reconnaissance the trio decided to enter the building, a single-storey prefabricated structure, by cutting their way through the roof. Goods would then be secured by rope and hauled up to the roof, to be slid down a ladder and into a van.

Jack and his chief cohort, Tom, had visited the firm during working hours on several occasions to check on the firm's security arrangements, particularly the alarm system, and to gain an impression of the general layout of the firm. This was achieved by driving into the premises in Jack's van, and strolling around looking slightly lost while clutching a handful of what appeared to be delivery notes. On being challenged they merely waved their notes and mentioned the name of a prominent transport depot near by, whereupon they were politely redirected (see Maguire 1982, pp. 115–16).

Both Jack and Tom were highly confident as they had enjoyed some success in recent weeks plundering warehouses laden with Christmas goods. Yet for both men this promised to be 'the big one', and the only foreseeable problem was the need to recruit one other man to position himself at the base of the ladder receiving and loading goods into the van. Henry was regarded as 'a good worker with no bottle'. A large man in early middle age, his reputation as a steady, small-time thief had been seriously damaged when he stepped up a rung into armed robbery. As the driver of a get-away vehicle used in a raid, a wave of hysteria and a bout of diarrhoea almost cost three of his colleagues 5–10 years and a fourth man, a parolee, considerably longer.

However, Tom was the key figure in the warehouse theft and other similar enterprises. His gymnastic ability was outstanding, earning him the nickname 'the cat', his party piece being a back somersault on to a pub's bar. His abilities were valued and respected, and the only drawback in working with Tom was his tendency to drink heavily before going to 'work'. However, this could result in quite spectacular athletic feats, and fences, gates, and walls proved no obstacle and his feline nickname stuck. The cat, albeit an inebriated cat, was a good thief. Shortly before Christmas, the van carrying the three men parked outside the warehouse at about two o'clock in the morning. Jack swiftly wielded his bolt-cutters, the gates swung open, Tom drove in, whereupon an elaborate Swedish padlock of Jack's secured the gates, rendering the warehouse and its occupants secure from unexpected intrusion, such as passing police or security firms. Once safely inside the compound the three men quickly assumed their allocated roles with Jack and Tom working on the roof with the bolt-cutters, and Henry passively waiting for the loot to come sliding down the ladder.

The anticipation, particularly for the two senior protagonists, was great for all of their combined efforts over the past six months were about to pay off handsomely. For Jack the 'big one' meant being able to purchase a truck, and establish himself as a self-employed transport contractor. Not that this would mean a cessation of his deviant activity, merely that the status of being legitimately employed as a lorry-driver would both maintain his entrepreneurial status, and widen the scope of his potential criminal activities.[3]

As soon as the roof was dealt with, much to Jack's horror, Tom fell straight through the hole. Jack had always maintained a steady professional attitude to his trade, never drinking more than a 'stiffener' before going to work, and he had often tried to deter Tom from imbibing before a job. Consequently, Tom's sudden descent into darkness did little to allay the apprehension that Jack had felt earlier when Tom had raucously sung all the way from the pub to the target. However, 'the cat' dropped only some 10 feet before his fall was broken by several gross of paper lampshades packed in cardboard boxes piled about 20 feet high.

On making his way to the floor, Tom, with the aid of a torch began to check the contents of the warehouse, and within a couple of minutes a pensive Jack heard a shriek of delight from below. Quickly the beam from his torch picked out Tom holding a pair of curling-tongs and a personal cassette-player. The warehouse was full of small electrical appliances, light, easily transported, and, most importantly, with Christmas imminent, easily marketed. All the trio now required was a couple of hours of unhindered hard work for a good Christmas, and possibly an enhanced life-style.

The ecstatic 'cat' continued triumphantly to stalk the floor periodically shouting 'hair-dryers', 'tongs' etc. up to Jack on the roof. Tom then stopped calling out, and Jack heard no movements from the darkness below. Shining his torch on to the floor, Jack eventually

---

[3] This type of enabling criminal action is what Polsky has termed 'moonlighting': 'The purpose of moonlighting is not merely to provide more income but to provide it in a way that allows you to keep your primary job, the one you prefer' (Polsky 1971, p. 91).

picked out Tom staring at a cluster of tea-chests in the far corner of the warehouse. 'Whisky', said Tom quietly. 'What?' 'Whisky,' the cat wailed, 'fucking whisky.'

Whisky and Christmas. The possible financial repercussions of such a cocktail were rapidly discussed, a decision reached and relayed to Henry. There were 25 tea-chests stamped and bonded as miniature bottles of Scotch whisky. They were to be lifted by rope on to the roof, slid down the ladder, and once inside the van transported to the 'cat's' lock-up. The long haul began. Jack lay prone and pulled using all his considerable strength.

Jack. My fucking arms felt like they was bursting. But all I could think of was the fantastic fucking result we were going to get.

Eventually all the cases were in the van, the 'cat' scuttled up the rope, and the trio drove to Tom's lock-up:

Jack. Feeling like we was leaving Wembley with the fucking Cup.

After unloading, Henry was dropped off and Jack and Tom retired to Tom's flat for a celebratory drink.

Jack. You just can't explain what it's like to 'do one'. Like it's unbelievable to be in a gaff full of gear, and it's yours to do what you like with. You are the boss, no questions.

After some half-hour of constant replays of the night's action, it was decided to return to the lock-up and open one of the cases, 'just to make us feel good'. Tom broke the steel bands binding the first case and slowly prized the lid.

Jack. Bibles.

D.H. Bibles?

Jack. Bibles, fucking Bibles.

Another case was assaulted, then another, revealing dozens of blue bound bibles.

Jack. Tom was still pissed, so he sat down and grinned. I didn't know whether to laugh or cry. We dropped them in the river, but first I took one each for the kids, you know to put next to their bed on Christmas morning. I thought under the circumstances like it was the right thing. Trouble was, Christmas morning, when they opened them they was written in fucking Polish!

Pregnancy-kits, bibles, and big money provide for the jump-up the tangible results of entrepreneurial enterprise. Yet the real reward for Jack is those culturally sanctioned characteristics of independence and autonomy that go to formulate his inheritance. As Jack himself so cogently notes 'No guv'nor can afford my wages.'

4. The 'I'm a business man'

In the three previous examples of entrepreneurial types, I have stressed the prevalence of an entrepreneurial style that pervades an entire culture. However, due to their position in the labour market the possibilities for entrepreneurial action for these three types are by necessity deviant and/or criminal. The 'I'm a business man' provides within the parameters of East End culture, a bridge, a crucial link between these preceding types and those for whom entrepreneurial activity can be linked to legitimate, that is non-criminal, activity.

Chester

Chester arrives at one of 'his' pubs within half an hour of lunch-time opening. He greets the landlord warmly and his greeting is reciprocated usually by a free drink. Chester is immaculately dressed, his attire is a crucial prop of his daily performance. Indeed, if he paid income tax he could probably claim a tax-free clothes-allowance. 'Casual, but smart, that's me. Some people reckon that I am flash, but I'm not, not really. It's a matter of self-respect'. Dressed in slacks, a double-breasted navy-blue blazer, white shirt, college tie, and discretely expensive shoes, Chester would not look out of place in any yacht-club bar, or exclusive gentlemen's club. Yet this vision of conservative decorum is somehow flawed by what looks like several hundredweight of gold around his neck, fingers, and wrists:

Chester. The tom [jewellery], well it's me. I do like a bit of gold. I can't resist stopping to look in a gold-shop window. It's a good investment. A friend of mine does a good deal, makes me up rings, anything; if your interested ...

The pub is Chester's place of business. He operates only from the pub; it is his office. The nature of his business varies, changing with altered economic circumstances. It includes central-heating installation, double-glazing, cavity-wall insulation, TV repairs, carpet-fitting, video-tape rental, furniture removals, building work, etc. Any one or a combination of these or similar trades can be Chester's business. Scorning pints of beer in favour of some beverage more commensurate with his status, such as a gin and tonic or a bottle of one of the more expensive lagers, Chester utilizes the pub's private phone (not the pay phone) to conduct his business. Often partners or customers will arrive in person to seal a deal, and negotiations will continue long after offical closing-time. On the face of it, Chester is a sharp, successful young entrepreneur who is willing and able to switch his resources around in response to economic whims and the general ebb and flow of the market.

A Card therefore I Am

Chester has no capital, no premises, no employees, and no business, yet he is quick and proud to define himself in preliminary introductions and at subsequent meetings in the following manner: 'I'm a business man'. Chester provides connections: he is 'in business' to connect clients to practitioners, and it is this role as an agent to which he applies his entrepreneurial ability. His status as a business man is maintained by the flaunting of what are perceived as the essential and universal accoutrements of the successful business man, affluent clothes and accessories, extensive business contacts, and a pack of assorted business cards. Sometimes the cards will represent a projected business venture in which he has some stake, sometimes the card has been handed to him by a business acquaintance. On occasions he will receive a sum of money for introducing a client to a fellow business man; other occasions may generate nothing more than goodwill and cultural reinforcement, the stuff of 'supportive interchange' (Goffman 1971, pp. 62–94). For while profit is the dynamic behind the 'I'm a business man', the *raison d'être* of his existence is the acquisition and maintenance of status, status as defined not by the norms of commerce, but by the combined experiences of generations of East Londoners. As Henry comments: 'He is demonstrating that he has a vast hinterland of social relationships, a veritable network of "people in the know" who have both the influence and the ability literally to "produce the goods"' (Henry 1978, p. 96).

Chester provides a service, and that service relates to the pool of goods and services available within the culture, and as he does not actually possess the skills to implement the trades and professions himself, he has made it his business to acquire the requisite knowledge of a vast range of other people's business and then to function as a community data bank of valued wisdom. 'Most importantly he indicates that the network can be put to the service of the person wanting or needing the goods' (Henry 1978, p. 96).

As a free-lance broker of goods and services Chester is not required by his clientele or his associates to distinguish between legal and illegal business, and as with Jack the extent of his involvement in criminal activity depends very much upon the risk factor of a particular enterprise rather than any consideration of morality. Due to his unique position on the labour market, Chester is able to apply his skills to a range of situations, the scope of which encompasses those illegal activities that require presentational skills and verbal dexterity as opposed to the physical commitment of a thief or robber. The 'I'm a business man' applies his occupationally accrued skills to confidence tricks, selling cut-price jacuzzis, and most spectacularly to the 'corner game' in equal measure. An example of the latter activity would be to be contracted to commit an illegal act such as grievous bodily harm or murder, convince the client that the contract has been fulfilled, and receive full payment. Meanwhile the 'victim' remains unharmed and unaware of such machinations. The client then has to decide whether to contact the police and alert them to the fraud, thereby risking a charge of conspiracy, or deal with the matter privately.

Perhaps a more typical example of the corner-man's art is, for instance, to position himself inside an electrical shop, posing as an assistant. When a prospective customer enters, he will offer to acquire the goods cheaply either via a staff discount or theft for perhaps half the retail price. Then after relieving the customer of a large sum of cash he will arrange a meeting some half an hour later at a mutually convenient spot. Again, the mug is 'cornered' for when no one appears with his video or washing machine, to resort to the police amounts to admission of both criminal action and incompetence.

For Chester all these activities, legal and illegal, are legitimate and viable, if spasmodic, methods of acquiring income. Often the opportunities for such enterprises will be sparse, yet this does not in any way detract from his self-definition, how he regards his various money-making activities in the context of East End culture. 'I'm a business man' may be his only connection with what bourgeois society might regard as the legitimate transactions of commerce or finance. Yet in exploiting the perverse tradition of East End economics, Chester is merely acknowledging the manipulation, exploitation, and greed that are the dynamics integral to all enterprises that pursue profit. His merging of legal and illegal methodology into one neutralizing or justificatory term 'business' exposes the essentially parasitic nature of entrepreneurship. Indeed,

Chester, in displaying quite openly his high regard for business activity, and his insistence on the 'business man' label is more candid in his articulation of the true nature of free enterprise than those entrepreneurs who have pursued a more conventional business career. For it is the status of business man that provides the key to the attraction of East End entrepreneurship, and for Chester his presentational style is often the only obvious clue to his entrepreneurial aspirations.

The 'I'm a business man' provides a touchstone for those aspiring to entrepreneurship. He links the illegal entrepreneur to the legal entrepreneur, and stresses the importance of formal status that refers both to the East End's cultural inheritance, and to the East-Enders' ambivalence towards bourgeois hegemony as it is manifested in the holy grail of free enterprise.

5. The Small Business Man

The rhetoric of business provides justifications for actions and more specifically functions as a neutralizing technique for illegal action. For the small business man the rhetorical function of commercial language is of no less importance. Structured upon a model of conventional business, the small business man carries out his commercial activity normally with a minimum of capital investment. As a self-employed mechanic, he may have no assets other than his tools, and perhaps a lock-up garage materially to distinguish him from other categories. As a plumber, his tools and some suitable transport will mark him out. The main distinguishing feature of the small business man, however, is his utility of commercial language to establish with others his identity, his self-perception being that of someone who is bonded, no matter how tenuously, with the world of private enterprise.

He has applied his entrepreneurial inheritance to gaining the skills necessary to acquire the status of a trade—plumber, mechanic, builder—and to gaining a market for his skills. These entrepreneurial skills are applied in a legally normative manner, in tune with the market economy, yet in a form that is in accord with the vagaries of East End culture. As a consequence, the small business man is not regarded by fellow denizens of East London as being unusual or involving himself in behaviour contrary to expectations.

Terry

Terry is a 34-year-old electrician, married with three young children, who has been self-employed for four years. He served a four-year apprenticeship with a London local authority and stayed with the council for a further eight years, before briefly taking employment with one of the few large factories in the area, and then setting up a business of his own.

Terry married in the mid-1970s and his wife, inevitably a local woman, immediately fostered an objection to him returning home from working on building sites in a grimy state, and began putting pressure on Terry to find a cleaner occupation. This pressure must have found favour with Terry, for he soon began to find fault with his trade, and adopted a stance that was conspicuously upwardly mobile. The two most notable manifestations of his stance were the 'selling' of his hobby, the renovation of old cars, the remuneration from which contributed to the second notable change in his life-style, a move to a remote housing estate in semi-rural Essex.

Terry became a commuter travelling 35 miles a day to and from his home and various building sites. His estate in the mid-1970s housed an almost itinerant mixture of tradesmen and white-collar workers, who used the cheap property of mid-Essex as a staging-post between East London and a 'semi' in Billericay. There was an unsettled feel about his estate as house prices escalated and young families moved on. Terry was quite rootless and he needed an identity that was as removed from the squalor of his childhood as was his double-glazed home. For a while he toyed with the idea of moving house again, but after commuting to work for a while, his wife gave up work in 1976. Coupled with a slump in his earnings due to a cut-back in the council's building programme, their income plummeted and moving house was no longer an option. Several people had approached Terry about setting up a business but his wife objected and Terry supplemented his lost overtime earnings by doing 'privates' at the weekend.

The pressure towards upward mobility finally proved to be too much in 1978 and Terry donned a suit to become an assistant site agent for a large firm of builders. However, he 'never liked being a guv'nor's man, telling other geezers what to do'. After eight months he took his suit off and explored the lumpen option by getting a job shift-working as a maintenance electrician at Fords of Dagenham. His wife accepted Terry's step back into overalls on the grounds that he would earn more money at Fords, indeed he could in 1980 earn over £200 per week. But the unique pressures that were brought to bear by working a three-shift system were considerable and he disliked not being able to see much of his family. He left Fords after just eighteen months, and despite pressure from his wife, began work with a building contractor installing electric systems on a piece-work basis.

However, by this time the social make-up of the estate had become easily identifiable, for the housing market had peaked and subsequently stabilized. The inhabitants of Terry's estate by 1979 were working-class East-Enders at the lower end of the tradesman's pay-scale, often self-employed or doing contract labour, and most were under 45 years of age. The availability of an exclusively working-class reference group served to reinforce Terry's original cultural influences. On the estate men went to work early in the morning in second-hand Cortinas, old vans and boiler suits, returning ten hours later to a meal cooked by a wife who had spent the day doing housework and caring for children under the age of 5, or waiting for a child to be born. The distance from London ruled out low-paid clerical work in the City as a viable financial option for most women. Consequently upward mobility often meant a reaffirmation of traditional sex roles for most of the couples on the estate, thereby regurgitating one of the essential elements of working-class culture, male economic hegemony. Children played in the street as they had in Canning Town and Poplar in the 1950s, before rehousing and heavy traffic had all but eliminated pre-pubescent street culture. The daytime presence of adults in the streets engendered a sense of security as well as a measure of control (Cohen, 1972). There was indeed a true sense of community that is not merely a reworking of a golden age of working-class culture, so much as a pragmatic response to the problems instigated by alienation that are experienced in many areas dominated by modern housing schemes.

At this point Terry's working day found resonance with both his home life and his experiences in his community. He was again living in an exclusively working-class environment, dominated by those traditional views of gender, work, and child-rearing to which he had been exposed as a child. The reaffirmation of Terry's status as a husband/father and craftsman gave him the confidence to exploit his entrepreneurial inheritance, and in 1981 Terry took the plunge, and became a business man.

Terry. Best thing I ever did. It was always there in me mind and I could have done it earlier; I had enough chances. I suppose it was Fords that did it. It was easy work; always got a kip on nights. It's not that, it's just that, well now I've got no guv'nors, that's what I like.

The break with employee status in order to become self-employed was always a feasible option, and was engineered in order that Terry might exercise an element of autonomy over his working day that is not necessarily linked to improved monetary reward. For as he is quick to point out when evaluating his income, the unpaid holidays, insurance premiums, and other considerations provide a net figure not dissimilar to the equivalent sum earned by an employed 'on the cards' tradesman. Terry used his entrepreneurial inheritance to gain control over his daily grind, becoming responsive to the market yet willing and able to negotiate with those who continued to affect, but not shape, each of his working days.

6. The Skilled Escapee

This section is concerned with skilled employees whose entrepreneurial direction is dominated by the special skill that they have derived from their experience in the workplace. One consequence of their application of these skills is enhanced monetary reward, and the subsequent ability to move out of the exclusive working-class environment, eastwards into one of the cultural buffer zones of Redbridge or Havering where escapees from the East End rub shoulders with the indigenous middle-class inhabitants of suburbia.

The escapee's primary concern is his flight from blacks, poor housing, poor schools, and dangerous streets. The enabling mechanisms of escape from these perceived threats are to be found in entrepreneurial activity, mechanisms which, in the escapee's own eyes, are manifested in qualities of wit and resourcefulness that were preordained in a bygone age and forged in poverty. However, most modern escapees have not experienced poverty, yet these cultural resources are regarded as an essential inheritance of an age in which traditional culture and cultural expression were formed to cope with poverty which in turn mark out durable characteristics of the East End's expanding environment. Bob is an escapee.

Bob

Bob works for a large company as a lift engineer and comes from a background of market people, scrap-metal dealers, and rag-collectors. As a child he had worked in all these trades and has retained his willingness to turn his hand to any money-making enterprise. However, his main source of extra income is derived from fitting extra telephone extensions to existing connections. Indeed, many local residents have a telephone in most of the rooms of their house. In this way one can see how Bob's entrepreneurial status is governed by the special skills and knowledge that are derived directly from his occupational status.

For instance, Bob was booking a table at a local restaurant and as he was leaving the manager, noticing Bob's yellow van asked if he had 'come to fix the phone'. Bob explained the purpose of his visit, but sensing an opportunity to cash in offered to fix the manager's phone privately. Before the manager could 'talk money' on completion of the work Bob said, 'Right that will cost you two free dinners on Sunday'.

The skilled escapee is well placed on the labour market to exploit the skills acquired in his occupation. Bob in particular is well placed as, like many other East-Enders of his generation, he has no formal qualifications and acquired his current status by exploiting family connections in his chosen trade after a long, rather 'haphazard' apprenticeship in a variety of jobs requiring manual dexterity. As a consequence Bob is able to apply himself to an impressive array of tasks and this adaptability enhances his marketability, thereby providing an ideal arena for the exposition of entrepreneurship.

Bob. When they was pulling down all the old houses I used to get everything from them . . . I got to know these blokes who went around after the people moved out and boarded up the windows . . . they used to put big padlocks on the doors. Anyway I got chatting and they gave me a key. I give 'em a few bob like, and I used to go in and take what I wanted. I had all me central heating that way. I just used to go in with some gear, make it look official . . . Sometimes we used to be just coming out of a house just as the builders were smashing down the back door with sledgehammers to get what they wanted.

Bob here can be seen to be applying his entrepreneurial skill, and combining this with his occupational skills and status to derive profit from what might appear to be a situation unlikely to prove advantageous, i.e. a derelict house.

The Way We Were

Bob's successful exploitation of his entrepreneurial inheritance has made it possible for him to move out of the culturally homogeneous

East End, and into one of the buffer-zone boroughs that form East London's eastern boundaries. For the escapee, entrepreneurship provides both the material and ideological foundation for the escape and for the maintenance of a culture that is identifiably working-class within the expanding environment of the buffer zone. As Rose has noted the individual can 'within the limits permitted by the culture define for himself somewhat new patterns suggested by the variation among the old ones' (Rose 1962, p. 14).

The escapee will find himself and, most importantly, his family exposed for the first time to middle-class culture. Indeed, this exposure is very much the price to be paid for environmental mobility. However, in the workplace the escapee experiences no alteration in his perspective, for the working environment that is defined by his position on the labour market has not altered with a change of residence. The central concerns of the workplace remain constant. It is in his immediate residential environment that elements of the parent culture are questioned, as the expanded environment stretches the culture's breadth of perspective to breaking-point. The symbolic structures that members bring to the immediate environment of the buffer zone are no longer obviously or unanimously appropriate. For the buffer zone is not a mono-cultural social place, as professional people and middle-class commuters also inhabit this first phase of suburbia and it is these groups, and not blacks or the urban poor that constitute the primary threats to the family life of the escapee East End entrepreneur.

The escapee exists in a state of siege. For the first time he and his family are exposed to middle-class culture, and as East London is so culturally insular, the shock to the escapee on entering the buffer zone is considerable. While he is protected by day from the most corrosive effects of bourgeois culture it is the family unit that is required to respond to an expanded environment, an environment that finds its parameters in the buffer zone. It is feasible for East End culture to sensitize itself to an expanded environment that contains elements of an alien culture, and changes in the economic infrastructure along with spasmodic influxes of immigrants have inspired East Londoners to acquire a cultural style that is both absorbent and expansive. However, the buffer zone contains cultural elements that are not only alien, but in cases of over-exposure potentially destructive to escapees. For material wealth has taken their sponge-like sensitivity to the expanding environment to saturation point, and certain potential changes can no longer be absorbed. When this occurs, the escapee looks inwards and backwards, for to maintain working-class cultural hegemony in the home, historical reinforcement of traditional culture is of paramount importance.

Skilled Escapees Don't Eat Quiche

Confronted by middle-class culture for the first time in the form of neighbours, the escapee is faced with assimilation or reaffirmation. To assimilate is to overburden the parent culture and take on focal concerns of the middle classes, thereby threatening the continuity of the parent culture. The way of life of the escapee family is dominated by a version of traditional working-class culture that is all the more rigid for being under a state of siege. In the buffer zone, class conflict is not articulated in the workplace or in the neighbourhood, but in the home, where men attempt to resist middle-class cultural subversion by imposing an exaggerated version of working-class culture derived from a notion of a 'golden age' of East End community.

Male offspring of the escapee, in particular, are imbued with this potent imagery as they are not exposed to the harsh realities and demands of East End entrepreneurship, the very forces that provided their fathers with the tools of escape. They do not have to work in the markets after school, sort rags, or sell seafood from a stall. Additionally, the employment market has changed drastically in the last twenty years, no longer permitting unqualified individuals to move from job to job picking up skills informally. Therefore to maintain the life-style acquired by their father's entrepreneurial activity, formal educational qualifications are required, along with a massive shift in attitudes by the escapees regarding the value and viability of educational achievement. Therefore in middle age the escapee, a self-educated man who spent much of his childhood, as in Bob's case, sorting rags, and now living in a house worth six figures, is asked to adopt characteristics of an alien culture, a culture to which the parent culture has by historical precedent always been opposed.

The escapee child whose cultural inheritance does not make accommodation for academic achievement beyond the three Rs, yet whose material environment is distinctly middle-class, is subjected to a major socio-economic contradiction. The child is reared in a materialistically affluent environment, devoid of any overt conflictual content. He is unaware of the negative and rigid influences of class, and without the rigours that formulated the parent culture that he has inherited, the child is not endowed with the culture's traditional resilience. Nor can the child develop his father's entrepreneurial skills, as market forces increasingly dictate shifts away from those traditional trades and skills that form the foundation of the inherited culture.

The street-market where Bob worked as a child was closed fifteen years ago, the small workshops of carpenters, cabinet-makers, and the likes are long gone, and the docks, the springboard and primary generator of the entrepreneurial inheritance, are now derelict. The escapee child leaves school and enters the job-market without the advantages of those core economic determinants of entrepreneurial culture, and he realizes then the reality of being working-class. After living in the buffer zone, fed a remorseless diet of distilled working-class culture, the youth is poorly prepared for the dole queue or lowly paid work that offers little opportunity of achieving either the high standard of living to which he has become accustomed, or of maintaining his father's occupational status. The most feasible option that emerges is to rely heavily upon the material affluence of the escapee culture to compensate for the failure of adult life to live up to expectations; inherited wealth compensates for both the constant crisis of capitalism and the lack of gritty deposits in a culture so finely decanted as to lose all real substance.

It is not education alone that offers an instrumental cultural option to the escapee, it is one of a number of threats to which the escapee and his family must seek an appropriate response. For in the buffer zone the escapee family comes under constant pressure from middle-class culture. Female middle-class inhabitants of the buffer zone have educational qualifications, careers, utilize child-minders and nannies, have partners who carry out household chores, and eat unusual food. Indeed, to the besieged escapee family, the everyday sights and sounds of mundane bourgeois existence are incoherent and are received with a cautious animosity. This is particularly apparent in the case of the escapee housewife, her primary function being the provision of food for the rest of the family. For her, a whiff of garlic or curry will inspire a tentative investigation that is designed in such a manner as to inspire confirmation and reinforcement of her family's traditional tastes and requirements.

Doris. You like that spicy food, like foreign food? Yeah, me and Debbie, we do, but Bob he won't touch it. No, he won't eat nothing, like out of the way. I made a quiche once and me and Debbie had to eat the lot ourselves.

In the buffer zone, where pine-clad walls meet flock wallpaper, the escapee will react powerfully to any perceived threat to traditional working-class culture; for instance, contact with individuals who scorn a traditional Sunday lunch (see Douglas and Isherwood 1978, pp. 114–16). As in many other similar households, this meal has acquired the status of a fetish, stemming from poverty-stricken times when Sunday represented the only day of leisure available to working men (not non-working women), the Sunday lunch-time meal being probably the only time that the entire family would all be present in one room. This meal represented the bread-winner's ability to 'keep a good table', and became a ritual event as father carved the most expensive food available, roast meat. Stories of housewives of the 1930s saving their housekeeping money in order to provide traditional Sunday fare are numerous, yet in modern times the Sunday lunch would appear to be little more than an expensive cultural throw-back (see Roberts 1973, pp. 109, 115–16).

The five-day, forty-hour week and improvements in the nutritional content of the working-class diet, no longer lend pivotal importance to Sunday lunch, or to the leisure afforded by the sabbath. For most families Sunday leisure is little different from the leisure they enjoy the rest of the week, the only notable difference being that the weekend provides adequate time for excess. Meat and vegetables are no longer eaten exclusively on the sabbath, yet the symbolic importance of a Sunday lunch featuring roast meat and a specific collection of vegetables is still considerable, particularly for the besieged escapee.

As a symbol of prosperity, family unity, and historical continuity, the Sunday meal represents the tangible evidence of the escapee and his wife's ability to work together. The result is a celebration every Sunday lunch-time of the successful collaboration of the rigid sex roles that provided the cash and enabled the purchase of food and the preparation of a 'special' meal. This is a celebration of a man's ability to provide adequate cash for the family's needs and of a woman's place being outside of the local Pakistani delicatessen, looking in.

That this ritual has been appropriated from another age lends a clue in the identification of the escapee's major strategy in resisting envelopment by middle-class culture. The escapee appropriates certain key aspects of what is regarded as an unambiguous 'golden age' of working-class culture, the 1920s and 1930s, and emphasizes them as regressive touchstones of cultural identity. So for Bob it's meat today and meat tomorrow, and garlic is a type of Irish football. Yorkshire pudding, however, is to the palate what 'Sing along a Max' is to the ear.

Knees up Mother Thatcher

When a community is under siege, it must look inward to itself for hidden resources that might provide ammunition or sustenance. Yet it is not only munitions that are sought by the besieged, for they must above all identify and emphasize those aspects of their culture that are oppositional to those of the enemy, thereby bolstering morale and stiffening the sinews of the besieged in an effort to resist the aggressor. If this process of moral armament does not occur spontaneously, as it appears to have done during the blitz on London during the Second World War, propaganda will attempt to create these essential characteristics artificially. These characteristics are then mythical, and as Silverstone has noted: 'Myths ... are sacred histories and as such they function to express and to maintain the solidarity of the social group' (Silverstone 1981, p. 54).

The escapees are under siege from bourgeois culture, they are threatened with extinction, and are forced, as they can hardly leave the shelter of their flock-wallpapered fortress without surrender (e.g. to pine-clad walls, foreign cars, foreign food, higher education etc.) to strengthen their resolve to resist by resorting to propaganda strategies, strategies that attribute mythical characteristics to key elements of East End culture. These characteristics will emphasize the true origins of the culture and stress the uniformity of action which is seen to be appropriate for continuity. Therefore in delving into the past the escapee is seeking to legitimize his rejection of the bourgeoisie by stressing how different the two cultures are, and within the escapee's citadel, through the incantation of ancient rituals, a form of working-class hegemony is established that is constricted only by the four flocked walls of the family home.

The escapee has distanced himself from the parent culture and as a consequence has put himself at risk. Within the East End proper, participants are not at risk as bourgeois culture has barely penetrated, therefore they are not under siege and have no need to resort to the mythic as a form of resistance. 'Where the participation of the individual in the social group is still directly felt, where the participation of the group with the surrounding groups is actually lived—that is, as long as the period of mystic symbiosis lasts—myths are meagre in number and poor in quality' (Bruhl 1926, quoted in Silverstone 1981).

However, in the buffer zone the solidarity that was a taken-for-granted factor of daily life in the 'homeland' is stretched and threatened by the very presence of middle-class culture, and myths become a vital tool in the structuring of strategies of resistance, a crucial link with an inheritance, and a bond with a culturally pure and therefore indomitable past. Crime was non-existent; policemen hard but fair; teachers stricter; beer stronger; every schoolboy went scrumping apples (London must have been one large orchard); people knew how to entertain themselves; young men boxed in the street; few went to school in shoes; men were men and women were women (see Pearson 1983). So Chas and Dave became rich by cruelly characterizing clothing and pub songs of the 1920s and the 1930s, and the escapee attempts to enter a mythic world that might bolster his resolve to resist his neighbours by involvement in ritual action. The escapee creates a space where cultural regurgitation is a natural consequence of attempts at communal problem-solving by the utilization of mythic devices.

At weddings, christenings, engagement parties, and at any comparable ritual event the escapee will dig deep in an attempt to disinter elements of traditional culture that can be presented as a reincarnation of the golden, unambiguous days of the 1920s and 1930s. That these ritual occasions celebrate only selected aspects of East End culture, such as solidarity and community, and not the enabling characteristics to which those admirable qualities were a response, such as poverty, unemployment, and disease, is illustrative of the rational and instrumental nature of parties and sing-songs as rituals that provide controlled and limited expression of unproblematic and essentially supportive images of working-class life.

Social clubs in the buffer zone will regularly have 'Cockney Nights' where the 'Beau Belles' (*sic*) perform traditional songs dressed as Pearly Kings and Queens. Besieged escapees with in many cases high incomes will group together and organize weekend excursions to holiday camps, and a recent addition to the refrigerated chests of local freezer-centres features frozen pie-mash and liquor, ideal for the microwave cooker.

While traditional values and norms of working-class culture are contradicted by the middle-class who share the buffer zone, the escapee can, by involvement in ritual action, relive the golden days of the past (minus rickets and tuberculosis) and resist the culture of his neighbours. Through ritual behaviour the symbolic values of the escapee's social life are invigorated and receive the power to prevent change by functioning as periodic *aides-mémoire* of their common cultural world (see Appendix): 'the mythological allusions, the references to ancestors and culture heroes from whom this magic has been received ... Tradition ... gathers in great abundance around magical ritual and cult' (Malinowski 1948, p. 55).

Bob responded with almost prerehearsed vehemence to a middle-class couple who were expounding the virtues of child-minders, education, and men and women sharing the responsibilities of child-rearing.

Bob. Well, yeah that's the way some people would do it and it might work, but we've done it the old-fashioned way, the old way. We've brought up three good kids and I think we're a happy family anyway.

The escapee has stretched the possibilities of his entrepreneurship to the limit, and due to his relatively favourable position on the labour market it has taken him a considerable distance. Yet for the continuity of working-class culture he must acknowledge the limitations of his abilities, and reach back into a mythical past beyond the parameters of the contemporary buffer zone.

7. The Holding Élite

The 'holding élite' are those individuals who have applied their entrepreneurial ability to acquiring positions on the labour market that are relatively exclusive, and as a consequence they are able to secure high pecuniary reward for their labour. As a consequence they are 'holding folding', are in possession of money. The combination of their capital, and the means by which they accumulated it, establish this group as distinct from the besieged escapee, although in many cases they will occupy an adjacent social space. The élite have no need to delve into the past for reinforcement of contemporary culturally defined action, for they are not under siege, their position on the labour market is strong, and they enjoy a confidence in their own status that stems from their entrepreneurial inheritance, yet is firmly entrenched in the realities of the market and the utility of cultural collateral.

The élite gain entry to their trades by means of a variety of formal and informal inductive processes. For instance, the London cab-driver is required to undergo an intensive course of study, 'the know-ledge', and pass all the various oral and practical examinations before being awarded his licence. This process is torturous, necessitating the trainee to spend many hours driving around London on a moped learning the designated routes, and it takes considerable tenacity and application to learn the 468 'runs' designated by the 'Blue Book' and the 15,842 streets in a six-mile radius of Charing Cross, before the trainee becomes a full-fledged cab-driver. During this process he must find a way of supporting himself either through part-time or full-time work that leaves sufficient time to study, and certain jobs are well suited to those 'on the knowledge'. For instance, market porters can earn good money from midnight to five or six a.m., thereby leaving sufficient daylight hours to study. However, this job and others like it require those seeking employment to possess a considerable degree of entrepreneurial ability, as these occupations are highly prized and are acquired normally through the cultivation of personal or familial contacts. On successfully being awarded his licence numerous possibilities present themselves that rely upon the ability of the 'cabbie' to apply his entrepreneurship in pursuit of profit and autonomy. One area of Redbridge, part of the buffer zone, is known locally as 'Green Badge Alley', due to the number of cab-drivers residing in the trim 1930s-built semis.

Cab-driving requires entrepreneurial ability to gain entrance to the trade, to learn the trade, and successfully to engage in trade. The cabbie negotiates with others to form companies, share ranks, and divide London into trading areas. The exclusivity of the trade nurtures the entrepreneurial spirit, and the pecuniary rewards of the trade reinforce the plausibility of working-class entrepreneurship. Yet the 'holding élite', due to their success in both monetary terms and in terms designated by the parent culture, are able to negotiate and bargain with the middle classes of the buffer zone in such a manner as to make bourgeois culture unproblematic. For unlike the escapees, the élite have a confidence in the entrepreneurial culture, and therefore in themselves, that is derived from historical precedent but not dominated by a homogenized and over-stylized version of their inheritance.

The boundaries of entrepreneurial action, legal or illegal, are as I have argued, defined by an individual's position on the labour market, and the 'holding élite' occupy a position that is, due to its exclusivity, so favourable that they are able to extend the parameters of working-class culture beyond that of other groups featured on the entrepreneurial scale. There is for the élite no limit to the social world that is open to techniques of negotiation, and the application of these techniques and other key aspects of entrepreneurial culture extend the scope of working-class influence way beyond the ghetto-like boundaries of the East End and its buffer zone.

Danny

Danny is in 'the print'; he is a skilled craftsman working in what remains at the time of writing the hub of Britain's printing-trade, Fleet Street. Despite his formal status as an employee, Danny, due to his high wages, and the entrepreneurial ability that both enabled entrance to the trade and sustained him in the buffer zone, warrants his status as a member of the 'holding élite'.

On leaving school, Danny served an apprenticeship with a local engineering firm, then thanks to the cultivation of key contracts he acquired the necessary union membership and joined the maintenance staff of a national newspaper.

Danny. I remember that first week's wage-packet. Before I went on the print I was doing well taking home £13 a week. That week on the print, I remember walking towards the station coming home, I had 60 quid in me pocket.

Danny, now in his mid-forties, lives in an exclusive area of the buffer zone, surrounded by business men and taxi-drivers. He works just three days a week, and if he needs 'a few bob extra'—for instance to pay for his family's annual vacation abroad—he will work one or two night shifts. His earnings are phenomenal and his spending power immense. Yet his entrepreneurial skills are constantly exercised and not allowed to wane, for this would enable East End culture at the peak of its market responsiveness to grow flabby, precipitating a total collapse of proletarianism as it is practised by a working-class élite.

For Danny there is no limit to the range of possibilities that might be exploited by the application of his finely honed entrepreneurial skills. At work within and without his trade union he is constantly involved in various processes of bargaining and negotiation over pay and conditions with his employer and shop steward, or with work-mates swapping and bartering shifts and hours. Danny, due entirely to favourable market position, has a great deal of control over his working day, choosing when he works and how hard he works, depending not on the demands of his employer, but upon how much money he wishes to earn.

Out of working hours Danny has the spending power to exploit the market, and the cultural collateral to drive a bargain. For instance, he decided to use his considerable free time to build an extension to his house. This involved not only a realignment of the skills he applies to his craft, but also the application of his entrepreneurial skills to the acquisition of materials. For despite his spending power, Danny was prepared to negotiate with local road-repairers when he needed sand, and with any other contact that he was able to nurture during the course of the building. For the essence of the 'élite's' entrepreneur-ship is to be found in the application of the entrepreneurial inheritance to the skilled consumption of goods and services. It is seldom necessary for Danny to commit criminal acts, and apart from the almost routine trade in stolen goods that is so much a part of East London's economic life, illegality is not a crucial characteristic of his day-to-day existence.

However, for Danny everything is negotiable and there are few aspects of social life from which Danny is barred. His children are encouraged to exploit the educational facilities of the area as education does not pose a threat to the self-confident family life of the 'holding élite'. Entrepreneurial ability is, as Danny recognizes, a useful tool in any economic milieu and educational qualifications merely provide an alternative avenue of market exploitation.

Danny. Yeah, I took Billy [son] down to Cambridge at the weekend. Nice place, I got it worked out the college he's going to go to. What is it, Kings? Yeah, with the choir. Always had a nice voice Billy. Yeah, King's, that will do, he can bring his washing home at the weekend, just up the motorway, handy.

The key concerns of Danny as the father of a prospective candidate for a place at Cambridge University are identifiably working-class yet have been mediated by the requirements of a middle-class institution. However, if his son does not acquire the required A-level grades, it is not unknown for ambitious fathers to make donations to needy colleges in return for a prestigious place for their offspring in a venerable seat of learning. As I have already intimated, for Danny everything is negotiable.

The Ultimate East End Entrepreneurial Story

Danny. See this lump on me neck? I'm going to have it cut off. It's a 'locomo' or something, yeah that's it, it's African [laughs]. No it's a fucking nuisance really, I have to take a 17-collar it got so big. I used to 'ave one on me forehead ... Anyway, I went to the doctor and he give me an appointment for the hospital.

So the doctor comes in and I'm lying on the bed and he has a look at the lump and says he's going to cut it out, sends the nurse out to get the instruments. So he's fucking about looking at me and I says 'Er, you do vasectomies 'ere do you?' So he says, 'yeah'. So I says, 'well I fancy one, who do I see? I don't want no queues or nothing'; so he says 'Well, I do 'em. If you like I'll do it now.' So the nurse comes in and I'm laid out bollock naked. So he says 'Right nurse we're going to top and tail him' [laughs]. I had me head done on the NHS and the vasectomy comes to £25.

Anyway I goes into work that night, bandy-legged with a couple of stitches in me head. The manager sees me and comes out, asked me what happened, thought I was in an accident. So I said, 'I've had a vasectomy. It was deep rooted.' He still don't believe me.

John. Wonder that the doctor never give you a haircut while he was at it.

The self-confidence and belief in the sanctity of the negotiatory process that is illustrated in this story is considerable, and it does highlight in an exaggerated fashion how members of a working-class entrepreneurial élite are able to chisel out a niche for themselves within capitalism. It is a niche that is not reliant upon a siege mentality, formed upon the rotting corpse of a dead culture, but upon the belief that all aspects of life including major institutions and professions (and few are more daunting than the medical profession) are subject to negotiation.

Summary

It is my argument that denizens of East London, by virtue of their action being ascribed to a common culture, can be understood in terms of their use of an essentially entrepreneurial inheritance. I have attempted in this chapter to show how members apply entrepreneurship to their day-to-day lives, and how entrepreneurship emerges as the core characteristic of East End culture. In doing so it has been my intention to highlight how members operate with varying degrees of competence within the entrepreneurial framework, and how the nature of their entrepreneurial activities will be attuned to their position on the labour market.

Throughout this chapter I have referred to both legal and illegal acts as being similar types of action distinguishable by varying risk factors and the consequential invocation of sanctions. Or as Veblen writes incisively in an attempt to parallel crime and business: 'The ideal pecuniary man is like the ideal delinquent in his unscrupulous conversion of goods and persons to his own ends, and in a callous disregard for the feelings and wishes of others and of the remoter effects of his activities' (Veblen 1924, p. 237).

The varying degrees of competence displayed by members does in many ways parallel the extent of their illegal activity, with those at the élite end of the scale having little necessity for risky acts of blatant criminality. They are able, by exploiting their favourable market position, to acquire pecuniary and status advantages from a more conventional, if slightly perverse reading of capitalist ideology. While, for instance, Danny shares a culture with Jack and both ascribe to the utility of entrepreneurship as a means of confirming their common inheritance and of acquiring collateral both cultural and monetary, 'he is unlike him in possessing a keener sense of status and in working more far-sightedly to a remoter end' (Veblen 1924, p. 237).

At the time of writing Jack's son is about to make a court appearance charged with actual bodily harm. Danny's son is well on the way to Cambridge.

8

Recruitment, Presentation, and Paper: The Organizational Context of Detective Entrepreneurship

Those characteristics of East End culture that serve to provide a historical frame for action while making possible the application of seemingly incongruous linguistic and presentational styles have parallels in the culture and working practices of CID officers. As argued in Chapters 2 and 3, the CID has an essentially organizationally deviant persona forged by its idiosyncratic and ambivalent relationship with the state and by the subsequent demands made upon the 'department' regarding covert policing.

I will argue that the detective's appropriation of entrepreneurial cultural devices also serves other purposes. Primarily it functions to distance as much as possible the detective branch from the formal administrative restraints of the uniform branch. More importantly, it provides a readily available and potent source of attractive linguistic and presentational styles that the officer can rework, tailor, and customize to fit his own personal and social needs.

Before we can approach these cultural functions of detective entrepreneurship and those presentational styles that serve to enhance their policing function I have, for the purposes of this chapter, concentrated upon how officers gain entrance to the CID, how they deal with paperwork, and how they present themselves in court, as these are key elements of CID work.

The CID makes up 14 per cent of the Metropolitan Police's full staffing complement. They are an élite by virtue of historical precedent, occupational requirements, and internal organization, and it is the élite status of 'the department' that is crucial in understanding the new recruits' perception of CID work as a highly desirable specialism. The PSI report claimed that 50 per cent of new recruits to the Met expressed a desire to join the department (Smith and Gray, Vol. 3, 1983, p. 178) and the report goes on to suggest that it is the more active, ambitious, and better qualified officers who express an interest in CID work. The authors support this claim by reporting that 62 per cent of detectives compared to 30 per cent of uniformed officers expect to sit sergeants' exams (Smith and Gray 1983, p. 180).

However ambitious an officer may be to join the CID, membership of 'the department' is gained only after a period of initiation that characteristically combines elements of ritualistic formality with patronage and individualistic entrepreneurial action.

Front Door

Until recently prospective CID officers served for a minimum of two years as detective aides. The aides were junior members of 'the department' who carried out all the basic tasks expected of full-blown detectives. As trainees they had to excel for, with demand for places being so high, competition under the old aide system was intense. Usually assigned to deal with low-status crimes, aides were assessed according to the volume of their arrests and subsequent successful convictions. One officer described how he and a fellow detective-aide had gained prominence by 'nicking anybody. If it moved, nick it.'

Aides also dealt with paperwork and presented themselves in court all the time observing and, by necessity, mimicking established officers who ultimately were to be arbiters of an aide's suitability for CID selection. A Detective Inspector explained how, as an aide, he had failed a selection board before good fortune had offered an opportunity to apprehend, after a violent struggle, an armed robber. Within three days he had successfully passed a rapidly formed selection board. The aide system was a form of apprenticeship (Wilson 1968, p. 283) designed to introduce the aide to the skills, practices, and mysteries of detective work, while retaining the CID's control over recruitment.

Since then, entrance to the CID has been achieved via the Crime Squad. Set up to deal with a wide range of crime, these squads comprise uniformed officers in plain clothes who have no specialist training. The officers are predominantly young and ambitious to join the CID and they are directly supervised by CID officers.

Predictably, perhaps, most detectives who had experienced the old aide system are dismissive of crime squads and, in particular, the standard of recruit the squads supplied for 'the department'. The principal criticism is that the squads operate as units, continuing the militaristic operational methodology of the uniform branch, therefore cosseting the officer from the individualism of detective work. As an experienced DI commented: 'When I get someone new I don't let him do anything, go anywhere, without someone holding his hand who knows the ropes.'

Crime squad officers are also restricted in their experience of paperwork and this, coupled with their limited crime experience, means that under the contemporary system of recruitment, new entrants to the CID are often totally lacking in experience of autonomous activity in a 'real' crime setting.

Back Passage

Despite alterations to the procedural rituals associated with entrance to the CID certain requirements and expectations remain constant. A detective in charge of an East End crime squad vividly described the type of officer that he is looking for as potential CID material: 'Someone who will talk to me. I will give him half the information and expect him to get the other half . . . can he go out and get his own work?' Within this broad frame of reference, potential CID recruits are expected to show considerable skill at communication within a CID-imposed rubric of autonomy. Yet, more importantly, they must achieve results and be certain that their CID managers are aware of their achievements; they must get themselves noticed. One way of doing this is via arrest figures—the aforementioned 'nick anybody' technique. Indeed, the PSI report stresses the similar pressure that is brought to bear upon aspiring detectives in both the old aide and the contemporary crime squad systems (Smith and Gray 1983, Vol. 4, pp. 59–61).

In spite of his theoretical control of CID supervision and recruit selection, it is difficult for a uniformed Chief Superintendent competently to perform his formal duties due to the unofficial chain of command that has now rooted itself in the crime squad (Van Maanen 1983, p. 391). The Detective Sergeant, despite the uniform branch's organizational claims to the contrary, functions as a filter through which crime squad officers must pass if they wish to join the CID. 'While they are with us, I let it be known whether or not he is any good, and this gets back unofficially to an Area Board, who are all uniform. They make the final selection for CID.'

Once the move from crime squad to CID is made, a period of

probation, including a formal course, must be negotiated, but the crucial phase is crime squad work, for it is here that the officer learns to acquire information and make cases (Erikson 1981) and it is in crime squad that the officer learns to envelop himself in the ambience of patronage and binding ideology of 'the department's "Invisible Church"' (Simmel, cited in Van Maanen 1980, p. 308). In turn, the crime squad officer must develop an obtrusive competence, acquiring an entrepreneurial persona that can turn small cases into big cases, criminal damage to burglary, a single case of shoplifting into a multiple charge involving offences taken into consideration (Erikson 1981).

The acquisition of these entrepreneurial qualities is a prerequisite for any potential CID recruit. When selecting the next generation of detectives, the incestuous 'department' utilizes crime squads as occupational incubators where protégés are selected according to their uncanny resemblance to those who sired them: the unsuccessful return to uniform. Moulded in the image of his creator, the new CID recruit is required to adapt to the occupational priorities of 'the department' and his time is divided mainly between the office and the policed environment. Yet it has been noted that the bulk of cases brought to the attention of the CID are straightforward, requiring minimal investigation (Steer 1980). As Greenwood *et al.* (1977, p. 225) indicate: 'The vast majority of clearances are produced by the activities of patrol officers, by the availability of identification of the perpetrator at the scene of the crime, or by routine police procedures.'

I Could Have Been a Judge but I Never Had the Latin

The ultimate expression of a police officer's skill as a crime-fighter is located in the courtroom. The officer's appearance in court is, even in the most petty of cases, the culmination of a series of organizationally significant events the ultimate objective of which is a satisfactory performance by the officer or officers in court, followed by a 'result'—a successful conviction. While elsewhere I have utilized the game analogy to describe and analyse certain crucial aspects of police and, more specifically, CID behaviour (Chapter 9), there are drawbacks to extending games imagery to the courtroom. As Black (1954), quoted in Carlen, indicates in discussing the implications of the game metaphor when applied to warfare: 'The chess metaphor ... used to illustrate war emphasizes the game of skill features while it suppresses the grimmer ones' (Carlen 1976, p. 94).

Carlen proceeds to point out that the game-playing metaphor relies upon informal rule-usages and as a consequence formal constitutive rules that 'define, revoke or enforce informal rules' are under-estimated, ignoring both the context in which these rules were constituted and their authorship. Just as vital is the game metaphor's assumption of conflictual interests or what Carlen terms 'adversary justice' (Carlen 1976, p. 95). This raises the crucial issue of defining a 'good result' in the light of a multitude of conflictual interests, dependent upon a finite number of circumstances. For instance, a defendant, whether guilty or not, might in the light of the case against him be realistically expecting a heavy fine. In this case, the imposition of a light fine would indeed be a result for the defendant. However, for a first-time offender convinced of his innocence, the same light fine might be an unacceptable imposition. Similar examples of relative notions of good or bad results can be cited for all the principal courtroom players. The police in particular entertain varying definitions of a good result, depending not least of all upon the relationship that evolves between officers and accused during the course of the complementary processes of investigation and prosecution (see Baldwin and McConville 1977).

If the relationship has evolved into a business collaboration, the accused may offer information, pliability, perjury, or a guilty plea in exchange for the dilution or dropping of charges, future immunity from arrest, or a sympathetic rendering of both evidence and previous criminal convictions. The criteria for a good result change with each individual context, suggesting that the rules are similarly amenable to alteration according to the personnel, venue, and match conditions specific to each game.

The courtroom is the arena for a game with only one possible loser, and to propagate the game myth is to conspire both with the legal profession and with the police for it is in their interest to present the legal process as a contest in which the most able player wins. The rhetoric of gamesmanship plays a prominent part in the police version of their court activities and, as the main burden of the preparation and presentation of cases falls to the CID, members of 'the department' are able to justify their courtroom activities in a similar manner to that of their routine investigative work.

The infinite variations on the 'good result' theme, and the multitude of variables that might affect the final score, lend the game metaphor to those social forces that stage, invigilate, and judge the contest. So often those elements that affect the actual playing of the game are omitted, thereby making a fetish of winning and emphasizing the ineptitude integral to losing. While the result of a court case is greatly dependent upon factors activated outside the arena of the courtroom, the individual judicial episode cannot be concluded until all parties have presented a performance—a performance reliant upon a rehearsed script with a few well-defined areas for ad-libbing. While Goffman has acknowledged that all the world is not a stage (1975b, p. 1), it is difficult to comprehend even the most minor of courtrooms as anything other than theatres, for as Carlen (1976, p. 32) has noted: 'Rhetorical presentation of legal and judicial personnel is managed within the courtroom through utilisation of the supportive props and scenic devices of the temporal and spatial conventions, as well as through collusive interprofessional showmanship.' Consequently I shall apply a theatrical or dramaturgical, metaphorical scheme to my analysis of the CID in court, for it is the detective's essential sense of performance that enables officers to depart from the routine ambiguities of detective work to emerge as agents of legality in the form of judicial theatrics.

The CID in Magistrates' Courts—Repertory Justice

Magistrates' courts are noisy, confusing, ramshackle places, where the various performers are aided by the stage whispers of experienced members of the cast. Actors are often nervous and hesitant, particularly an accused making a first appearance in court who does not know where to stand or how to respond verbally to court officers. These actors need expert and sympathetic prompting for the production to proceed. For inexperienced uniformed police officers, prompting is more problematic for, despite cursory training in court procedure, mistakes are made and the officer, physically isolated in the witness-box, is reliant upon the good temper of the clerk of court for guidance. Uniformed officers' performances in court are routine and robotic. Evidence in particular is presented in a stilted, mechanical manner with little stylistic or tonal variation. The overall impression is that of a servant of the court, a spear-carrier with a walk-on part, the courthouse butler serving evidential sustenance to the principal players.

The routine coming and going of players throughout the court's proceedings is occasionally enlivened by the guest appearance of a detective. In the manner of Lord Olivier plunged into 'rep', the CID officer makes impressive entrances and exits, his performance smooth, precise, and flexible, not easily thrown by awkward questions or unexpected developments. Moving easily around the court, the detective's presence is in stark contrast to the militaristic obtrusiveness of the uniformed officer. Detectives display a deep knowledge of the 'ceremonial courtesies of complimentary address and reference' (Carlen 1976, p. 31).

Their precise rendition of evidence in particular is unhindered by errors in their physical placement, or by addressing magistrates in an incorrect or incoherent manner. Detectives, unlike many of their uniformed colleagues, tend to answer solicitor's questions correctly, through the bench, and constant rehearsals of court performances produce a level of presentation that enables a rapid, trouble-free invocation of formal rules. These constant rehearsals generate around the officer an aura of competence and confidence that enables him to deal with magistrates as senile relatives, displaying to the bench a respectful, yet not totally serious demeanour. Evidence is presented with precision in a clear, unwavering voice, injecting a clear-cut formality to a rather informal setting. Detectives take to the witness-box with the air of salesmen about to present a business communication package to a gullible board of directors. With the expressionless profile and the measured pauses of an actor trained in the method school, evidence is 'sold' and questions, no matter how inane, are answered with a mixture of reverence and menace, giving added weight to the sales patter.

At ease with solicitors, both in court and backstage, the CID officer drives a hard bargain in negotiations concerning pleas, bail, and sentences. He is often the individual upon whom the outcome of a case rests, and his entrance into the magistrates' court marks a raising of the court's status and, by association, a boost for the potency of magisterial justice. As Thespians of note, CID involvement in a magistrates' court places a truly professional stamp on what is at best a semi-professional production, superimposing another more worldly frame upon the mundane mechanics of the magistrates' court.

The CID in Crown Court—West End and Broadway

Crown Court provides the true stage for the talented socio-legal Thespian and, as I have argued above, by merit of constant rehearsal and occupational necessity, the detective is extremely adept at treading the boards of justice. However, it is crucial to note that, whereas in the magistrates' court the CID officer shares top billing with JPs, in a Crown Court the starring role is taken by members of the legal profession and the detective takes a supporting role. The most prominent role for a CID officer in a Crown Court is that of a straight man for the prosecution counsel, feeding the barrister with lines by way of facts and written statements. Despite the routine nature of this task, good stage technique is essential. Experienced detectives answer any questions from counsel directly to the judge and many officers in the presence of a jury will pause and establish eye contact with a juror before making a particularly important point during an evidential soliloquy.

The experienced CID officer after years in repertory is able to function unobtrusively in court as the lesser half of a double act with prosecuting counsel. Seated immediately behind the prosecution, the officer controls the flow of documentation to the barrister, passing notes and making whispered asides to his partner as the need arises. The detective's main risk of being upstaged emanates from the defence counsel and, as most cases require little or no detection, the onus on the prosecution lies with the competent documentary and verbal presentation of evidence. Consequently much of the defence counsel's task concerns the dissection of CID-prepared statements in the quest for anomalies or contradictions, and their subsequent exposure when the officer is in the witness-box. The cross-examination of the police by the defence centres upon documentation prepared by the detective, seizing upon any incongruity and stressing the importance of competent paperwork. While this cross-examination is seldom gentle, it is only when a detective appears to have been incompetent that defence counsel becomes anything but gentlemanly. The exposure of bureaucratic incompetence or documentary deception provokes the defence's castigation and ridicule.

For instance, an otherwise faultless performance by a DC in a case involving drugs was flawed by the defence's discovery that the accused had omitted to put his signature next to an answer that the CID claimed he had given to a question posed by the DC during an interview. The defence claimed that the officer had concocted the answer; the officer's only recourse was to claim that the lack of a signature was due to an oversight, an error on his behalf. The defence counsel was able to appeal to the jury that the officer was at worst a perjurer, at best an incompetent, and hinted in his summing-up that he was probably an incompetent perjurer. The defendant was acquitted.

Crucial errors of performance then can stem from case-preparation which forms the basis of a sound rehearsal. Insufficient or lax rehearsals will provoke a hostile response from the defence barrister, while, conversely, solid, competent case-preparation will be acknowledged by the defence in the form of a routine cross-examination of a sympathetic and respectful nature. Generally the CID and the legal profession rely upon each other for a smooth-running performance, and support each other in the manner in which a Gothic arch lends support to a structure, its strength emanating from the pressure that each side of the arch imposes on the other.

CID officers are comfortable and at ease in court, displaying a finely honed procedural sense. Occasionally mistakes are made, scripts are misread, and cues missed, yet the competent detective will bluff his way through, accepting prompts from the prosecution counsel and acknowledging his error to the judge in some mildly sycophantic stage whisper. Competent performers often anticipate questions about to be posed by counsel and occasionally correct briefs on matters of detail in a bold, purposeful but respectful manner.

While CID officers move confidently around the court and its environs, uniformed and crime squad officers are edgy and uncertain both on stage and backstage. Overly subservient in court, their evidence tends to be consistently robotic, and they often omit to address the judge. They appear fearful of fellow Thespians and nervously cling to each other in adjacent canteens, while CID officers can be observed in canteens and nearby pubs in the company of barristers, both prosecution and defence, thus acknowledging the elasticity of the judicial theatre's parameters. For even during the intervals between performances of Shakespearian tragedies, Macbeth might be found in a convenient saloon bar relaxing over a pint of beer with Macduff.

The moral identity of the CID officer as it is manifested in court is determined by the knowledge of other significant actors concerning the detective's abilities and capacities to exert power in social situations beyond the immediate environment of the courtroom. The business of the court constantly refers to interaction manifested beyond the legally sanctified atmosphere of the court, and the expression of this non-judicial universe through the competent utility of legal rhetoric is crucial to a successful performance. The task of the CID officer is to switch from the rhetorical utility of working-class speech and presentational strategies which typify much of his working day, to the expression of legal rhetoric that marks his performance in court.

The police officer is regarded by the court as a 'professional witness' (English and Houghton 1983, p. 89) and the CID by merit of specialized training, occupational priority, and depth and frequency of rehearsal, represent in the witness-box those elements that define professionalism—'freedom, dignity and responsibility' (Carr-Saunders and Wilson 1933). It is an essential element of the detective's performance to portray these characteristics and, in doing so, conform to established scripts and utilize legal rhetoric to reinforce the audience's preconceived expectations of plot development.

Paper

A recent report claims that 35 per cent of a divisional CID officer's time is spent dealing with clerical and administrative matters (Smith and Gray 1983, Vol. 3, p. 39). The presentation of competently written documentation is a central factor in the assessment of an officer's capabilities made by a detective's immediate superiors. Paperwork provides a tenuous link between the actions of detectives and the law, and the skilful presentation of evidence on paper can bridge the gap between the mystical workings of 'the department' and the abstract legal mechanics of due process. Failure to perform successfully on paper could put pressure upon colleagues and damage the prospect of gaining a result in court. Predictably, officers make great play of the irrelevance of much paperwork and the boredom entailed in carrying out administrative duties (Shapland and Hobbs 1987). However, paperwork represents more than a large portion of the detective's working day; it functions as a reinforcement of the presentation of detective work as essentially dramaturgical. Through paper, the detective sifts and marks 'the selective presentation of behaviours for public view' (Manning 1977, p. 23).

Paperwork is the means by which the CID presents itself as bureaucratically organized, shrouding the 'situationally justified' motivation of much of its activity (Manning 1977, p. 103). The documentation of detective work marks out certain activities as meaningful and interesting, enabling the CID to project an image that provides a rationale for action. The reality of detective work, and more specifically of detective–'criminal' encounters as they are manifested in court, is then a reality filtered through paperwork and marks the crucial link between the largely unsupervised autonomous activities of individual officers and the legally sanctified notion of due process as manifested in the wider criminal justice system.

Despite their repeated claims that paperwork restricts their real function as 'thief-takers', the effort and expertise required in the construction of a crime file in particular is considerable. The co-ordinating of not only the paperwork but also the sifting and ordering of responses to management rules and directives that underlie this documentation is a skilled and very precise process (see Shapland and Hobbs 1987; Chatterton, forthcoming). The disparity between what officers say about paperwork and how they actually processed paper (see Cruse and Rubin 1973) should not be totally disregarded, for as Manning and van Maanen (1978, pp. 5–6) have noted, officers assess themselves in terms of activity that is a comparative rarity within the police organization, and do not take credit for some often highly important activities that are actually of great significance when evaluating the function of the police. As Chatterton (forth-coming) has indicated: 'Much so-called "administration" and "paper-work" is as much policing as handling a domestic dispute, searching for a lost child, chasing a burglar, etc.'

While officers constantly articulated reinforcement of Manning's view that paperwork was 'dirty work' (Manning 1980, pp. 220–1), senior officers in particular were expert in reconstructing police-related action on paper. These officers also regarded the supervision of such reconstructions as crucial to the harmony and smooth operation of their office and the imposition of informal sanctions or 'fines' was a common response to incompetent paperwork skills. As a Detective Inspector explained: 'so it costs him a bottle of Scotch. If I was to let it go, in the long run it might cost him and the rest of his mates a lot more than that.'

Co-operation with colleagues in the collaborative reconstruction on paper of events that took place within the enacted environment requires negotiating skills and entrepreneurial ability, for decisions made on the street may have precipitated legal infractions that would invalidate cases and propagate suspicion, unrest, complaints, transfer to uniform, or suspension, and possibly lead to criminal proceedings being brought against conspiring officers.

Successful detectives 'make' cases in the same manner that business entrepreneurs make money, and the correct processing of cases is heavily reliant upon the medium of paperwork. However, paperwork requires the public expression of personal knowledge, the sharing organizationally of a previously exclusive discrete wisdom, body of information, or internalized record of significant occurrences. This knowledge may not coincide with organizational rules or legal statutes, and consequently the need for colleagues' collaboration is paramount in its literary expression. Great care then is taken in formulating reports so that information is presented on paper in such a manner as to verify the legitimacy of the activities of all concerned. As Manning (1980, p. 227) has noted: 'The information is cast in an invisible code because it is not formulated in a way that can be independently verified by supervisors.'

For the detective, paperwork, particularly that pertaining to the construction of a case, or to a record of his activities, demands the nurturing of special collaborative writing skills unique to 'the department'. Collaborative alliances often promote trading relationships among officers, favours are owed, and the successful detective is able to negotiate a good deal by recruiting documentary support for his paperwork without paying over the odds.

Dangerous Paper

Certain documentation renders the detective vulnerable and the experienced detective deals with this paperwork in the appropriate manner. For instance, the diary that records an officer's on-duty whereabouts can 'disappear', or be stored in a safe place as an insurance against repercussions, although it is forbidden to remove the diary from the office. An officer, in the comfort of his own home, showed me a collection of his diaries covering his activities over several years and, on casual perusal of the documents was able, from memory, to differentiate between the information in his diaries and what 'really' happened. Paperwork is generally regarded as an organizational restraint upon the otherwise autonomous actions of detectives and these restraints can be either bypassed, as with the 'lost' diaries, or resisted via collaborative trade-offs with colleagues.

While not all paperwork is of such a crucial or dangerous nature, most of it does refer, albeit circuitously, to decisions made by the detective within the enacted environment, and provides a potential enabling tool for supervisors and managers to evalutate officers' performances (Manning 1980, pp. 220–31). Supervisory constraints upon the CID are seen to emanate from the uniform branch who have assumed divisional command of both branches. The association made by CID officers between paperwork and the uniform branch is vital in reinforcing the detective's belief that his uniformed colleagues are more concerned with petty restraint than with 'real crime'.

The physical context in which paperwork is dealt with serves to compound both the petty rigidity of the uniform branch and the associated irrelevance of paperwork for, when a detective is at the office he is not working, that is dealing with crime. The office is merely a place 'where one does trivial things, personal business and makes short-term arrangements' (Manning 1980, p. 222).

In the action-orientated working day of the detective, where various priorities make conflicting demands upon the officers' time, paperwork can always wait, and a backlog of paperwork is regarded by most members of the department as an a priori sign of a good detective and a boost to his image as a thief-taker. Further, it is one of many contradictions of CID work that paperwork is regarded as 'dirty work' (Hughes 1963, p. 23), despite its crucial function as a filter of police activity, maintaining strategic links with courts. Consequently the importance of paperwork is manifested in the begrudging commitment of massive man-hours.

A Business Address: The Enacted Environment of the CID

The PSI report estimates that 17 per cent of a CID officer's day is spent contacting or interviewing witnesses or informants outside police premises and a good deal of this time was deemed to have been spent in pubs. The authors qualify this figure by emphasizing the self-reported nature of their survey and claim that 17 per cent may be an underestimate (Smith and Gray 1983, Vol. 3, p. 175). Later the authors point out that alcohol, whether consumed in pubs or in the office, is integral to conventional CID work. Indeed, my own observations would suggest that the PSI report contains a gross underestimate of CID time spent in pubs, and that alcohol provides a strategic prop in the dramaturgical presentation of the urban detective. A sufficiently high regular intake of alcohol functions as an embalming fluid, preserving a deviant rebellious image of detective work, the resultant longevity of which outlasts periodic attempts at reform.

Most CID officers join the department early in their careers while still in their twenties (Smith and Gray 1983, Vol. 3, p. 177). Imported from the provinces and after a few years living with other police constables, probably in a section house, the novice CID officer will soon find himself isolated in a pub or club, for it is here that he is expected to nurture contacts. In an environment such as East London where even the most basic manual occupation necessitates trading and negotiatory skills, individuals experience a close proximity to capitalism, and the language and ethics of conventional commercial activity have been appropriated and realigned to assist in the interpretation of everyday life. Consequently everybody is 'doing the business'. Into this electric, wheeler-dealer atmosphere comes the young CID officer who, like the East-Ender, has inherited a nonconformist deviant culture that values entrepreneurial ability and utilizes the argot of capitalism within the boundaries of trading relationships. Consequently the conversation in any East London pub will eventually turn to business, commodities, availabilities, and prices. It is only a matter of time before the young detective, cut off from his regional inheritance and alienated from the rules and methodology of the uniform branch, will be asked what he has to sell. For, as Fielding (forthcoming) notes: 'Because of the paradox of discretion in police-work (those lowest in the organisation have most discretion) that audience will very often be those directly involved, its citizens ... rather than supervisors or others to whom the police are formally accountable.'

9

Trading Places—Symbiotic Control
and Occupational Imagery

> ... the game between detectives and criminals can be generalized
> to public interaction in urban life.
>
> Sanders (1977, p. 21).

Entrepreneurship is an increasingly attractive option in times of
economic crisis, and detectives are not immune to those attractions.
Sharing much of their working environment with working-class
entrepreneurs, some of it is bound to rub off on the detective and this
is increasingly likely when much detective work is in itself entrepreneurial.

This chapter will not refer directly to police corruption. Other
authors, in particular Punch (1985) and McVicar (forthcoming), have
more to say on this subject than I. My concern is to present an
account of a specific style of police work and its relationship to a
specific economic and cultural order. My argument is that it is to the
latter that we must look in understanding the former.

Van Maanen (1978, p. 322) has noted that 'deceit, evasiveness,
duplicity, lying, innuendo, secrecy, double talk and triple talk mark
many of the interactions in police agencies'. This description accurately describes many of the characteristics of the 'working personality' (Skolnick 1966) of detectives. For within the boundaries of
East-Enders' culture, certain linguistic constraints related to entrepreneurial activity are replicated, and by virtue of their replication
can be 'translated into accounts of motivating by members' (Cressey
1962, p. 452). Motives here are treated as 'typical vocabularies' (Mills
1940, pp. 904–13) and if a culture can be regarded as a system of
listing, categorizing, and ordering motives, this system then lends
itself to those who are subscribers. Both the CID and East-Enders
store a vocabulary, linguistic constraints that serve to 'actually propel
them and legitimate their activity' (Taylor 1979, p. 151).

In the East End of London the adoption of local vocabularies serves to remove the CID officer one step further away from the bureaucratically controlled universe of the uniform branch, and apparently aligns the detective with those for whom the vocabulary and strategies are 'natural'. As a Detective Sergeant explained: 'If they're going to have a go at me I'm going to be first and whack 'em. And if I'm going to kick a door in at five in the morning I'm going mob-handed so if anyone catches a right-hander, it's not me, or one of my lads.' The officer was an ex-grammar school pupil, the son of a business man, and was brought up in a sedate seaside town on the south coast.

The social encounter that is most common to CID officers is that which brings him into contact with working-class culture, and in the East End of London this means close contact with an entrepreneurial cultural style. It is this potent cultural influence that determines the presentation of the officer as a trader: 'He phoned me up and wanted help, wanted to know what a-going equipped might be worth to him. But he had nothing for me, nothing to tell me. So I says, "Jacko, you come back to me when you've got something to deal. For me it's business".'

Detectives were sources of information and occasionally, to those who were regularly 'at it' or 'in at the heavy', instigators of irritation and misery. Individuals would often ask for favours and assistance with police-related problems that they, their friends, or their family were experiencing (Fielding, forthcoming). For in accordance with the area's market economy issues were dealt with informally without resorting to contact with bureaucratically defined organizations. Consulting a CID officer was the legal equivalent of a 'cash only' deal—no VAT, no due process. However, unless the East-Ender had something to trade no deal was forthcoming. When one man's younger brother was arrested in connection with a robbery he consulted a detective, a drinking-partner of several years' acquaint-ance: 'What have they got, nothing solid have they? He never did it. He's not at the heavy; shooters not his thing. What have they got?' When this potential 'client' was asked to 'put up' names, he declined and the transaction was aborted.

The cost–benefit approach to policing is reliant upon a state of mutual reciprocity, which is characterized by neither side controlling the other (Rock 1973, p. 197). As Muir has noted, reciprocal relation-ships are informed by commerce (Muir 1977, pp. 47–8), and I became aware of several instances where law-breakers were assisted or ignored by a detective, and as a result the officer's potential as a trader was considerably enhanced. The following story, which is worth relating at some length, is an example of such positive assistance.

A Bit of Business

Peter is a 'jump-up' and not a very good one at that. Buying and selling, a bit of thieving.

Peter. I'd make more dosh [money] selling my arsehole than I do with all this ducking and diving.

Pub Landlord. Not in this drinker. I have trouble selling dry roast peanuts.

Peter is an amiable man with few pretensions. He, like many others, scrapes a living and his contacts with the police have been minimal, limited to minor indiscretions as a youth, and the intervention of the crew of a patrol car in a family argument one Christmas Eve. However, when he telephoned me late one mid-week evening he was about to set in motion a chain of events that were going to introduce Peter to a very special kind of community policing.

Peter had been contacted by a relation of his who periodically took to theft as a means of supplementing his wage as a school-caretaker. Peter was accustomed to this man trying to sell a whole range of items, but this time instead of school chalk, toilet paper, or gallon bottles of disinfectant he was selling antiquarian books. We met the next evening at Peter's lock-up garage. He pulled out two battered cardboard suitcases.

Peter. I couldn't resist it. He's only done a museum. Yes, a museum. Course everything's belled up and he's creeping about all these fucking statues and that in the middle of the night. His bottle's starting to go. He never knew what to do. I mean what do you fucking have in a museum full of belled-up old shit?

More as a gesture of desperation than anything else, the man jemmied the door of a cupboard that had no alarm attached. He grabbed the contents and left. On his safe return home he was profoundly disappointed with his haul, cursed his luck, and proceeded to attempt to off-load a dozen antiquarian books on to his friends and relations. Peter bought the lot for £25.

Peter then embarked on a course of self-education based on the pragmatic demands of the market-place that would gladden the hearts of most conservative educationalists. He visited libraries all over London and learnt about antiquarian books and their market, he studied prices, even the relative merits of renovation in an effort to gain some expertise on the subject.

Over about six months he sold all of the books but one.

Peter. It's my fucking enigma, Dick. The others were easy. Just went out to the sticks, Cheltenham, or somewhere and knocked 'em out to a local bookseller. Easy, you don't get top price but it's a drink. Besides, there's no risk. I was getting 25, 40 quid for a book worth a ton [£100] in an auction, no trouble, no questions asked. But this little fucker's . . . years old. Come to more than a drink, a take-away, and a piss up the wall on the way home. This is the big one, this is a fucking enigma.

Cousin Max and his Knowledgeable Associates

Peter's cousin Max had attended a grammar school at the age of 11 years and a Borstal at 16 years.

Peter. Always the bright spark, Max wanted to be a journalist, a writer when we was kids. Did well at school and a bit at Borstal later on, but it was like whatever he done he was lucky. My mum called him Jack Shit 'cos he was lucky like.

In his late teens and twenties Max tried various occupations and businesses, including insurance salesman, milkman, plumber, thief, and rag-and-bone man. He was in many ways an upwardly mobile 'jump-up merchant', certainly more financially successful than most, and showed great skill in buying and selling until in his early thirties the local police captured him shortly after he had taken receipt of an entire lorry-load of menswear that was originally destined for a well-known gents' outfitters. His eighteen months in an open prison were not wasted.

Max neither smoked nor drank alcohol, and his ability to replenish the inmates' stocks of both these valuable commodities brought Max to the attention of an extremely influential, professional criminal who was serving the last few months of a sentence he had received for extortion. Max had impressed the older, more experienced man and the two became firm friends and business partners sharing the profits they made from smuggled cigarettes and lemonade bottles containing vodka.

When Max emerged from prison he was considerably richer than when he went in, and his new associate arranged for Max to take over a used-car business in Hackney. From then on there was no looking back, and this led to considerable resentment from Peter, as it was he who had stolen the ill-fated consignment of menswear that sparked Max's ascendancy:

Peter. I thought I was lucky to get away with it, like I felt sorry for the bastard. When he got put away I was gutted. Now he's got a house, two motors, a gaff in Spain . . . pound notes. All 'cos I was prick enough to park a hookey lorry with . . . written on the side outside his lock-up.

It was to Cousin Max that Peter turned in dealing with his enigma.

Peter had attempted to sell his goods to numerous dealers but their high value turned many prospective buyers off: 'You want £2,000 for an old book? No book is that fucking old.' He could not possibly risk going to a specialist dealer or auction house for fear of detection and for several months tried without success to persuade various market-traders, publicans, builders, and the odd academic to purchase his goods. He turned reluctantly to Max whose ascendancy had been viewed by Peter with a mixture of awe and resentment. Max's initial response over the telephone was promising and he remarked that a building firm in which he had an interest had recently renovated the premises of a prominent art dealer, but Max, before he renewed the dealer's acquaintance, insisted on viewing the goods.

Peter took the goods to his cousin's house where Max apparently concurred that the book was indeed very old, and agreed to consider its purchase. After several weeks Peter was becoming twitchy, insisting that Max's apparent caution was symptomatic of his cousin's reluctance to share his ill-gotten gains with other members of the family. As a result I listened to many hours of Peter's reminiscences of childhood when Max had apparently enjoyed good fortune virtually since birth.

Eventually Max contacted Peter, and while confirming his interest in the book, showed some caution regarding its origins. However, he agreed to meet Peter in a pub in Hackney, and Peter suggested that as it promised to be a good night out I might like to attend.

Max, who arrived with his business partner, was exceptionally good company. A mild-mannered man who sipped Perrier water, his well-cut suit stood out from the logos and blousons adorning the bulk of the clientele. As the evening progressed Peter was becoming agitated for the real purpose of the meeting was not touched upon. Around ten o'clock we were joined by Doug who, apart from his taste in heavy gold jewellery, shared Max's sartorial style and blended comfortably into the company. Within twenty minutes of Doug's arrival Max broached the subject of 'our bit of business'. He explained that he had checked out the market and that his contact in the art world was happy with the price. The only drawback was the chance of detection. Max felt that such a valuable item must have precipitated 'the scream going up', and that the police could easily trace the book.

Max. It's not like a load of shirts, is it Pete? I mean you cut out the labels and knock 'em out anywhere, on a stall, anywhere there's no way of tracing them. And who is going to bother? But this, when it went missing it must have brought a lot of attention on the thieves. It's a bit iffy.

Max's partner agreed, and Peter's explanation of how the book had been stolen echoed implausibly around the table. Peter was clearly upset at being reminded of what should happen to a consignment of stolen shirts, and it seemed that the evening was about to end rather abruptly. At this point Doug intervened and said that if Peter would care to write down the details of the book he would check to see if it was on any stolen lists. Aghast, Peter looked to Max who smiled benignly and assured his cousin that it was a good idea. Peter scribbled the details on a scrap of paper as the colour rushed from his face, and handed the note to Doug who left saying that he would not be more than half an hour.

Peter. Why didn't you say he was Old Bill? How come he's here anyway? You winding me up?

Max attempted to placate Peter that Doug was 'as good as gold' and that after dealing with him for many years Max was now owed several favours.

But Peter was not having it: 'You should have said. He don't owe me fuck all.'

The next forty minutes were spent in virtual silence as both Peter and Max's partner switched from lager to whisky. Max divulged little concerning the details of his collaborations with Doug, although it was apparent that his local station was in another part of the East End. I have no way of knowing what kind of checks Doug made, but options exist for officers, if they have adequate descriptive detail, to draw upon collated information regarding both crime and stolen goods. On his return Doug appeared pleased to announce that (for reasons unknown to me), the book was not on any list. Max was pleased, Peter still wary, and Max's partner drunk, but the details of the deal were agreed, and Doug seemed almost sanctified at being able to make people happy.

Doug to my knowledge received no money in recompense, Max has since gone into property development, and Peter still unmolested by the forces of law and order recently invested £200 in a batch of ladies' blouses.

While the positive assistance rendered by the detective in the above story may be unusual, more common is the absence of action—the 'turning of a blind eye' to blatant criminal action as a coping mechanism. On another occasion a conversation in a pub between a detective and two active villains was interrupted by a man selling a van-load of stolen gramophone records. Not realizing the identity of the detective, the thief pressed home with a persuasive sales pitch. The detective turned his back and took two short steps along the bar away from the haggling while his two companions attempted to deter the seller who appeared to be genuinely insulted at being snubbed by men with whom he had obviously dealt in the past. The CID officer excluded himself from what was evolving into a serious confrontation by engaging me in a conversation about football, and eventually the only way to deter the zealous seller was for the two men physically to take the record-dealer aside, and urgently inform him of their drinking partner's identity. The dealer retreated, the detective reverted to his original position at the bar, and the trio hesitantly resumed their conversation—not, however, before the hapless record-seller, in an attempt to regain some composure, had returned to the bar and bought us all a drink, claiming in the detective's hearing that: 'Course they ain't all iffy really. I bought them at the auctions' (see Niederhoffer 1969, p. 64).

In this instance, the officer had utilized discretion by choosing not to police a situation in anticipation of receiving information of a higher status at some future date from his drinking companions. As Muir has indicated, in reciprocal relationships the officer demurs from implementing his coercive power in exchange for a range of rewards (Muir 1977, p. 274). However, the detective also has relationships with superior officers, who can also offer rewards of status, promotion, and continued employment in the department in exchange for the attainment of organizational goals. It is crucial to stress that I am not casting the detective as an urban cowboy living close to the precipice of criminality in order to dispense a form of natural justice (Manning and Redlinger 1977, pp. 147–66; Laurie 1970, p. 243). Rather, that integration into the occupational entrepreneurial culture of East London is a response to the organizational environment of policing (see Harris 1973).

Turn-taking

Despite the detective's use of policed vocabularies, 'the job' demands results and results are achieved by nominating individuals to 'take their turn'. Turn-taking is a CID strategy of policing that has developed in response to organizational demands, and by shrouding the process in the language of inevitability, responsibility rests not with the detective but with fate. The 'villain' is unlucky, but an early morning visit from 'the department' is never totally unexpected. It is merely another aspect of 'the game'. As Newman cogently indicates: 'Such moves were almost like a game the CID played with the felonry, both parties being aware that sooner or later the spotlight of police attention would swing in their direction' (Newman 1984, p. 51). But behind the game analogy lies a central state organization whose brief is the maintenance of law and order and the apprehension of felons. Emergent from this formal organizational design come 'schemes of interpretation that competent and entitled users can invoke in yet unknown ways whenever it suits their purpose' (Bittner 1965, pp. 249–50).

Turn-taking is one such scheme of interpretation that is manifested in the enacted environment of the CID as rhetoric, yet despite the rhetoric, the activities of the CID are dominated by formal organizational demands. As Newman (1984, p. 52) maintains: 'Whatever the reason prompting the CID's actions, at the bottom of the line there was always a clear-up rate, which they strove to keep as high as was reasonably expected. Within the general rate detectives were obliged to keep their own numbers up and justify their existence.'

The rhetoric of turn-taking serves to shroud any acknowledgement of organizational, and by association uniform-branch, hegemony, and is instrumental in maintaining CID mythology. By relieving the CID officer of responsibility for his activities, the detective is able to maintain his ambiguous position in the saloon bar, and reinforce his image as an autonomous entrepreneur of law and order, dealing in justice, unhindered by organizational demands. An analogy can be drawn between the detective's utility of the law and the role of the dice in Rhinehart's novel *The Dice Man* (1972). Rhinehart throws dice in order to decide upon courses of action; choice is therefore negated for it is the arbitrary fall of the dice that determines action, rendering the thrower bereft of culpability. Consequently the dice is an agent of fate, and motivation can be defined simply as, 'What the dice dictates I will perform' (Rhinehart 1972, p. 59).

It is essential that the CID officer maintains, by the skilful use of rhetoric, an essentially deviant identity based upon deliberately ambiguous presentational strategies that serve to distance the department from the formal organizational regions that direct detective work. Turn-taking is one such rhetorical device, serving as a means of camouflaging the contemporary subservience of the CID to the hegemony of the uniform branch.

Beyond the Pale

Random policing also distances the detective from considerations of fairness or formal justice, yet in one category of crime the detective can dispense with the rhetorical utility of working-class vocabularies and devices such as turn-taking. This form of crime includes certain categories of assault and murder. In investigating these crimes, detectives resort to a formal role of overt policing and the ambiguities of going native are dispensed with, for public, mass media, and organizational pressure are brought to bear and a 'result' in the form of an arrest and successful conviction is demanded. Particularly in the investigation of murder, officers are direct and to the point in identifying themselves and in the public expression of their aims. For instance, after a recent bizarre murder, a member of the public was telephoned by a Detective Sergeant and the conversation proceeded as follows:

DS. Hello, is that Mrs . . .

Member of the public. Yes.

DS. My name is Detective Sergeant . . . of . . . CID. I believe you are professionally acquainted with . . .

Member of the public. Yes.

DS. Well, I am afraid Mr . . . is dead, and I am conducting a murder inquiry. I believe that you have some knowledge of the family. Is there any information that you can give me that may be of help?

Murder, in particular, offers an opportunity for detectives to confront 'evil', the worst kind of crime, and enables the CID officer to escape the tensions brought about by the random policing of turn-taking; he no longer pretends to have any affinity with the organizationally imposed goals of management, for murder incites demands for action that coincide with the unambiguous implementation of police power in response to society's wrath.

Murder is perceived by the CID officer as a 'pure' crime, untainted by the ambiguities involved in the routine investigation of 'normal' crime. Murder constitutes a step beyond the parameters of day-to-day urban life, and as a consequence, represents an opportunity for the detective to respond in a manner that stresses and enhances his police role, while licensing the officer to apply his entrepreneurial skills in a manner that may appear clumsy and heavy-handed. As an experienced DC explained at the conclusion of a murder case: 'We just tugged anybody we fancied and sat on them a bit. We knew he ran with a gang. Eventually, one of the gang gets religious and decides to cleanse his soul.'

Murder provides the detective with a licence for action that would prove awkward and unprofitable if implemented during the investigation of 'normal' crime. The detective's proximity to evil affords the officer a potency or quality that is exclusive to those who are routinely confronted with violent death and its aftermath. In murder investigations the detective limits his negotiating skills to dealing with suspects and with individuals who are suspected of being involved in other crimes. Citizens not suspected of crime are not subjected to negotiatory techniques; the liberal use of the word 'murder' is usually sufficient to inspire co-operation (Sanders 1977, 173–9).

Unarmed Combat

'Watch out, here comes plod', or 'oops, it's the filth', does not necessarily indicate a detective's incompetence in his choice of attire or even that he has big feet. What such comments do indicate is that the equilibrium of a given social setting has been seriously affected by the presence of individuals who wear their uniforms as contradictory visual styles. Particularly in casual clothing, CID officers look anything but casual, for they are working, lurking, and getting results, and are licensed to dress in civilian clothing by a militaristic organization informed by an oppositional ideology. Consequently, the rhetorical device of plain clothes is often identified by the opposition—the policed—as a uniform, albeit in the form of a heavily camouflaged battledress.

Experienced CID officers are aware of their uniform and are adept at exploiting their high visibility and obtrusive presence to the full, utilizing the rhetorical device of plain clothes in accordance with organizational goals as defined by their uniformed superiors. The CID officer can exploit the policed culture's accurate interpretation of the function of plain clothes, and in doing so exhibit the true nature of much CID rhetoric and demystify detective work. For despite the 'mirror image' (Manning 1980, p. 67) that detectives have developed in relation to the entrepreneurial culture, it is an apparent contradiction of CID work that their covert or undercover role is exaggerated, while the policed environment is so clearly marked out as to include identifiable CID officers in its cast of characters. The stylistic convention adopted by detectives does not ultimately bear on the work itself, but on the detective's idealized and egocentric notion of his own role in an idealized but ultimately alien culture.

Most of a detective's working day is spent in the company of individuals who are fully aware of the identity of the officer, and anonymity is undesirable, or at worst counter-productive. The CID's enacted environment can be closely compared to that of professional boxing, where opponents tend to know each other, periodically are incapacitated by suspension, injury, or retirement, and vacant licences are taken up by a steady flow of new participants and young contenders into 'the game'. Surveillance and other covert activities are not as crucial as fictional accounts of detective work would have us believe; on the contrary, the essence of CID power lies in their skill in utilizing working-class vocabularies, both linguistic and presentational, to enhance their police function. This function, in common with the uniform branch, is largely a symbolic one. However, in the case of the CID, the essence of the officer's power as a symbol of the state's ability to intervene (Manning 1977, p. 105) is not to be found in a uniform or helmet, but in the manner by which the policed can identify their appropriated vocabularies as blunt-edged rhetoric.

As one CID informant declared: 'Sometimes everybody should

know who you are—front them, then they either walk out or they start giving chat across the bar. It's what you call unarmed combat'.

Scarred Faces

Unlike the narcotics officers in Manning's *Narc's Game* (1980) most CID information-gathering is carried out in brief spurts and involves interaction with actors who are fully aware of the detective's identity. Informants are aware of the detective's use of various rhetorical devices, and regard the CID officer simply as a more devious version of his uniformed counterpart. The relationship between detective and informant hinges upon the ability of the officers to coerce those with information to divulge it, and while I was aware of individuals who had voluntarily offered information in exchange for monetary inducements or for rewards offered by insurance companies, it was claimed that this was comparatively rare: 'I would go to normal people who are committing crimes and kick a few doors, kick up enough hassle' (see Reiner 1985, pp. 120–1).

In pressurizing informants, the detective abandons any pretence concerning his merging into the social milieu of the locality. His very obtrusiveness enhances his eloquence, and vocabularies are transformed into coercive verbal and visual forms that become instrumental in the attainment of police-orientated goals. 'You don't go for just anyone, you only go for them who are committing crimes, and if they're at it you make it impossible for them to continue their normal business without getting pulled. They can't carry on with an unmarked car outside their house twenty-four hours a day ... in the end they have to come to us to continue.'

Gleaning

Not all information is gained by coercive or even negotiatory means. Occasionally a detective will be required to 'chat up' or 'con' citizens into unknowingly relaying to the officer crucial information. This method is comparatively subtle, and requires the detective to utilize local vocabularies in an attempt to merge into the social landscape. However, this requires great skill and its success is dependent upon the officer's accurate identification of the potential informant as a 'punter' who is not equipped to identify the detective's appropriation of vocabularies as a rhetorical device. As an example of this process it is worth drawing attention to an incident that occurred while I was accompanying Harry, a self-employed plumber, who was working as a subcontractor on a redevelopment scheme. One afternoon a smartly dressed man in his mid-thirties entered the flat where Harry was working, greeted us, and stood in the middle of the living-room looking around. He explained that he was thinking of buying one of the flats and started to walk around the rooms. He was extremely friendly and asked several questions pertinent to a potential property buyer. He asked eventually about the quality of the plumbing materials and whether or not they were expensive, and it was at this stage that he established prolonged eye contact with Harry, whose voice became flat and cold as he answered non-committally. Eventually the man turned away and walked into the kitchen, and as he did so Harry turned to me and mouthed 'Plod'. Sure enough the man's next questions when he returned concerned whether or not materials were stolen from the site, and how much were the central-heating boilers worth? Harry now kept his back turned to the questioner as he fixed a radiator to the wall and responded in semi-articulate grunts. The man left and Harry told me that some boilers had gone missing over the course of the previous weekend. The following day he was called to the site office where he was formally questioned by the 'flat-buyer', a Detective Sergeant.

The detective had mistaken Harry, a competent and highly experienced buyer and seller of stolen goods and occasional petty thief, for a 'punter', a stereotyped honest citizen, ill-equipped to interpret his rhetorical image construction as covert police activity (see Baldwin and Kinsey 1982, p. 69). Harry could not pin down how he had identified the officer, just that '. . . he weren't right. He was too slippery, sort of smooth. Anyway, what sort of flat-buyer wants to know the price of copper a foot, or fucking rad valves.'

For this detective it appeared that, far from everybody being 'at it', potentially culpable for a range of crimes, only certain types of person committed crime, and apparently Harry was not a criminal type equipped to play the detective's game. Consequently the officer failed successfully to use East-End linguistic style as a covert policing device, and Harry, as an actor in the policed environment, was competent in the utility of his native vocabulary and was able to identify the detective's activities as rhetorical, as efforts to establish a rapport based upon common linguistic constructs and cultural background. Inevitably, then, mistakes made during his initial contact with Harry led to failure and the detective resorted the next day to what was to prove a fruitless questioning session, a session that could also have been carried out had the officer been in uniform. This calls into question the function of much CID work; it is an issue that has been partially acknowledged within the Metropolitan Police, with the recent innovation that has handed over the investigation of low-level theft, in some areas, to the uniform branch (see Eck 1979).

Into Clothes

The transfer from the uniform branch to the CID marks an escalation of the police officer's power and represents a deliberate switch in his function from mundane to crucial aspects of policing, from the maintenance of order to thief-taking. However, a contrary view of detective work is expressed by Manning in his description of the work of narcotics officers: 'boring, unsystematic, cat-as-catch-can, and focused on obtaining immediate rewards and arresting low-level users' (Manning 1980, p. 262). Investigation of burglary, petty theft, and cheque frauds seldom requires a covert police presence; the detective will not be required to carry out these routine inquiries *incognito* unless exceptional circumstances should arise, for instance, when covert surveillance is carried out; although for this purpose officers peering through a slit in a 'nondescript' vehicle could be dressed in full ceremonial uniform for all the effect it might have on their police function. Interviewing witnesses, interrogating suspects, and visiting the scene of the crime all require the detective to utilize an 'honest' presentational strategy, the officer identifying and presenting himself as a policeman. Going 'into clothes' (Rubinstein 1973, p. 399) represents a way of elaborating the uniform branch's stock of rhetoric, thus enhancing the police role by the adoption of a discrete uniform based on the visual style of the policed culture, the function of which is the provision of a distinct and specific image.

The policed, particularly in environments sensitized to a police presence, identify the linguistic and visual presentations of these vocabularies as metaphors for police activity. However, as I have intimated, this metaphysical function of CID rhetoric is acknowledged by experienced detectives, and is regarded as a positive and productive instrument of police work. Rhetoric serves to reduce the distance between the detective and the policed culture, only to the point of increasing the potency of the detective and therefore enhancing the probability of him 'getting a result'. For it is within the capabilities of the CID to bargain with bail or sentences, to exercise discretion in making arrests, and generally to impose sanctions, both negative and positive, that can affect the social and economic well-being of the policed culture. The 'trade-offs' and 'fit-ups' (see Burrows and Tarling 1982; *Observer*, 13 July 1986) are part of the CID game, which is played within a commercial framework. The function of CID rhetoric is to convince the players that the parameters of the game are 'real' in that the law has constructed boundaries of behaviour over which it is forbidden to cross. This game can be played only when both sides are willing to conform to an image of law and order as interpreted by the CID's rhetorical devices: 'villains moan about fit-ups, promises of bail, verbals and we play along and fit them up. But if they go too far and really try and fit me up, then in court I might let slip a bit of their previous. So both sides know the rules.'

As in most sports, the organizers justify the rules in terms of a rhetoric that seeks to legitimize the 'extra-curricular' activities of the players. For instance, a useful analogy might be found in an analysis of professional ice hockey, where the National Hockey League provide one set of rules (rhetoric), while the continued prosperity of the sport is reliant upon the players' adherence to a pragmatic, more violent code (Atyeo 1979). However, the CID are not merely players, they are a branch of the referees' association also, and have close links with both the sport's national body and with the promotional entrepreneurs who stage the events. If the CID did not wear the correct kit and dressed in the same manner as the referee nobody would play against them.

Symbolically Filthy

In emphasizing the instrumental rupture between the CID and the policed culture, I am stressing how the police utilize vocabularies, both linguistic and presentational, and transform a specific working-class inheritance into a rhetorical device. CID rhetoric serves to reinforce the symbolic presentation of the detective as a pragmatic exponent of the law, proficient in the use of street language and dramatic techniques that when combined generate the image of what Muir (1977) in the context of uniformed policing, has called 'the street-corner politician'. Unlike the patrol officer, the detective's sole function is to 'get results' necessitating the arrest and conviction of felons. This simplistic task-definition removes the detective from the mundane world of school-crossing patrols, dealing with found property, and other service roles, and also from general order maintenance that requires a combination of policing techniques ranging from pacification to violence. As Muir (1977, p. 271) notes, 'calming an apprehensive or resentful populace is a problem common to presidents and patrolmen alike'. 'Getting a result' requires qualities found in very few politicians save the most wise and ruthless totalitarian dictatorships. Negotiation tends to be accompanied by threats, and the origins of this potential for coercion lies within the CID and not the policed culture.

The relationship between the CID and the policed is in the final analysis one-sided. For rhetorically the detective can create an impression of transactions between the CID and those they regard as criminal as reciprocal arrangements founded upon mutually profitable legitimate business relationships, the currency of which is information. However, the ability of CID officers to glean information by threatening the implementation of a variety of coercive devices, of which legitimate police action such as arrest is but one option, suggests a peculiar economic structure indeed. The rhetoric of the CID acknowledges in practice the one-sided nature of the relationship, and the appropriation of East End vocabularies serves merely to emphasize the role of CID officers as holders of a symbolic torch of law and order that emits a heat to which the detective is frequently immune.

Both the East-Ender and the CID officer are able to conceive of each other in terms of common essences, and as Katz (1975, p. 1371) observed this mutual identification can be located in repetitious references being made to a common 'inherent factor'. Business serves to provide a reference point for the location of a common moral identity: the entrepreneur. The detective who espouses East End language and style in an overt manner may be thought to possess such latent powers of coercion, deception, and detection that his obtrusiveness be regarded as intrinsic to his policing style and function. Similarly East-Enders who cannot be identified as having committed an offence may be regarded by officers as especially astute in camouflaging this criminality.

These complementary qualities of police power and criminality are regarded as existing independent of observable behaviour (Katz 1975, p. 1371). They are imputed essences deemed to exist beyond the actions of individuals and interpreted as immutable states of being rather than as flexible adaptive responses to environmental, cultural, and organizational stimuli. The assumptions that precede the imputation of essences can be located in the imputee's cultural location. For the CID officer this means a consideration of the autonomous entrepreneurial occupational culture of 'the department'. The assumptions that precede the East-Ender's imputation of police potency to the detective can be located in the recognition of the CID's distillation of the East-Ender's heritage in the form of a tanglible, blatant rhetorical style that is of limited utility in terms of efficient policing. However, this filtering of style produces a stylistic format that constitutes a moral licence that rationalizes the detective's separateness from the uniform branch and its encumbent restraints, and assists in neutralizing the officers from the possible consequences of poor performance and low clear-up rates. As Katz (1975, p. 1378) indicates: 'Agents request relief from ordinary obligations to their principals in appreciation of the special claims deviants make on them'.

When uniformed officers invoke formal rules in a periodic attempt to standardize CID practice and performance, the detective can claim that 'you don't catch villains in church.' 'Thieves don't work 9 to 5.' Or most tellingly, 'it takes one to know one.' The assumption that because of his perpetually obtrusive presence the detective has some special competence (Katz 1975, p. 1381) in the urban malaise is not exclusive to the East End, and has parallels all over the Western world (see Ruhm 1979, pp. 8–18). However, the uniqueness of both East End culture, and CID occupational culture, and in particular the isolation of both groups from day-to-day normative restraint, make their mutual identification all the more crucial, for the imputation of charisma to CID officers decreases the detective's moral commitment to policing strategies that are derived from due process.

The CID and Cultural Accountability

The day-to-day activities of the Metropolitan CID officer are subjected to only minimal institutional restraints. The 'key resource' (Holdaway 1983, p. 22) for the CID officer is the occupational culture, and it is of paramount importance, if the culture is to be comprehended, to locate the source of those essences that serve to construct the moral identity of 'the department'. These essences are provided by East End culture, and it is this culture to which detectives are accountable for the maintenance of their power. It is power that is founded upon the mutual imputation of deviant and charismatic essences.

The effectiveness of the CID is difficult to measure. The Commissioner's Report for 1985 shows a clear-up rate of 17 per cent and Steer (1980) and Mawby (1979) suggest that 25 and 23 per cent respectively of the clear-up rate involves what Reiner (1985, p. 122) calls 'real detective work'. While it is feasible to assess the effectiveness of the uniform branch according to various preventative-based criteria (Kelling *et al.* 1974; Clarke and Mayhew 1980) the effectiveness of detectives is inevitably linked to the clear-up rate. 'Real detective work', however, does put great store upon local knowledge as a prime factor in successful investigation (Burrows 1986). Local knowledge and associated negotiatory skills are useful in 'arranging' t.i.c.s (offences taken into consideration) (see Mawby 1979; Steer 1980; Burrows and Tarling 1982; Burrows 1986). My own observations suggest that despite the claim to local knowledge made by most CID officers, they are often comically lagging behind the East End non-police entrepreneurs in their understanding of the market-place. One such shortfall was made apparent to me when a group of hard-boozing detectives sat drinking into the small hours in a pub, while above them on the second floor was the hoard of stolen whisky the theft of which they were 'busy' investigating. They were amongst the minority in the neighbourhood of people who had no knowledge of the loot's whereabouts.

The effectiveness of the CID in East London can be assessed in terms of the department's contribution to maintaining a unique local order. A 'bedrock of effectiveness' (Reiner 1985, p. 123) in terms of clear-up rates exists, yet in the East End of London the style of detective work so neatly matches the indigenous culture in terms of commercially defined precepts and market-orientated unpredictability that it is facile to deal with the detective's effectiveness in an orthodox manner. The true measure of the detective's effectiveness rests in his acquisition of local stylistic conventions while maintaining a level of order that is acceptable to the community, a community whose relationship with the law is matched in terms of ambiguity by its relationship with the market-place.

The relationship between the CID and the East End functions as an informal model of community policing. Culturally rather than legislatively accountable to their public, the CID are ever-present potential obstacles to action in the community, a community upon which the detective is reliant for the provision of his operational style. In turn this operational style amounts to a caricature of East End culture to the extent that the policed can identify in the detective their own deviance and by association are able to attribute charismatic essences to both the police and to the policed.

The key to the CID's importance in maintaining order lies in their imputation of deviant essences to the denizens of the East End, the consequent recognition of their own deviance, the imputation of charismatic essences to the East End, and the acceptance of the East-Ender's imputation of mutually exclusive essences of deviance and charisma to himself. The role of the East End detective then is defined by the East-Ender, for it is his language and style that provides the cultural tools for the detective to operate, albeit as an agent of state control. As Alderson (1979, p. 161) has remarked: 'the role of the police in a given community can be defined by the law, by senior police, by junior police or by the community itself'.

However, the East End has taken indigenously defined policing a step further by the provision of a legitimizing rhetoric for entrepreneurial police action that additionally defines the parameters of the area's own activities. The East End's adoption of commercial language is an impudent appropriation of key elements of the dominant economic structure. Yet its function as an accommodating device excludes any attempt at radically altering the structure. Likewise the symbiotic relationship between the East-Ender and the CID rests upon the same ethos of accommodation rather than resistance. The language of legitimate business commodifies law and order, creating an informal cultural consensus, as well as a policing style that concurs with the expectations of the area's denizens, with requirements of the state, and the whims of the market-place.

The Symbiosis of Control: Policing in the Vernacular

> The existing relations of production between individuals must necessarily express themselves also as political and legal relations.
>
> Marx, quoted in Bottomore and Rubel 1963, p. 92

CID policing is congruent with the social order of the East End. The ambiguity of East End culture rests with the area's peculiar relationship with capitalism. The East End, while embracing the basic ethos of capitalism, is ambivalent towards both the normative social relations suggested by capitalism and to the enabling ideological framework upon which capitalism rests, notably the consumption of goods and the acquisition of private wealth.

Domestic order is maintained by the market, or more specifically by the denizens' responses to the opportunities provided by the market to implement their entrepreneurial inheritance. The East-Ender is neither antagonistic nor compliant to state control. He is realistic about the chances of any criminal act being detected and adapts his response to the market accordingly. Burglar alarms, guard-dogs, the technology of property protection, and the fickle transience of the market-place provide the main obstacles to those individuals who consider property crime as a normative source of income. The police in general, and—considering the low clear-up rate for most normal crimes—detectives in particular are mere periodic irritations. As Barry explained sagely, 'they can be a fucking nuisance. They got a job to do, so long as they don't do it too well, so long as they play the game.' The relationship between the denizens of East London and the CID is symbiotic, appropriately based upon the trading of moral identities. The sharp entrepreneurship of the East-Ender provides, when appropriated and reworked by the detective a potent occupational front that distances him from the restraints of the administratively bound uniform branch. The adoption of such a front also equips the detective with a stylistic format that neatly dovetails with the individualistic entrepreneurship demanded by the formal detective task as well as with the pervading culture that he encounters in the enacted environment of detective work. The control aspect of symbiosis is manifested in the status afforded to the detective by East-Enders, and the implication of the detective's appropriation and overt utility of East End style is that he is fully conversant with the origins and implications of the style's instrumentality. Thereby the detective is imbued with the twin moral identities of entrepreneur and agent of state power; his normative ineptitude combines to construct a symbol of charismatic urban competence and control whose coercive potential is all the more formidable for its apparently erratic and arbitrary utility.

Postscript: Back to the Future

Here in Docklands you are succeeding in shifting the centre of gravity of London's economy back east. For a century, businesses have been moving their locations ever westward. Now, many of tomorrow's businesses want to locate in East London, close to the financial and commercial centre of the city.

Lord Young, Secretary of State for Employment, 16 April 1986

Recently market forces have imposed unprecedented pressure upon East London, and as a consequence the area's inheritance and its relationship with the City of London has been reinforced at a rate matched only by escalating property values. At the time of writing the three inner East End boroughs of Hackney, Tower Hamlets, and Newham boast a total of over 50,000 registered unemployed with an aggregate unemployment rate of approximately 25 per cent. The highest unemployment rate of the outer London boroughs is to be found in the outer East End, in Barking and Dagenham where the figure stands at 11 per cent.

The knock-on effect of unleashed market forces has grave consequences for East-Enders in terms of health; the number of deaths from tuberculosis is six times the national average (GLC 1985b). Over 16 per cent of dwellings in Hackney and over 12 per cent in Tower Hamlets and Newham are classified as unfit for human habitation, and over 10 per cent of East London's denizens are living in overcrowded conditions (GLC 1985b). Approximately 25 per cent of pupils leave school with no formal qualifications, only one in twenty pupils in Hackney gained five O-levels or above (Harrison 1983).

However dispassionately one tries to evaluate life in East London, whatever measure of urban blight is used, the area emerges as a poor, hard, mean place in which to survive. The unemployment, poverty, and general deprivation certainly bear comparison with any area of Britain or indeed Western Europe, yet the most striking characteristic of the East End is the scale of the problem. In the three inner East End boroughs over half a million men, women, and children must survive not only the long-established, almost routine, onslaught inflicted over centuries by a fickle market-place. The population now finds itself the focal point of an attack that is unprecedented since the blitz of the Second World War in terms of its viciousness and irrevocable damage inflicted.

The London Dockland Development Corporation (LDDC) is the tool that will take the East End into the twenty-first century and back to the Victorian era. Set up in 1981 by a Conservative administration, the LDDC's brief was to bypass local government and, coinciding with the final closure of the Royal Docks, promote private developments such as the Isle of Dogs Enterprise Zone, an airport in the Royal Docks, massive private development schemes, a water-sports centre, two earth satellite teleports, and an artificial ski-slope at Beckton. The closure of the East End's docks and wharfs released large amounts of land close to the City of London just at a time when the City was on the verge of expansion. Hence we have Canary Wharf, the biggest development scheme in the world, with an estimated 12 million square feet of office space.

The Enterprize Zone (EZ) has been at the forefront of the often bizarre onslaught. The EZ was designed to attract private investment to the Isle of Dogs by relaxing planning controls and offering immunity from local rates until 1992. The LDDC bought land at public expense, prepared it for development, and sold it off to private developers at less than half the cost. By making the area attractive to private investors many developers have shown an interest in coming to the area, and some parts of Dockland are now (1987) changing hands at £5 million an acre. With no rates, low rents, and little or no planning restrictions the forces of capital have been unleashed, and East-Enders can do little but sit, watch, and be squeezed out. The type of industry coming to Dockland in general, and the EZ in particular, has not provided jobs for East-Enders nor is it likely too in the future. An independent study reported in 1984 that there had been a net loss of jobs. The type of jobs being attracted to Dockland are unlikely to meet the needs of the local work-force, the incoming occupations overwhelmingly favouring professional and white-collar workers (Tym and Partners 1984).

For every job lost in the docks, there were three lost in dependent industries such as manufacturing, transport, and service industries. This has had a devastating effect on the East End, as Ted Johns, a prominent Dockland activist and himself a redundant river-worker, has noted: 'the fact that the land values rise in the Docklands, it simply means that the land that is occupied by the dole queue is worth £5,000 more now than it was five years ago. It doesn't make any difference to that dole queue'.

In 1986 of the 1,400 new jobs created in the EZ 28 had gone to local people. The LDDC and EZ in particular offer little respite to East-Enders; for instance, the bizarre 'Stolport'—a short take-off airport in the Royal Docks, a scheme that was 'sold' by the LDDC in terms of the 4,000–5,000 jobs it would create (GLC 1985a)—has created something less than a jobs bonanza. The latest estimate by the contractors themselves is that the airport operating at maximum capacity would generate from 359 to 464 jobs, and of these one-third would be specialist occupations such as pilots. A prospective employer trawling the jobcentres of Bethnal Green, Whitechapel, Poplar, Plaistow, or Canning Town would have as much success were he or she recruiting shepherds. 'In fact both the GLC and local groups showed that the airport would lead to the displacement of jobs from the docks. There were over 50 firms employing 700 people within the dock walls and of these jobs it was estimated 100 would be directly affected by the airport, with a further 300 affected by potential expansion of the airport' (GLC 1985a, p. 22).

As aircraft negotiate Newham's tower blocks to land in what used to be the Royal Victoria and Albert Docks, East-Enders will have to do in 'Stolport' what they will be forced to do in the rest of the East End—they will perform their traditional role, they will serve the City. The offices and high-tech workshops will bring the educated, the well trained, the middle classes into the East End on a scale that the area has never experienced. Between 1971 and 1981 managers and professionals increased in Hackney, Newham, and in Tower Hamlets, and although these figures are still low in comparison with the rest of inner London (managers and professionals in the three boroughs make up only 9 per cent of the total population (1981 census)), it does nonetheless mark a shift, a dark, emerging bruise of middle-class settlement on the body of Britain's working-class city.

In Hackney middle-class incursion has taken the form of seepage from its more affluent North London neighbours, and bourgeois settlement has manifested itself in the gentrification of much of the borough's private housing stock: 'Teachers, lecturers, social and community workers no longer able to afford houses in more fashionable Islington, began to move in but not enough to alter more than marginally the basic social make-up: in 1981 owner-occupiers still accounted for only the 16% of households in Hackney, against a national average of 55%' (Harrison 1983, p. 181).

However, in Tower Hamlets with the highest percentage of council housing in England (82 per cent), middle-class colonization is a more complex issue, and the consequences potentially more devastating. The existing private housing stock in Tower Hamlets is considerably better served by public transport than in Hackney. Consequently, city workers have begun to move into property adjacent to Bethnal Green, Bow, and Mile End tube stations. Predictably property values have escalated far beyond the reach of the indigenous population, the waiting-list for council property has lengthened, and overcrowding, poor health, and the insidious overwhelming pressure of East End survival is compounded still further. Yet in the south of the borough, in Docklands itself, the nature of bourgeois colonization is palpably different. Here gentrification abounds in its most bizarre form, and somehow 'real' East-Enders must make sense of it.

When it first started, when they started moving in I thought they was fucking mad. I spent the last five years I was in the dock counting the days to get out, and I thought if somebody is stupid enough to want to live in an old warehouse, then best of luck. But now I go back to see family and you realize just how much money was involved, and you think I spent a life in that dock for a bad back and now . . . it's all gone changed like we was never there (68-year-old retired docker).

Warehouse conversions in prime riverside locations have been at the vanguard of private housing developments in Poplar, Wapping, and the Isle of Dogs, with new property reflecting both the new-found chic image of the area and the cost of building on concrete as opposed to green-field sites. The native community in this area are being squeezed out, for with nine out of ten of the population of the Isle of Dogs living in 1960s-built council accommodation they are unable to participate fully in the 'Metropolitan Water City of the 21st Century' unless it needs cleaning or decorating. As Pawley (1986, p. 14) notes, 'the ultimate fate of all the council housing on the island must be to drift rapidly into the £200,000 riverside private sector, either through individual house sales or nifty deals converting tower blocks into complexes of high-rise businessmen's pads.'

When Canary Wharf is completed and the rates 'holiday' finishes in 1992, Tower Hamlets could be the richest borough in London in terms of income, but with its present overwhelmingly working-class population being rapidly undermined and impoverished by the move-ment of capital into the area, the borough is likely to need every penny it collects in rates. A recent leader of Tower Hamlets council explained that during and after the development of Docklands 'East-Enders will do what they have always done'—serve the City. How-ever, it is unlikely that too many will be providing a service from a prestige riverside residence, for the name of the game is and will be 'profit' and the only way to make money out of council houses is to sell them. 'If Canary Wharf goes ahead and creates a kind of Hong Kong Central on London's river there will be no periphery of decaying council housing. All of it will be sold. In the eye of history, the departure of the welfare state from London's docklands will appear to have taken place directly after the abandonment of the docks' (Pawley 1986, p. 14).

In Newham, the development of Docklands has taken an altogether low-rent, down-market turn. The huge area of the Royal Docks is at the time of writing virtually deserted. The plush execu-tive-style developments further west have not replicated themselves in Canning Town, North Woolwich, or Silvertown, and this until recently heavily industrialized area is a virtual wasteland. Transport and education provision is appalling in this area, huge factories and food-processing plants are left to crumble, and the general feeling of isolation in a borough with 107 tower blocks is exacerbated daily as individuals try to come to terms with urban desolation on a grand scale. As the population of South Newham shrinks, so owner-occupiers have colonized what was known until recently as 'Beckton Marshes', an enormous conglomerate of private development. Yet despite having property values considerably lower than any other part of Dockland, few locals have taken advantage of the 'varied designs, excellent quality, interesting courtyards, attractive land-scaping' (LDDC 1985). Perhaps Billy, a 35-year-old lorry-driver's recollections of Beckton are rather more conservative: 'When I was a kid you never ever went to Beckton. There's no buses, nothing there. The only time I went was to play football on the marsh by the dumps, but it was always flooded. You'd have matches till Christmas, then a stray dog would have a piss in the goal mouth and it was waterlogged till Easter.'

Whether it is the indigenous population's concern with the water-level or with house prices, few East-Enders are settling in Beckton. In a recent survey 265 households were interviewed, and only 17 per cent of heads of households moving into new private homes in Newham had been on council waiting-lists. Seventy per cent were white-collar workers. 'In other words these households were typically young marrieds, first-time buyers . . . The typical jobs included junior professional/clerical style white-collar jobs' (GLC 1985b).

The long-term ripple effect of this new settlement of lower-middle-class households in Newham takes two forms. First, the entire area—the largest of the East End boroughs with a population of over 212,000—experienced rises in house prices of approximately 104 per cent between 1983 and 1987. Second, this new housing, which provides accommodation predominantly for individuals working in the West End and the City has created an informal new political constituency. For as the 'natives' move out of south West Ham away from Silvertown or Canning Town they take with them their traditional political allegiances, and as a consequence the Labour vote deteriorates and the Conservative vote steadily climbs as each new phase of private housing is released. Analysis of the June 1987 general election voting figures shows that Newham South took a massive swing away from Labour, and that over the last two elections the Labour vote has disintegrated from 19,600 to under 13,000. This is the constituency that gave Britain its first Labour Member of Parliament.

The East End—Inner City on Ice

What the City of London wants it takes, and in the 1980s it wants more space. Deregulation of the City has led to a vast growth in its function as a primary financial centre, and East London is being used to provide land, some spectacular views of the river, and a vast pool of largely unskilled manual labour to build and service the City's new annexe. The East End, as I have stressed throughout this book, has always had a rather peculiar relationship with capitalism, but now central government is exploiting that relationship to the full, and by direct intervention in municipal government and the manipulation of crucial funding by way of fantastic levels of subsidy to private enterprise, the East End is now being used as a flagship for a 'new' Great Britain Ltd.

The fact of the inner city in the 1980s, the facts of unemployment, poor housing, inadequate education, poor health, etc. are not unique to East London. What is unique is that the government has scrapped many of the central functions of democratically accountable local government, thereby actively encouraging the development of a specific economic base and a concomitant community. By making part of the inner city safe and profitable for the middle-class to live and work in does nothing but add to the staggering load that is placed upon the vast majority of the area's inhabitants. Once market forces have gained momentum there is little to stop them. The simplistic message of Docklands will undoubtedly prove to be addictive to those that dabble in the most dangerous of addictive substances, greed: 'Why don't we do it in all the old industrial areas of this country? Why don't we rebuild provincial Britain? We know how to do it; it's a question of just making your mind up to get on with it' (Michael Heseltine MP, ex-Minister for the Environment 1979–83).

Abandon democracy, artificially raise land-values, attract property speculators, and high-tech and low labour-intensive businesses, then the residents of the inner city will become invisible from the Stock Exchange, their scent will not carry to the Bank of England. The indigenous population of the inner city will be on ice, and if they can't program a computer, sell commodities, drive a taxi, clean floors, or generally lick the hand of the beast that keeps them in place they must be controlled, restrained if not by markets, then by more subtle means.

The CID and Detecting Change

It is perilously simplistic to construct models of cultures that do not take into account possible variations in action that subsequently undermine the structural connotations of the overall argument. These variations may in the case of the working-class be familial, residential, or occupational and, as I have argued, these variations will emanate from economic diversity. In the case of occupational culture, however, the key resource is the enacted environment, and as these environments will inevitably vary, diversities within seemingly homogeneous occupational groupings are inevitable. This is certainly the case in policing, where organizational, regional, and national diversification in addition to occupational specialization make the term 'occupational culture of the police' problematic. A rural beat-officer in Devon, an urban patrol officer in Chicago, and a detective in London's East End will certainly have some functions in common.

Most notably they will all be charged with order maintenance, even though the form of this order and the cultural and legislative foundation upon which it is based will not necessarily be identical. Certainly any attempt to identify and tease out 'core characteristics' (Reiner 1985, pp. 87–103) will become problematic for as Fielding (forthcoming) has noted: 'Police are not disembodied and culture free, but are more or less imbued with values and norms evident in their milieux'.

Authority would appear to be a common characteristic apparent in all police agencies, yet the plethora of options available to the police in wielding this authority may hamper further attempts to lump together disparate forms of social control, unless the task is to locate and dissect one of the more manifest of variables that is distilled through the occupational culture. The circumstances of police work provide the key to understanding the informal practices and style that constitute subcultural adaptation.

In Chapter 9 I indicated that much CID activity, despite the utility of East End stylistic conventions as a policing device, is reliant upon the criminal law, albeit in the overall context of the market-place. As I have stressed in the previous section, the future of the East End is one of *déjà vu* rather than progress, peripheral changes hardly warranting a shift in the long-standing central cultural props of East End life. Likewise for the CID the market-place is constant, the policed environment in essence has not been subjected to radical change. Nor has the organization of the CID, but what has altered is the law, the legislative parameter of a 'good result'. Yet, as I will briefly argue, these changes have served to widen the existing rifts between the uniform branch and the CID, and to deskill detectives in a manner that draws further parallels with the East End.

The Police and Criminal Evidence Act of 1984 (PACE), according to many provincial policemen, is a punishment for the 'sins of the Met', 'i.e. that the Act had only become necessary because of behaviour in the MPD that did not occur in county forces' (Maguire 1988). By focusing upon these aspects of the Act that seek radically to alter detention and questioning procedures (Parts IV and V) changes in key aspects of police methodology can be observed to have taken place despite the prevailing occupational culture. Amongst other issues the Act has sought to regulate procedures for the detention and interviewing of prisoners, and has created the Custody Sergeant to supervise these procedures.

A major consequence of this legislation has been that detectives, if they seek contact with a prisoner, must first negotiate a member of the uniform branch who has sole responsibility for the well-being of the prisoner in accordance with the Codes of Practice.

It used to be so easy we took it for granted. Someone would get pulled, and you could have a little chat. No don't laugh, it would be a chat, because you just want to know what's going on. Is he pissed, pissed off, chatty, a shithead or what? But now red tape's in the way, I've got to get round some wooden-top. He might be a good bloke, a mate, probably been in the department, but make him a Custody Sergeant and he has to record everything. So no little chats (Detective Sergeant).

The 'little chat', or as described by Irving (1980) 'first reconnais-sance', has taken on, according to the Codes of Practice, the status of an interview, i.e. any face-to-face contact between the suspect and the investigating officer (McKenzie and Irving 1987).

Unless he can find a compliant custody officer the detective must abandon informal negotiatory technique, any contact must be logged, and more importantly any interview must be recorded verbatim in the form of contemporaneous notes. This has led to a deskilling of detective work in that the investigator or his 'scribe' must con-centrate on the physical task of writing, resulting in a stilted, frag-mented conversation that negates the flow that is typical of regular verbal exchanges. Interrogation becomes a mechanical task and 'the skill (or art) of interrogation has . . . disappeared under the unaccus-tomed burden of contemporaneous note-taking' (McKenzie and Irving 1987, p. 8). Further, 'arrest totals and detection rates have fallen generally since the implementation of PACE' (Maguire 1988).

Detectives have not only been deskilled but to an extent emascu-lated by PACE. As the rules governing detention have become more rigid, 'fishing expeditions'—detaining for interview individuals in the hope of obtaining information—are less regular outings. As Maguire (1988) explains,

If in the past, a uniformed officer saw a known burglar acting in a mildly suspicious manner, he was likely to take him to the station, giving the CID a pretext for a long interview about his and others' recent movements. Now, however, there might not be sufficient evidence of an offence for detention to be authorised by the custody officer. And even if there was, the person would have to be charged, giving little leeway for the kind of interview they want.

Consequently offences taken into consideration are likely to wane while 'prison write-offs' resulting from interviews with convicted prisoners are likely to increase (Burrows 1986).

The net effect of PACE, certainly regarding detectives, is (a) to confirm the rift between the CID and uniform branch by giving crucial gate-keeping powers to the latter; (b) to deskill the detective by introducing the unwieldy practice of contemporaneous notes, and formalizing interview procedures; and (c) considerably to stifle the flow of information available to detectives by tightening the criteria for the detention of prisoners.

Consequently the emphasis of detective work is focused yet further away from the police station, uniform branch, supervision, and the formal conventions of due process. The view firmly held by many CID officers that their 'real' work is somewhere 'out there', 'on the street', or 'in the pub' is confirmed. Informal methodologies carried out away from the police station become almost reified; the 'challenge to the CID . . . to develop other investigation strategies outside the interview room' (Maguire 1988) is met by the reinforcement of time-served strategies of autonomous action emphasizing entrepreneurship as an appropriate policing device for the foreseeable future.

Conclusion

The economy and the subsequent cultural responses that the local economy in particular generates are the key variables in comprehending both working-class culture and subsequent attempts to control it. However, working-class culture itself is a very specific response to a particular composite of economic variables, and as a consequence regional variations will abound. Recognizing these variations serves to enhance the inherent richness and depth of working-class culture. For it is as patronizing to present working-class life in simplistic blanket terms, or in 'terms of a discrete sociological variable' (Clarke et al. 1979, p. 14), as it is naïve to present policing as a homogeneous activity carried out by individuals who are immune to both the ambiguities of the organizational structure and to the contradictions inherent in the policed environment.

Strategies that work are unlikely to be discarded, and recent changes in East London's economy have served to confirm entrepreneurship as an enduring strategic device. Likewise for the CID, changes in the law and subsequent organizational and occupational responses have reaffirmed entrepreneurship and underlined the importance of the East End as a cultural touchstone for detective work. There will, of course, be regular moral panics when someone oversteps the mark, or simply commits the cardinal sin of getting caught, e.g. 'Detective Accused of Bribes Scandal' (*Newham Recorder*, 18 June 1987). But the dealing will continue, and for the most part the level of dealing will remain low, often non-criminal; the enduring attraction of entrepreneurship to both East End culture and CID occupational culture lies in its essential utility as a problem-solving device. While market forces continue to create problems that are mere variations on the constraints imposed upon successive generations of East-Enders, entrepreneurship will remain a relevant strategy. Until it is proved to be redundant 'Doing the Business' is likely to continue as a sound investment for the future.

At 4 p.m. on a hot, sticky Saturday afternoon the pub should have closed an hour ago, but there are about fifteen men, women, and children gathered in the saloon bar chatting, watching horse-racing on television, and drinking champagne. A young woman proudly announces that her small child has just taken her first steps and the baby girl obliges with an encore among the cigarette-ends to the general approval of the semi-inebriated clientele.

It is just ten days since a general election, and a government with the redevelopment of the inner cities at the vanguard of its electoral campaign has been re-elected. I am spending the afternoon celebrating the good fortune and business acumen of Geoff who yesterday completed the sale of a consignment of stolen goods at a profit of over £6,000.

We toast Geoff for the umpteenth time as he apologizes that 'this shit's not your Moët, or your Lanson for that matter, is it? I mean it's not the same. I mean I miss the dryness. I do like a drop of Moët.'

He had debts of just under £3,000 and his windfall will be invested in a second-hand truck.

As the pub opens at 5 p.m. we spill out on to the pavement leaving behind two men sitting next to the juke-box in their underpants and socks singing 'Viva España', while a young woman drains her glass and picks a baby's dummy up from the floor. Outside in the street the concrete radiates the day's oppressive heat and a storm is brewing; Geoff remarks that rain would clear the air, and smugly drives away in an old pick-up truck towards Poplar.

Appendix: Nostalgia Rules— Hokey Cokey?

Thing is there's nothing for the young. People come here to die.
But as long as you got your health what good's money?

The taxi-driver at Clacton station seemed to encapsulate the town's confused state. As a resort Clacton does not have too much to offer: Butlin's has closed, there's a pier, amusements, a pebbly beach, the North Sea, and Don Maclean in *Summer Showtime*. But what it has got are caravans, thousands of them. Regimented avenues of sheet-metal punctuated with toilet blocks and chip shops.

I am met at the entrance of 'Valley Farm' by 12-year-old Jason and an all-pervading stench of stale fat that emanates from the chip shop and hangs over the site like cordite over a battlefield. Jason guides me to the section of the camp set aside for touring caravans, and this is where the caravans of Bob and his mother-in-law, Lil, rest neatly side by side. Both caravans are kept on a farm in Essex for fifty weeks of the year, their sole function being the forty-mile trek to Clacton for the last two weeks of August.

The site is clean and tidy, yet cramped. The numerous flower-beds and neatly manicured lawns serving to heighten the Lilliputian impression of a man-made universe in miniature. Inside, the caravan is immaculate and just like home, only the Constable print, flock wallpaper, and reproduction telephone on an onyx base are missing.

Bob and his family, like most of the site's residents, are East-Enders. A skilled building-worker Bob supplements his wage by installing kitchen extensions for grateful neighbours. The site is full of families like Bob's—Mum, Dad, two kids, granny, and a five-year-old Cortina. Mum and Gran are well permed, whilst Dad and the kids are embossed with the motifs of expensive-designer casual wear. This is an affluent working-class community. Many have escaped the East End for a semi in the buffer zones of Redbridge and Havering, where they reside in a state of cultural siege, wedged as they are between the 'Pooters' and those Jews whose grandparents escaped from the Pale of Settlement via Stepney a century ago.

Terry is an ex-docker who used his severance payment to set up as a jobbing builder. A couple of nights ago he entertained fellow campers with an impromptu belly-dance in the early hours.

Terry. Me, I don't drink, not with this fucking headache.... Who needs to go abroad with weather like this?

Caravan doors are left open and kids play in and out of the toilet-block as neighbours invite one another over to share their patio furniture and drink canned lager of uncertain national origin.

Terry. We used to go hopping as a kid. Tin hut, everything in the hopping pot. It was like when we was evacuated, never give a fuck. All that fresh air and a sing-song.

On the beach we sit staring towards Belgium, while behind us the occupants of 'Edelweiss', the beach chalet with the four horseshoes over the door, brew tea, filling the air with paraffin fumes. Graham, a 33-year-old lorry-driver, has spent his last ten holidays in a caravan at Clacton.

Graham. Everybody's so friendly, no aggro. It's the way things used to be before the niggers moved in.

Indeed this is white man's territory, only among the parties from children's homes are black faces discernible. 'Its true,' insists Bob basking in the sun, 'people down here are great; it's like they get away from home and they're different people. No Pakis or nothing. It's great.'

Meanwhile, while swimming Jason has found an enema-kit floating ominously amongst seaweed.

At 4 o'clock we leave the beach and return to the camp as Lil has to change her clothes and queue for the early evening bingo session. After fish and chips bought from the shop next to the Roaring Donkey pub, we prepare ourselves for the evening. My hosts go to the camp club every night, arriving as bingo finishes around 7 o'clock. You have to get there early as competition for seats is fierce. Making our way to the club, it becomes apparent just how much of a 'home from home' the camp is. This is particularly true of the section reserved for static vans, where many retired couples and mothers with children spend the entire summer. One man has brought his lawn-mower on holiday, and is busy reducing the parched grass to a urine-coloured stubble, while his wife applies a watering-can to their rose-bushes.

We join a queue of about fifty people outside the club eagerly awaiting the bingo session to end, and as we funnel through the doors we enter a vast, cavernous structure about ten years old. Once through the huge foyer we are in an aircraft hangar of a dance-hall-cum-bingo parlour, six-seater bench-seats of municipal uniformity facing each other in rows of fifty, and there are three rows on either side of a huge dance-floor with a small stage at the far end. The periphery of the club is studded with kiosks and adjacent attractions; the 'kiddies' disco', amusement arcades, a burger bar, and a sweet-shop. We claimed seats next to Lil who missed the jackpot by two numbers.

On our way to the bar Bob repeats his belief in the friendliness of our fellow inmates, a belief that hardly coincides with the scenes that unfold around me, scenes that closely resemble shots from a film of third-class passengers aboard the *Titanic* as frightened and confused immigrants scramble for space on too few lifeboats. People are pushing and shoving, herding kids called Debbie and Wayne from one congested bench-seat to another. Jackets and cardigans are strategically placed in an effort to reserve seats for those unwisely arriving a full 15 minutes after opening time. Kids are crying and parents braying as one bearded man sits in his stockinged feet, his shoes placed provocatively on the seat opposite.

Three deep at the bar, Bob continues to extol the virtues of the place: 'People are so friendly here Dick, you can't help but enjoy yourself.' The beer is cheap, one sip and I know why—the Roaring Donkey has pissed in it. On the journey back to our seats some 50 yards away, I cannot help but notice how uniformly miserable the gathered throng appear. By now the place is packed, all seats are taken, and the aisles are ruled by sprinting kids in jog-suits. There is a general air of resolute boredom as Bob, whose optimism is un-wavering, bobs around in a valiant attempt to resist the mood of pervading doom.

Someone is tuning a snare-drum on stage, and a young man in an adjacent seat slaps his young son, evidently too gently for his wife who snatches the child from the tattooed arms of her husband to deliver a rasping forearm smash to the side of the boy's head. The wailing child breaks free from the grasp of his attacker, takes two strides on to the dance-floor, and faces his parents in a pugilistic stance, the damp patch on his groin spreading wider and darker.

Soon the resident band takes the stage to a groan of recognition from the audience. Dressed in red shirts and black polyester flares, the lead singer is a fat, fiftyish man sporting a Bobby Charlton hairstyle. He is also our compère and, so rumour has it, the camp's Entertainment Manager. Sarah, a demure young woman in a black trouser-suit, is the featured singer and the ageing quartet launch into 'Country Roads'. The bass player, toupee perilously askew, thumb plucks while the organist produces vast surging chords that roll like waves over the admirable Sarah who smiles and gestures into the middle distance, oblivious to both the enveloping din and to the two small girls who are sitting at her feet playing with her high-heeled sandals.

The 'grande finale' of the weekly talent contest is scheduled to begin at 9.30, but meanwhile the drummer who bears a striking resemblance to our compère, is introduced as 'Uncle Lenny' who will 'look after the little ones'. Spurred on by the florid Uncle Lenny, children stream on to the dance-floor and the musicians lurch into an over-long medley of the very worst of 1960s' pop. The deafening roar of the band's renditions of 'Lily the Pink', 'Simon Says', and 'March of the Mods' brings forth little girls of seven or eight dressed in fashion that had bypassed their mothers, while crop-haired boys with ear-rings goose stepped across the floor in grey jogging-suits. Periodically grandparents in acrylic cardigans are cajoled into joining the kids for a brief, condescending gyration before returning stony-faced to their tables. A quick rock-and-roll medley and an eight-year-old skinhead dominates the floor with an impromptu Kung Fu exhibition, while all around skirmishes break out as parents attempt to round up defiantly laughing children for a return to the caravan. Two-year-old Darren is hauled from the dance-floor for mugging a fellow infant hoofer. 'Come on kids,' says Uncle Lenny, 'dance like tin soldiers', and the high-stepping skinheads gleefully oblige.

Kiddie time over, Sarah sings a ballad from *Cats* oblivious to the mayhem surrounding her. She is concentrating upon a vision of fame and glamour far from Ron's roaring organ—Yarmouth perhaps? The very young kids have been driven out, and preparations are being made for the talent contest. Briefly a DJ takes over, and for the first time adults outnumber the kids on the dance-floor. All the females in our group dance in a tight circle around their handbags, à la Ilford Palais *circa* 1967.

Barry, a 20-year-old semi-pro musician from Dagenham, sits scribbling lyrics on a beer mat in preparation for the talent contest in which there are seven contestants, several of them identified as regulars recognized from previous years. The first is a man in his sixties, who, minus his top set of dentures, shambles on to stage in sandals, woolly socks, nylon shirt, and an ancient baggy brown cardigan with an 'Old Holborn' tin protruding from a sagging pocket. The previous week he had failed to win his heat and came to blows with members of the winner's family. Tonight, as before, he sings 'Underneath the Arches' in a sad mimicry of Bud Flanagan, to an abruptly respectful audience. A smattering of polite applause, and next is a woman in her mid-forties who looks like a gypsy in her black dress and flat shoes, hair unfashionably long, reminding me of a peasant woman from southern Europe. But this is Clacton, and when the band made a false start she glared at them disapprovingly before losing herself in a tale of bars and juke-boxes.

After a quick word with Uncle Lenny, Barry makes his way almost apologetically to the vacated organ and gives an impressive rendition of an old white soul classic. Next comes Sue, a short, bespectacled woman of around 50 with 'San Francisco', and a neatly dressed man of indeterminate years who sings in a deep baritone a version of 'Edelweiss' that, thanks to the singer's microphone technique, forces a draw with the roaring organ.

Fist clenched and torso contorted a young woman in her early twenties gives us 'One Day at a Time Sweet Jesus', ignoring the maverick Darren who is weaving across the dance-floor in search of the victim of his earlier assault. The final contestant brings groans from Barry who recognizes her from the club circuit. An attractive, heavily made-up woman in her early twenties, she stormed into 'Fame' winning a huge ovation from an almost animated audience.

The three judges, all volunteers from the audience, deliberated for no more than a couple of minutes before handing the result to our compère. A roll on the drums, third an embarrassed 'Fame', second 'Edelweiss', and our white soul casual from Dagenham is the winner. His booty is ceremoniously presented by the lovely Sarah. Back at the table the contents of the plastic bag are disgorged: two £2.50 vouchers for the camp shop, a sugar-shaker, and three butterflies mounted on hessian.

The docks are empty and the small workshops have been decimated. The East End's inheritance of casual labour and entrepreneurial style was forged of necessity and transmitted orally to successive generations, manifesting itself in a series of core cultural concerns that can appear redundant in the isolation of tower blocks and dole queues of Stepney, Bethnal Green, Poplar, and Canning Town. For these core concerns have their origins in the East End of the 1920s and 1930s and feature a particular image of solidarity as a pivotal characteristic; an image that like a Max Miller joke, or music-hall song, is orally transmitted and adapted to the requirements of the 1980s.

Holidays like those I have briefly described above are crucial in the confirmation and reinforcement of a culture constantly besieged by bourgeois society and market trends. At 'Valley Farm' we return to a golden age of ever-open doors, conversation, and street-life; of Chas and Dave and sing-songs, a place that is safe and predictable, basic yet compatible with the way we were before avocado bathroom suites, Lord Devlin, and containerization.

The family unit is confirmed at 'Valley Farm' when Joyce cooks a Sunday Lunch for fourteen in a four-berth caravan. The family eat in shifts and she finishes washing up at 5 p.m. too tired to eat.

Leaving the club to the strains of the Hokey Cokey, my impression is that of a cultural concentration camp or cockney theme-park. However, the inmates will all return to the hazards and contradictions of life in the working-class city, refreshed by a fortnight of solid reassurance that despite the car, house, and designer T-shirts, blood is thicker than Piña Colada.

Bibliography

Abrahamsson, B. (1971), 'Military Professionalism and Political Power' (Thesis) Stockholm.

Alderson, J. (1979), *Policing Freedom*, Plymouth: Macdonald & Evans.

―― and Stead, P. J. (eds.) (1973), *The Police We Deserve*, London: Wolfe.

Alin, J. and Wesker, A. (1974), *Say Goodbye: You May Never See them Again*, London: Cape.

Allason, R. (1983), *The Branch: A History of the Metropolitan Police Special Branch 1883–1983*, London: Secker & Warburg.

Andreski, S. (1961), 'Conservatism and Radicalism of the Military', *European Journal of Sociology* 2, pp. 63–51.

Anon. (1912), 'Sport and Decadence', in *Whitehouse* (1912).

Armitage, G. (1937), *The History of the Bow Street Runner 1729–1829*, London: Wishart.

Arnold, M. (1960), *Culture and Anarchy* (1889), ed. Dover Wilson, Cambridge: Cambridge University Press.

Ascoli, D. (1979), *The Queen's Peace*, London: Hamilton.

Atyeo, D. (1979), *Blood and Guts: Violence in Sport*, London: Paddington Press.

Bailey, D. M. (1981), *Children of the Green*, London: Stepney Books.

Baldwin, J. and Bottomley, A. K. (eds.) (1978), *Criminal Justice*, London: Martin Robertson.

―― and Bottoms, A. E. (1976), *The Urban Criminal*, London: Tavistock.

―― and McConville, M. (1977), *Negotiated Justice*, London: Martin Robertson.

―― and ―― (1978), 'The Influence of Sentencing Discount on Inducing Guilty Pleas', in Baldwin and Bottomley (1978), p. 116.

Baldwin, R. and Kinsey, R. (1982), *Police Powers and Politics*, London: Quartet.

Ball, J., Chester, L., and Perrott, R. (1978), *Cops and Robbers*, London: André Deutsch.

Banton, M. (1964), *The Policeman in the Community*, London: Tavistock.

Barnardo, S. and Merchant, J. (1907), *Memoirs of Dr. Barnardo*, London: Hodder & Stoughton.

Barnett, H. (1918), *Canon S. A. Barnett*, Vol. 1, Brighton: Robertson.

Becker, H. S. (1963), *Outsiders*, New York, NY: Free Press.

―― (ed.). (1964a), *The Other Side*, New York, NY: Free Press.

―― (1964b), 'Personal Changes in Adult Life', *Sociometry*, 27(1), pp. 40–53.

―― (1971), *Sociological Work*, London: Allen Lane.

Belson, W. (1975), *The Public and the Police*, London: Harper.

Bennet, R. (1977), 'The Conservative Tradition of Thought', in Nugent and

236   Bibliography

King (eds.), (1977).

Bennet, R., King, R., and Nugent, N. (1977), 'The Concept of the Right', in Nugent and King (eds.) (1977).

Berger, L. and Luckmann, T. (1967), *The Social Construction of Reality*, London: Allen Lane.

Bermant, C. (1975), *Point of Arrival*, London: Eyre Methuen.

Besant, W. (1901), *East London*, London: Chatto & Windus.

Beynon, J. (1983), 'Ways in and Staying in: Fieldwork as Problem Solving', in M. Hammersley (ed.), *The Ethnography of Schooling: Methodological Issues*, Driffield: Nafferton.

Biggs, R. (1981), *His Own Story*, London: Sphere.

Birch, J. G. (1930), *Limehouse through Five Centuries*, London: Sheldon Press.

Bittner, E. (1965), 'The Concept of Organisation', *Social Research*, 32, pp. 230–55.

—— (1967), 'The Police on Skid Row: A Study of Peace Keeping', *American Sociological Review*, 32, pp. 699–715.

Black, M. (1954), 'Metaphor', *Aristotelian Society Proceedings*, pp. 284–5.

Bloomberg, J. (1979), *Looking Back—A Docker's Life*, London: Stepney Books.

Blumer, H. (1969), *Symbolic Interactionism: Perspective and Method*, Englewood Cliffs, NJ: Prentice-Hall.

Board of Trade (1894), *Reports on the Volume and Effects of Recent Immigration from Eastern Europe into the United Kingdom*, London: HMSO.

Booth, C. (1889), *Labour and Life of the People*, London: Williams & Norgate.

—— (1902), *Life and Labour of the People*, London: Macmillan.

Booth, W. (1890), *In Darkest England and the Way Out*, London: Salvation Army.

Bordua, D. (1967), *The Police: Six Sociological Essays*, New York, NY: Wiley.

Bottomley, A. K. (1978), 'Bail and the Judicial Process', in Baldwin and Bottomley (1978).

—— (1979), *Criminology in Focus*, London: Martin Robertson.

Bottomore, T. and Rubel, M. (eds.) (1963), *Karl Marx: Selected Writings in Sociology and Social Philosophy*, Harmondsworth: Pelican.

Bottoms, A. E. and McClean, J. D. (1976), *Defendants in the Criminal Process*, London: Routledge & Kegan Paul.

—— and —— (1978), 'Bail Bargaining and Plea Bargaining', in Baldwin and Bottomley (1978), p. 82.

Box, S. (1981), *Deviance, Reality and Society* (2nd edn.), London: Holt, Rhinehart & Winston.

—— (1983), *Power, Crime and Mystification*, London: Tavistock.

Boyle, J. (1977), *A Sense of Freedom*, London: Pan.

Brake, M. (1980), *The Sociology of Youth Culture and Youth Subcultures*, London: Routledge & Kegan Paul.

British Journal of Sociology (1976), Special History and Sociology Issue 27(3), Sept.

Brodeur, J. P. (1983), 'High Policing and Low Policing: Remarks about the Policing of Political Activities', *Social Problems* 30(5), pp. 507–20.

Brogden, M. (1977), 'A Police Authority—the Denial of Conflict', *Sociological Review*, 25(2), May.

—— (1982), *The Police: Autonomy and Consent*, London: Academic Press.

—— (1987), 'The Emergence of the Police—The Colonial Dimension', *British Journal of Criminology*, 27(1), pp. 4–14.

Bruce, S. and Wallis, R. (1983), 'Rescuing Motives', *British Journal of Sociology*, 34(1), Mar.

Bulmer, M. (1980), 'Comment on "The Ethics of Covert Methods" ', *British Journal of Sociology*, 31(1), Mar.

Bunyan, T. (1977), *The Political Police in Britain*, London: Julian Friedmann.

Burgess, E. (1929), 'Basic Social Data in Chicago', in *An Experiment in Social Science Research*, ed. T. Smith and J. White. Chicago, Ill.: University of Chicago Press.

Burgess, R. G. (1984), *In the Field: An Introduction to Field Research*, London: Allen & Unwin.

Burke, E. (1906), *The Works of Burke*, Vol. 5. London: Oxford University Press.

—— (1968), *Reflections on the Revolution in France* (1790), London: Penguin.

Burke, K. (1950), *A Rhetoric of Motives*, Englewood Cliffs, NJ: Prentice-Hall.

Burrows, J. (1986), *Burglary: Police Actions and Victims' Views, Research and Planning Paper*, 37, London: Home Office.

—— and Tarling, R. (1982), *Clearing up Crime*, London: Home Office.

Buscombe, E. (1976), 'The Sweeney—Better than Nothing?' in *Screen Education*, 20.

Bush, J. (1984), *Behind the Lines: East London Labour 1914–1919*, London: Merlin.

Cain, M. (1973), *Society and the Policeman's Role*, London: Routledge & Kegan Paul.

—— (1979), 'Trends in the Sociology of Police Work', *International Journal of the Sociology of Law*, 7(2).

Campbell, D. (1979), 'Society under Surveillance', in Hain (ed.) (1979).

Camps, F. and Barber, R. (1966), *The Investigation of Murder*, London: Joseph.

Carlen, P. (1976), *Magistrates' Justice*, London: Martin Robinson.

—— and Collison, M. (eds.) (1980), *Radical Issues in Criminology*, London: Routledge & Kegan Paul.

Carr-Saunders, A. and Wilson, P. A. (1933), *The Professions*, Oxford: Oxford University Press.

Carson, W. G. (1971), 'White Collar Crime and the Enforcement of Factory Legislation', in Carson & Wiles (eds.) (1971).

—— and Wiles, P. (1971), *The Sociology of Crime and Delinquency in Britain*, Vol. 1, London: Martin Robinson.

Casper, J. D. (1972), *American Criminal Justice: The Defendants' Perspective*, Englewood Cliffs, NJ: Prentice-Hall.

Chadwick, E. (1842), *Report on an Inquiry into the Sanitary Conditions of the Labouring Population of Great Britain.*

Chambliss, W. J. (1971), 'A Sociological Analysis of the Law of Vagrancy', in Carson and Wiles (1971).

Chatterton, M. (1983), 'Police Work and Assault Charges', in M. Punch (ed.), *Control in the Police Organisation,* Cambridge, Mass.: MIT Press.

—— (forthcoming), 'Mouldy Files, Red Pen Entries and Paper that Bounces: Issues in the Supervision of Paperwork,' Paper given at Harrogate Conference on Policing Research, 1985.

Chesney, K. (1968), *The Victorian Underworld,* Harmondsworth: Penguin.

Chibnall, S. (1977), *Law and Order News,* London: Tavistock.

—— and Saunders, P. (1977), 'Worlds Apart: Notes on the Social Reality of Corruption', *British Journal of Sociology,* 28(2), June.

Clarke, J. (1976), in Hall and Jefferson (1976).

——, Critcher, C., and Johnson, R. (1979), *Working Class Culture: Studies in History and Theory,* London: Hutchinson.

Clarke, R. V. G. and Hough, J. M. (eds.) (1980), *The Effectiveness of Policing,* Aldershot: Gower.

—— and —— (1984), *Crime and Police Effectiveness,* London: HMSO.

—— and Mayhew, P. (eds.) (1980), 'Designing out Crime', London: Home Office Research Unit.

Clarke, S. (1977), 'Levi-Strauss's Structural Analysis of Myth', *Sociological Review,* 25(4), Nov.

Clarkson, C. T. and Hall-Richardson, J. (1889), *Police,* London: Leadenhall Press.

Clinard, M. and Quinney, R. (1967), *Criminal Behaviour Systems,* New York: Holt, Rhinehart & Winston.

Cloward, R. and Ohlin, L. (1960), *Delinquency and Opportunity,* New York, NY: Free Press.

Cohen, A. K. (1955), *Delinquent Boys,* Chicago, Ill.: Chicago Free Press.

Cohen, P. (1972), 'Sub-Cultural Conflict and Working Class Community', Working Papers in Cultural Studies No. 2, Birmingham: Centre for Contemporary Cultural Studies, University of Birmingham.

—— (1979), 'Policing the Working Class City', in B. Fine *et al.* (eds.), *Capitalism and the Rule of Law,* London: Hutchinson, pp. 118–36.

Cohen, S. (ed.) (1971), *Images of Deviance,* London: Penguin.

—— (1980), *Folk Devils and Moral Panics* (2nd edn.), London: Constable.

—— and Scull, A. (eds.) (1983), *Social Control and the State,* Oxford: Blackwell.

—— and Taylor, L. (1972), *Psychological Survival,* London: Penguin.

—— and —— (1976), *Escape Attempts,* London: Allen Lane, Penguin Books.

Colman, A. and Gorman, P. (1982), 'Conservatism, Dogmatism and Authoritarianism in British Police Officers', *Sociology,* 16(1), Feb.

Colquhoun, P. (1979), *Treatise on the Police of the Metropolis,* London: Joseph Maurman.

Corrigan, P. (1979), *Schooling the Smash Street Kids*, London: Macmillan.

Cox, B., Shirley, J., and Short, M. (1977), *The Fall of Scotland Yard*, Harmondsworth: Penguin.

Cressey, D. R. (1962), 'Role Theory, Differential Association and Compulsive Crimes', in A. M. Rose (1962), pp. 443–67.

Critchley, T. (1978), *A History of Police in England and Wales 1900–1966*, London: Constable. (1st edn. 1967.)

Cruse, D. and Rubin, J. (1973), 'Police Behaviour': Pt 1, *Journal of Psychiatry and Law*, 1, 18–19.

Daley, R. (1978), *Prince of the City*, London: Granada.

Damer, S. (1976), *Wine Alley: The Sociology of a Dreadful Enclosure*, in Wiles (1976).

Daniel, S. and McGuire, P. (1972), *The Paint House*, London: Penguin.

Delgado, A. (1979), *The Enormous File: A Social History of the Office*, London: John Murray.

Denzin, N. K. (1970), *The Research Act in Sociology*, London: Butterworth.

—— (1974), 'The Methodological Implications of Symbolic Interactivism for the Study of Deviance', *British Journal of Sociology*, 25(3), Sept.

De Polnay, P. (1970), *Napoleon's Police*, London: W. H. Allen.

Devlin, Lord (1966), *Report of the Committee of Inquiry into the Wages Structure and Conditions of Pay for Dock Workers*, London: HMSO.

Dickens, C. (1986), 'On Duty with Inspector Field', in N. Philip and V. Neuburg, *Charles Dickens, a December Vision*, London: Collins, pp. 26–41.

Dickson, J. (1986), *Murder without Conviction*, London: Sidgwick and Jackson.

Dilnot, G. (1929), *Scotland Yard*, London: Geoffrey Bles.

Dingwall, R. (1980), 'Ethics and Ethnography', *Sociological Review*, 28(4), Nov.

Ditton, J. (1976), 'Moral Horror versus Folk Terror: Output Restriction, Class and the Social Organisation of Exploitation', *Sociological Review*, 24(3), Aug.

—— (1977), *Part-time Crime*, London: Macmillan.

Douglas, J. (1971), *Understanding Everyday Life*, London: Routledge & Kegan Paul.

—— (1976), *Investigative Social Research*, Beverly Hills, Calif.: Sage.

—— et al. (1977), *The Nude Beach*, Beverly Hills, Calif.: Sage.

Douglas, M. and Isherwood, B. (1978), *The World of Goods*, London: Allen Lane.

Downes, D. (1966), *The Delinquent Solution*, London: Routledge & Kegan Paul.

—— and Rock, P. (eds.) (1979), *Deviant Interpretations*, Oxford: Martin Robertson.

—— and —— (1982), *Understanding Deviance*, Oxford: Clarendon Press.

Durkheim, E. (1964), *The Rules of Sociological Method*, New York, NY: Free Press.

Dyos, H. J. and Wolff, M. (eds.) (1973), *The Victorian City*, Vol. 2, London: Routledge & Kegan Paul.

Eck, J. E. (1979), 'Managing Case Assignment: The Burglary Investigation Decision Model Replication', Washington DC: Police Executive Research Forum.

Eckstein, S. (1975), 'The Political Economy of Lower Class Areas in Mexico City: Societal Constraints on Local Business Opportunities', in W. Cornelius and F. Trueblood (eds.), *Latin American Urban Research*, 5, London: Sage.

Eco, U. (1972), 'Towards a Semiotic Enquiry into the Television Message', UPCS 3, Birmingham: University of Birmingham.

Edwards, P. K. and Scullion, H. (1982), 'Deviancy Theory and Industrial Praxis: a Study of Discipline and Social Control in an Industrial Setting, *Sociology*, 16(3), Aug.

Emsley, C. (1983), *Policing in its Context 1750–1870*, London: Macmillan.

Engels, F. (1969), 'The Condition of the Working Class in England', (eds.) W. O. Henderson and W. H. Chaloner, Oxford: Blackwell.

English, J. and Houghton, R. (1983), *Police Training Manual* (4th edn.), London: McGraw-Hill.

Erikson, K. (1966), *Wayward Puritans*, London: Wiley.

Erikson, R. (1981), *Making Crime*, Toronto: Butterworths.

Fielding, N. (1981), *The National Front*, London: Routledge & Kegan Paul.

—— (1984), 'Police Socialisation and Police Competence', *British Journal of Sociology*, 35(4), Dec.

—— (forthcoming), 'Competence and Culture in the Police', Paper given at Harrogate Conference on Policing Research, 1985.

Fishman, W. (1979), *The Streets of East London*, London: Duckworth.

Fitzgerald, M., McLennan, G., and Pawson, J. (eds.) (1981), *Crime & Society: Readings in History and Theory*, London: Routledge & Kegan Paul.

Fitzpatrick, P. and Blaxter, L. (1975), 'Colonialism and the Informal Sectors', *Australian & New Zealand Journal of Sociology*, 11(3), Oct., pp. 42–6.

Foote, N. (1951), 'Identification as the Basis for a Theory of Motivation', *American Sociological Review*, 16, pp. 14–22.

Foran, W. R. (1962), *The Kenya Police 1877–1960*, London: Robert Hale.

Foster, J. (1987), unpublished Ph.D thesis, London School of Economics.

Foucault, M. (1972), *The Archaeology of Knowledge*, trans. M. Sheridan-Smith, London: Tavistock.

Frankenberg, R. (1973), *Communities in Britain*, Harmondsworth: Penguin.

Franklin, C. (1970), *The Third Degree*, London: Robert Hale.

Gartner, L. P. (1960), *The Jewish Immigrant in England, 1870–1914*, London: Allen & Unwin.

Gaskell, P. (1833), *The Manufacturing Population of England*, London: Baldwin & Craddock.

Gatrell, V. A. C. (1980), 'The Decline of Theft and Violence in Victorian England', in Gatrell, B. Lenman, and G. Parker (eds.), *Crime and the*

Law, The Social History of Crime in Western Europe since 1500, London: Europa.

—— (1987), 'Crime Authority and the Policeman-State 1750–1950, in F. M. L. Thompson (ed.), *The Cambridge Social History of Britain 1750–1950*, Cambridge: Cambridge University Press.

Gavin, H. (1848), *Sanitary Ramblings*, London: Churchill.

Geertz, C. (1963), 'The Impact of the Concept of Culture on the Concept of Man', in J. R. Platt (ed.), *New Views of the Nature of Man*, Chicago, Ill.: University of Chicago Press.

Gerth, M. and Mills, C. W. (1954), *Character and Social Structure in the Psychology of Social Institutions*, London: Routledge & Kegan Paul.

Gibbens, T. and Ahrenfeldt, R. (eds.) (1966), *Cultural Factors in Delinquency*, London: Tavistock.

Gill, O. (1977), *Luke Street*, London: Macmillan.

Glaser, B. and Strauss, A. (1967), *The Discovery of Grounded Theory*, Chicago, Ill.: Aldine.

Glaser, D. (1962), 'The Differential-Association Theory of Crime', in Rose (1962).

Glass, R. (1955), 'Urban Sociology in Great Britain', A Trend Report, *Current Sociology*, 4(4).

GLC (1985a), 'The Docks—London Industrial Strategy', London: Greater London Council.

—— (1985b), 'The East London File', London: Greater London Council.

Glover, D. (1979), 'Sociology and the Thriller: The Case of Dashiell Hammett', *Sociological Review*, 27(1).

Goffman, E. (1969), *The Presentation of Self in Everyday Life*, London: Allen Lane.

—— (1971), *Relations in Public*, London: Allen Lane.

—— (1975a), 'On Face Work', in Lindsmith, Strauss and Denzin (eds.) (1975).

—— (1975b), *Frame Analysis*, Harmondsworth: Peregrine.

Gorer, G. (1955), *Exploring English Character*, London: Cresset.

Gosch, M. A. and Hammer, R. (1974), *The Last Testament of Lucky Luciano*, Toronto: Little, Brown & Co.

Gouldner, A. (1968), 'The Sociologist as Partisan', *American Sociologist*, 3 (May), pp. 103–16.

—— (1971), *The Coming Crisis of Western Sociology*, London: Heinemann.

Graves, R. and Hodge, A. (1971), *The Long Weekend*, Harmondsworth: Penguin.

Greenwood, J. (1874), *The Wilds of London*, London: Chatto & Windus.

Greenwood, P. W., Chaiken, J. M., and Petersilia, J. (1977), *The Criminal Investigation Process*, Lexington, Mass.: D. C. Heath & Co.

Gwynn, R. (1985), *Huguenot Heritage*, London: Routledge & Kegan Paul.

Hain, P. (ed.) (1979), *Policing the Police*, Vol. 1, London: Platform Books.

Hall, P. G. (1962), *The Industries of London since 1861*, London: Hutchinson.

Hall, S. (1980), *Drifting into a Law and Order Society*, London: Cobden Trust.

242   Bibliography

Hall, S. *et al.* (1978), *Policing the Crisis*, London: Macmillan.
—— and Jefferson, T. (eds.) (1976), *Resistance through Rituals*, London: Hutchinson.
Halstead, F. (1970), *GI's Speak Out against the War*, New York, NY: Merit.
Hammersley, M. and Atkinson, P. (1983), *Ethnography Principles in Practice*, London: Tavistock.
Harring, S. L. (1979), 'Class Conflict and the Suppression of Tramps in Buffalo, 1892–1894', in S. I. Messinger and E. Bittner (eds.), *Criminology Review Year Book*, Beverly Hills, Calif.: Sage.
—— (1983), *Policing a Class Society*, New Brunswick, NJ: Rutgers University Press.
Harris, R. N. (1973), *The Police Academy: An Inside View*, New York, NY: Wiley.
Harrison, M. (1971), *London Beneath the Pavement*, London: Peter Davies.
Harrison, P. (1983), *Inside the Inner City*, Harmondsworth: Penguin.
Hatt, P. K. and Reiss, A. J. (eds.) (1951), *Urban Sociology*, New York, NY: Free Press.
Hawkes, T. (1977), *Structuralism and Semiotics*, London: Methuen.
Hay, D. (1975), 'Property, Authority and the Criminal Law', in D. Hay, P. Linebaugh, and E. P. Thompson (eds.), *Albion's Fatal Tree: Crime and Society in Eighteenth Century England*, London: Allen Lane.
Hebdige, D. (1979), *Subculture: The Meaning of Style*, London: Methuen.
Henry, S. (1976), 'The Other Side of the Fence', *Sociological Review*, 24 (Nov.), 793–806.
—— (1978), *The Hidden Economy*, Oxford: Martin Robertson.
—— (ed.) (1981), *Can I Have It in Cash?* London: Astragel.
—— and Mars, G. (1978), 'Crime at Work', *Sociology*, 12(2).
Hill, O. (1883), *Homes of the London Poor*, London: Macmillan.
Hill, S. (1976), *The Dockers*, London: Heinemann.
Hirschi, T. (1969), *Causes of Delinquency*, Berkeley, Calif.: University of California Press.
Hiscock, E. (1976), *The Bells of Hell Go Ting-a-Ling-a-Ling*, London: Artlington Books.
Hobbs, D. (1984), 'Fathers and Sons: Delinquency and Cultural Inheritance', in *Criminal Justice* 2(3), pp. 5–7.
Hobsbawm, E. (1968), *Industry and Empire*, Harmondsworth: Penguin.
Hoggart, R. (1957), *The Uses of Literacy*, London: Chatto & Windus.
Hohimer, F. (1981), *Violent Streets*, London: Star.
Holdaway, S. (1977), 'Charges in Urban Policing', *British Journal of Sociology* 28(2), June.
—— (ed.) (1979), *The British Police*, London: Arnold.
—— (1983), *Inside the British Police—A Force at Work*, Oxford: Blackwell.
Hollingshead, J. (1861), *Ragged London in 1861*, London: Smith, Elder and Co.
Homan, R. (1980), 'The Ethics of Covert Methods', *British Journal of*

Sociology, 31(1), Mar.

Horowitz, R. (1983), *Honor and the American Dream,* New Brunswick, NJ: Rutgers University Press.

Hough, M. and Mayhew, P. (1983), *The British Crime Survey,* London: HMSO.

Howarth, E. G. and Wilson, M. (1907), *West Ham,* London: Dent.

Hughes, E. C. (1951), *Personality Types and the Division of Labour,* in Hatt and Reiss (eds.), (1951).

—— (1958), *Men and their Work,* New York, NY: Free Press.

—— (1963), 'Good People and Dirty Work', in Becker (1963).

Hugill, A. (1978), *Sugar and All That: A History of Tate & Lyle,* London: Gentry.

Humphries, S. and Taylor, J. (1986), *The Making of Modern London 1945–1985,* London: Sidgwick & Jackson.

Humphreys, L. (1975), *Tea-room Trade: Impersonal Sex in Public Places,* Chicago, Ill.: Aldine.

Humphry, D. (1972), *Police Power and Black People,* London: Panther.

Hurst, K. (1973), 'Informal Income Opportunities and Urban Employment in Ghana', *J. Modern African Studies,* 2, pp. 61, 89.

Husbands, C. T. (1982a), 'East End Racism 1900–1980', *London Journal,* 8(1).

—— (1982b), 'The London Borough Council Elections of 6th May 1982, Results and Analysis', *London Journal,* 8(2).

Hutt, C. (1976), *The Decline of the English Pub,* London: Arrow.

Idle, E. (1943), *War over West Ham,* London: Faber & Faber.

Inciardi, J. (1980), *Radical Criminology,* Berkeley, Calif.: Sage.

Irving, B. (1980), 'Police Interrogation: A Case Study of Current Practice', Royal Commission on Criminal Procedure, Research Study, No. 2, London: HMSO.

Irwin, J. (1970), *The Felon,* Englewood Cliffs, NJ: Prentice-Hall.

Jefferson, T. (1976), in Hall and Jefferson (1976).

—— (1987), 'Beyond Paramilitarism', *British Journal of Criminology,* 27(1), Jan.

Jeffries, C. (1952), *The Colonial Police,* London: Max Parrish.

Jones, D. (1982), *Crime, Protest, Community and Police in Nineteenth Century Britain,* London: Routledge & Kegan Paul.

Jones, J. and Winkler, J. (1982), 'Beyond the Beat: The Facts about Policing in a Riotous City', *Journal of Law and Society,* 9(1), pp. 103–14.

Jones, T., Maclean, B., and Young, J. (1986), *The Islington Crime Survey,* Aldershot: Gower.

Katz, J. (1975), 'Essences as Moral Identities', *American Journal of Sociology,* 80(6), May.

Kelling, G. *et al.* (1974), 'The Kansas City Preventative Patrol Experiment', Washington, DC: Police Foundation.

Kettle, M. (1979), in P. Hain (ed.) (1979), pp. 9–62.

—— and Hodges, L. (1982), *Uprising,* London: Pan.

Kinsey, R., Lea, J., and Young, J. (1986), *Losing the Fight against Crime,*

Oxford: Blackwell.

Kitson, F. (1971), *Low Intensity Operations: Subversion, Insurgency, Peace Keeping*, London: Faber & Faber.

Klockars, C. B. (1975), *The Professional Fence*, London: Tavistock.

—— (ed.) (1983), *Thinking About Police: Contemporary Readings*, New York, NY: McGraw-Hill.

Kops, B. (1969), *By the Waters of Whitechapel*, London: Bodley Head.

Knight, S. (1976), *Jack the Ripper, The Final Solution*, London: Harrap.

Kray, C. and Sykes, J. (1976), *Me and My Brothers*, London: Everest.

Laing, D. (1969), *The Sound of Our Time*, London: Sheed & Ward.

Landau, H. (1984), *The Justice of the Peace 1679–1760*, Berkeley, Calif.: University of California Press.

Laurie, P. (1970), *Scotland Yard*, Harmondsworth: Penguin.

LDDC (1985), *The Royal Docks: A Framework for Development*, London: London Docklands Development Corporation.

Lea, J. and Young, J. (1984), *What Is to be Done about Law and Order?* Harmondsworth: Penguin.

Lemert, E. (1976), *Human Deviance, Social Problems and Social Control*, New York, NY: Prentice-Hall.

Letkemann, P. (1973), *Crime as Work*, New York, NY: Prentice-Hall.

Leventhal, A. (1973), *War*, London: Hamlyn.

Levi, M. (1981), *The Phantom Capitalists*, London: Heinemann.

Liebow, E. (1967), *Tally's Corner*, London: Routledge & Kegan Paul.

Lindsmith, A., Strauss, A., and Denzin, N. (1975), *Readings in Social Psychology*, Chicago, Ill.: Dryden Press.

Lipset, S. M. (1961), *Political Man*, London: Heinemann.

Lloyd, D. (1963), 'Enclosing Docks Further Decasualisation Plan', Leaflet.

Lofland, J. (1976), *Doing Social Life: The Qualitative Study of Human Interaction in Natural Settlings*, New York, NY: Wiley.

London, J. (1903), *The People of the Abyss*, London: Isbister.

McBarnett, D. (1977), 'False Dichotomies in Criminal Justice Research', in Baldwin and Bottomley (1978).

McCabe, S. and Sutcliffe, F. (1978), *Defining Crime*, Oxford: Blackwell.

Macintosh, M. J. (1971), 'Changes in the Organisation of Thieving', in Cohen (1971).

McClure, J. (1980), *Spike Island, Portrait of a Police Division*, London: Macmillan.

McCormick, D. (1970), *The Identity of Jack the Ripper*, London: Arrow.

McGee, R. G. (1973), *Hawkers in Hong Kong*, Hong Kong: University of Hong Kong Press.

McKenzie, I. K. and Irving, B. (1987), 'Police Interrogation', *Policing*, 13(1), Spring.

McKenzie, R. (1927), 'The Concept of Dominance and World Organisation', *American Journal of Sociology*, 33.

McVicar, J. (1979), *McVicar by Himself*, London: Arrow.

—— (1982), *Time Out*, 610, 30 Apr.

—— (forthcoming), *The Rotten Orchard*.

Maguire, M. (1982), *Burglary in a Dwelling*, London: Heinemann.

—— (1988), 'Effects of the "PACE" provisions on Detention and Questioning: Some Preliminary Findings', *British Journal of Criminology*, 21(1), Jan.

Maher, V. and Terkel, S. (1983), 'Vincent Maher', in Klockars (1983).

Mahoney, M. (1983), 'Dressed to Kill', *Time Out*, 687, pp. 12–14.

Malinowski, B. (1948), *Magic, Science and Religion*, New York, NY: Free Press.

Manning, P. (1977), *Police Work*, Cambridge, Mass.: MIT.

—— (1979), 'The Social Control of Police Work', in Holdaway (1979).

—— (1980), *The Narc's Game*, Cambridge, Mass.: MIT.

—— (1982), 'Organisational Work', *British Journal of Sociology*, 33(1), Mar.

—— and Redlinger, J. (1977), 'Invitational Edges of Corruption', in Rock (1977).

—— and Van Maanen, J. (eds.) (1978), *Policing: a View from the Streets*, Santa Monica, Calif.: Goodyear.

Mark, R. (1977), *Policing a Perplexed Society*, London: Allen & Unwin.

—— (1978), *In the Office of Constable*, London: Collins.

Mars, G. (1974), *Dock Pilferage*, in Rock and Macintosh (1974).

Marx, G. T. (1983), 'The New Police Undercover Work', in Klockars (1983), p. 199.

Marx, K. (1963), in Bottomore and Rubel (1963).

Matthews, R. and Young, J. (eds.) (1986), *Confronting Crime*, London: Sage.

Matza, D. (1969), *Becoming Deviant*, Englewood Cliffs, NJ: Prentice-Hall.

—— and Sykes, G. (1961), 'Delinquency and Subterranean Values', *American Sociological Review*, 26(5).

Mawby, R. (1979), *Policing the City*, Farnborough: Saxon House.

Mayhew, H. (1861), *London Labour and the London Poor*, 4 vols, London: Dover, facsimile edn. 1968.

—— (1950), *London's Underworld*, P. Quennell (ed.), London: Spring Books.

—— (1951), *Mayhew's Characters*, P. Quennell (ed.), London: Spring Books.

Mayhew (1952), *Mayhews London*, P. Quennel (ed), London: Spring Books.

Mead, G. M. (1934), *Mind, Self and Society*, C. W. Morris (ed.), Chicago, Ill.: University of Chicago Press.

Mearns, A. (1883), *The Bitter Cry of Outcast London*, Victorian Library edn. 1970, Leicester:Leicester University.

Melly, G. (1972), *Revolt into Style*, London: Penguin.

Merrick, T. W. (1976), 'Employment and Earnings in the Informal Sector in Brazil: the Case of Belo Horizonte', *J. Developing Areas*, 10, pp. 337–54.

Millen, E. (1972), *Specialist in Crime*, London: Harrap.

Miller, W. (1979), in Holdaway (1979).

—— (1977), *Cops and Bobbies*, Chicago, Ill.: University of Chicago Press.

Miller, W. B. (1958), 'Lower Class Culture as a Generating Milieu of Gang

Delinquency', *Journal of Social Issues*, 15.

Mills, C. Wright (1940), 'Situated Actions and Vocabularies of Motive', *American Sociological Review*, 5 (Dec.), pp. 904–13.

Morgan, D. H. J. (1981), 'Man, Masculinity and the Process of Social Enquiry', in H. Roberts (ed.), *Doing Feminist Research*, London: Routledge & Kegan Paul, pp. 83–113.

Morgan, J. (1987), *Conflict and Order: The Police and Labour Disputes in England and Wales 1900–1939*, Oxford: Oxford University Press.

Morris, T. P. (1958), *The Criminal Area*, London: Routledge & Kegan Paul.

—— (1983), *Lawbreakers and Lawmakers: The Politics of Social Control*, Inaugural Lecture, LSE.

Morrison, A. (1897), *A Child of the Jago*, London: Methuen.

Muir, jun. K. W. (1977), *Police: Streetcorner Politicians*, Chicago, Ill.: University of Chicago Press.

Mungham, G. and Pearson, G. (eds.) (1979), *British Working Class Youth Cultures*, London: Routledge & Kegan Paul.

Newham Docklands Forum (1983), *The People's Plan for the Royal Docks*.

Newham Monitoring Project (1984), *Annual General Report*.

Newman, G. F. (1984), *Law and Order*, London: Panther.

Niederhoffer, A. (1969), *Behind the Shield: The Police in Urban Society*, New York, NY: Anchor.

Norris, C. (1987), 'Policing Trouble: An Observation Study of Police Work in Two Police Forces', Ph.D. thesis, University of Surrey.

Nugent, N. and King, R. (eds.), (1977), *The British Right*, Farnborough: Saxon House.

Odell, R. (1965), *Jack the Ripper in Fact and Fiction*, London: Harrap.

Orwell, G. (1971), *The Collected Essays, Journalism and Letters of George Orwell*, Vol. 1: *An Age Like This 1920–1940*, Harmondsworth: Penguin.

—— (1974), *Coming up for Air*, Harmondsworth: Penguin.

Park, R., Burgess, E., and McKenzie, R. (1925), *The City*, Chicago, Ill.: University of Chicago Press.

Parker, H. (1974), *View from the Boys*, London: David & Charles.

Parker, R. (1981), *Rough Justice*, London: Fontana.

Patrick, B. and Terkel, S. (1983), 'Bob Patrick', in Klockars (1983), p. 257.

Patrick, J. (1973), *The Glasgow Gang Observed*, London: Eyre Methuen.

Pawley, M. (1986), 'Electric City of Our Dreams', *New Society*, 13 June.

Pearson, G. (1975), *The Deviant Imagination*, London: Macmillan.

—— (1983), *Hooligan*, London: Macmillan.

Pearson, J. (1973), *The Profession of Violence*, London: Panther.

Perkin, H. (1969), *The Origins of Modern English Society 1780–1880*, London: Routledge & Kegan Paul.

Phipps, A. (1986), 'Radical Criminology and Criminal Victimisation', in Mathews and Young (1986).

Piren, F. and Cloward, R. (1982), *The New Class War*, New York, NY: Pantheon.

Polsky, N. (1971), *Hustlers, Beats and Others*, Harmondsworth: Pelican. (1st edn. 1967.)

Prothero, M. (1931), *The History of the Criminal Investigation Department at Scotland Yard*, London: Herbert Jenkins.

Punch, M. (1979), *Policing the Inner City*, London: Macmillan.

—— (1985), *Conduct Unbecoming: The Social Construction of Police Deviance and Control*, London: Tavistock.

Quinney, R. (1970), *The Social Reality of Crime*, Boston: Little, Brown & Co.

Radzinowicz, L. (1948), *A History of the English Criminal Law and its Administration*, Vol. 1, London: Stevens.

—— (1956), *A History of the English Criminal Law and its Administration*, Vol. 3, London: Stevens.

Read, P. P. (1979), *The Train Robbers*, London: Coronet.

Reiner, R. (1978), *The Blue-Coated Worker*, Cambridge: Cambridge University Press.

—— (1984), 'Review of Simon Holdaway's *Inside the British Police*', in *Sociology*, 18(1), Feb.

—— (1985), *The Politics of the Police*, Brighton: Wheatsheaf Books.

Reith, C. (1938), *The Police Idea*, Oxford: Oxford University Press.

—— (1940), *Police Principles and the Problem of War*, Oxford: Oxford University Press.

—— (1948), *A Short History of the British Police*, Oxford: Oxford University Press.

—— (1956), *A New Study of Police History*, London: Oliver & Boyd.

Report of a Committee of Inquiry into the Major Ports of Great Britain (1962), Cmnd. 1824, London: HMSO.

Reynolds, G. W. and Judge, A. (1969), *The Night the Police Went on Strike*, London: Weidenfeld & Nicolson.

Rhinehart, L. (1972), *The Dice Man*, London: Panther.

Roberts, R. (1973), *The Classic Slum*, Harmondsworth: Penguin.

Robins, D. and Cohen, P. (1978), *Knuckle Sandwich*, Harmondsworth: Penguin.

—— (1984), *We Hate Humans*, Harmondsworth: Penguin.

Rock, P. (1973), *Deviant Behaviour*, London: Hutchinson.

—— (ed.) (1977), *Drugs & Politics*, New Brunswick, NJ: Transaction Books.

—— (1979), *The Making of Symbolic Interactionism*, London: Macmillan.

—— (1983), 'Law, Order and Power in Late Seventeenth and Early Eighteenth Century England', in Cohen and Scull (1983).

—— and Mackintosh, M. (eds.) (1974), *Deviance and Social Control*, London: Tavistock.

Rogers, P. (1972), *Grub Street: Studies in a Sub-Culture*, London: Methuen.

Rollo, J. (1980), in Hain (1979), pp. 153–208.

Rose, A. M. (ed.) (1962), *Human Behaviour and Social Processes*, London: Routledge & Kegan Paul.

Rose, M. (1951), *The East End of London*, London: Cresset.

Rubinstein, J. (1973), *City Police*, New York: Farrar, Straus & Ciroux.

Ruhm, H. (ed.) (1979), *The Hard Boiled Detective*, London: Coronet.

Russell, C. and Lewis, M. S. (1900), *The Jew in London*, London: T. Fisher Unwin.

Ryle, G. (1949), *The Concept of Mind*, London: Hutchinson.

Salamam, G. and Thompson, K. (1978), 'Class Culture and the Persistence of an Élite: The Case of Army Officer Selection', *Sociology Review* 26(2), May.

Salgado, G. (1977), *The Elizabethan Underworld*, London: Dent.

Samuel, R. (1981), *East End Underworld: The Life and Times of Arthur Harding*, London: Routledge & Kegan Paul.

Sanders, W. B. (1977), *Detective Work*, New York, NY: Free Press.

Schoen, D. E. (1970), *Powell and the Powellites*, London: Macmillan.

Schoenwald, R. L. (1973), 'Training Urban Man: A Hypothesis about the Sanitary Movement', in Dyos and Wolff (1973).

Scott, A. M. (1976), 'Who Use the Self-employed?', in C. Gerry and R. Bromley (eds.), *The Casual Poor in Third World Cities*, London and New York: Wiley.

Sellwood, A. V. (1978), *Police Strike 1919*, London: W. H. Allen.

Shapland, J. and Vagg, J. (1985), 'Social Control and Policing in Rural and Urban Areas', Report to the Home Office, Oxford: Centre for Criminological Research.

—— and Hobbs, D. (1987), 'Policing on the Ground', Working Paper, Oxford: Centre for Criminological Research.

Sherman, L. W. (ed.) (1974), *Police Corruption*, New York, NY: Anchor.

Shils, E. (1965), 'Charisma Order and Status', *American Sociological Review*, 30 (Apr.).

Silver, A. (1967), 'The Demand for Order in Civil Society', in Bordua (1967).

Silverstone, R. (1981), *The Message of Television*, London: Heinemann.

—— (1984), 'Review of Culture by Raymond Williams', *British Journal of Sociology*, 35(1), Mar.

Skolnick, J. (1966), *Justice without Trial*, New York, NY: Wiley.

Slipper, J. (1981), *Slipper of the Yard*, London: Sidgwick & Jackson.

Smith, D. J. and Gray, J. (1983), *Police and People in London*, Vols. 3 & 4, London: Policy Studies Institute.

Smith, H. L. (1939), *The History of East London*, London: Macmillan.

Sociology Review (1979), *The Analysis of Qualitative Data, A Symposium*, Nov.

Souza, P. R. and Tokman, V. (1976), 'The Informal Urban Sector in Latin America', *International Labour Review*, 114, pp. 355–65.

Spitzer, S. and Scull, A. (1977), 'Social Control in Historical Perspective', in D. Greenberg (ed.), *Corrections and Punishment*, Beverly Hills: Sage, pp. 265–86.

Stedman-Jones, G. (1971), *Outcast London*, London: Oxford University Press.

—— (1974), 'Working Class Culture and Working Class Politics in London', *Social History*, Summer.

Steedman, C. (1984), *Policing the Victorian Community*, London: Routledge &

Kegan Paul.

Steer, D. (1980), *Uncovering Crime—The Police Role*, London: HMSO.

Stonier, G. W. (1951), 'Review of M. Rose, *The East End of London*', *New Statesman and Nation*, 29 Dec.

Stow, J. (1755), *Survey of London 1598*, Vol. 2, 6th edn.

Styles, J. (1987), 'The Emergence of the Police—Explaining Police Reform in Eighteenth and Nineteenth Century England', *British Journal of Criminology*, 27(1), pp. 15–22.

Suttles, G. D. (1968), *The Social Order of the Slum*, Chicago, Ill.: University of Chicago Press.

Taylor, I. (1971), 'Soccer Consciousness and Soccer Hooliganism', in S. Cohen (1971).

—— (1981), *Law and Order: Arguments for Socialism*, London: Macmillan.

—— and Taylor, L. (eds.) (1973), *Politics and Deviance*, Harmondsworth: Penguin.

——, Walton, P., and Young, J. (1973), *The New Criminology*, London: Routledge & Kegan Paul.

——, ——, and —— (eds.) (1975), *Critical Criminology*, London: Routledge & Kegan Paul.

Taylor, L. (1976), 'The Significance and Interpretation of Replies: The Case of Sex Offenders', in Wiles (1976).

—— (1979), 'Vocabularies, Rhetorics and Grammar: Problems in the Sociology of Motivation', in Downes and Rock (1979), pp. 145–63.

—— (1984), *In the Underworld*, Oxford: Blackwell.

Thompson, E. P. (1974), *The Making of the English Working Class*, Harmondsworth: Pelican.

Thrasher, F. (1928), *The Gang*, Chicago, Ill.: University of Chicago Press.

Tobias, J. J. (1979), *Crime and Police in England 1700–1900*, London: Gill & Macmillan.

Turmin, M. M. (1950), 'The Hero and the Scapegoat in a Peasant Community', *Journal of Personality*, 19.

Tym and Partners (1984), 'The Potential for Future Docks: Use of the Royals', Report for the GLC.

Ure, A. (1835), *Philosophy of Manufacturers*.

Van Maanen, J. (1978), 'On Watching the Watchers', in Manning and Van Maanen (1978).

—— (1980), 'Street Justice', in R. Lundman (ed.), *Police Behaviour*, Oxford: Oxford University Press.

—— (1983), 'On the Making of Policemen', in Klockars (1983), p. 388.

Veblen, T. (1924), *The Theory of the Leisure Class*, new edn., London: Allen & Unwin.

Waddington, P. A. J. (1987), 'Towards Paramilitarism? Dilemmas in Policing Civil Disorder', *British Journal of Criminology*, 27(1), Jan.

Wambaugh, J. (1972), *The New Centurions*, London: Sphere.

—— (1978a), *The Choirboys*, London: Weidenfeld & Nicolson.

—— (1978b), *The Black Marble*, London: Weidenfeld & Nicolson.

Wambaugh, J. (1982), *The Glitter Dome*, London: Futura.

Warshay, L. M. (1962), 'Breadth of Perspective', in Rose (1962).

Webb, S. and B. (1927), *English Poor Law, the Last Hundred Years*, London: Longmans.

Weightman, G. and Humphries, S. (1983), *The Making of Modern London 1815–1914*, London: Sidgwick & Jackson.

Westley, W. (1970), *Violence and the Police*, Cambridge, Mass.: MIT.

Whitaker, B. (1964), *The Police*, London: Eyre Methuen.

—— (1979), *The Police in Society*, London: Eyre Methuen.

White, J. (1980), *Rothschild Buildings: Life in an East End Tenement Block*, London: Routledge & Kegan Paul.

—— (1983), 'Police and People in London in the 1930s', *Oral History*, 11(2).

White, R. J. (1950), *Conservative Tradition*, London: Kaye.

Whitehouse, J. M. (ed.) (1912), *Problems of Boy Life*, London: P. S. King.

Whyte, W. (1943), *Street Corner Society*, Chicago, Ill.: University of Chicago Press.

Wiles, P. (ed.) (1976), *The Sociology of Crime and Delinquency in Britain*, Vol. 2, London: Martin Robinson.

Williams, F. (1973), *No Fixed Address: The Great Train Robbers on the Run*, London: W. H. Allen.

Williams, M. (1982), 'The New Raj: the Gentrifiers and the Natives', *New Society*, 14 Jan.

Willis, P. (1977), *Learning to Labour*, London: Saxon House.

Wilmott, P. (1963), *The Evolution of a Community*, London: Routledge & Kegan Paul.

—— (1969), *Adolescent Boys in East London*, Harmondsworth: Penguin.

Wilson, J. Q. (1968), *Varieties of Police Behaviour*, Cambridge, Mass.: Harvard University Press.

Wirth, L. (1964), *The Ghetto*, Chicago, Ill.: University of Chicago Press.

Wolfgang, M. (1967), *Studies in Homicide*, New York, NY: Harper & Row.

Wolveridge, J. (1981), *Ain't it Grand (or 'This was Stepney')*, London: Journeyman Press.

Yablonsky, L. (1967), *The Violent Gang*, London: Pan.

Young, J. (1971), 'The Role of the Police as Amplifiers of Deviancy', in Cohen (1971).

—— (1976), 'Drugtaking, Reaction and the Subterranean World of Play', in Wiles (1976).

—— (1986), 'The Failure of Criminology: the Need for a Radical Realism', in Matthews and Young (1986).

Young, M. and Willmott, P. (1957), *Family and Kinship in East London*, London: Routledge & Kegan Paul.

Zangwill, I. (1893), *Children of the Ghetto*, 3rd edn., London: Heinemann.

Ziegler, P. (1969), *The Black Death*, London: Collins.

Zorbaugh, H. W. (1929), *The Gold Coast and the Slum*, Chicago, Ill.: University of Chicago Press.

Zweig, F. (1948), *Labour, Life and Poverty*, London: Gollancz.

Index